Betty Saw's
KITCHEN
SECRETS

TIMES BOOKS INTERNATIONAL
Singapore • Kuala Lumpur

The questions and answers were first published in
The New Straits Times, Malaysia, from 1992 to 1994.

© 1996 Times Editions Pte Ltd
© 2000 Times Media Private Limited
Reprinted 1996 (twice), 1998, 2000

This book is published by
Times Books International
an imprint of Times Media Private Limited
Times Centre, 1 New Industrial Road
Singapore 536196
Tel: (65) 2848844 Fax: (65) 2854871
E-mail: te@corp.tpl.com.sg
Online Bookstore:
http://www.timesone.com.sg/te

Times Subang
Lot 46, Subang Hi-Tech Industrial Park
Batu Tiga, 40000 Shah Alam
Selangor Darul Ehsan, Malaysia
Fax & Tel: (603) 7363517
E-mail: cchong@tpg.com.my

Printed in Singapore

ISBN 981 204 643 7

Foreword

Cooking has been more of a hobby than a vocation for me, and over the past 30 years I have learned a great deal through trial and error in my own kitchen. I have always had a strong desire to share my knowledge and enthusiasm for good homecooked food, and this has resulted in several books, appearances on television programs, and countless cooking demonstrations.

When I was approached by the *New Straits Times* to write a weekly column, I naturally accepted the invitation without hesitation, and in April 1992, the column "From Betty Yew's Kitchen" (now known as "From Betty Saw's Kitchen") was born. The column enabled me to reach an even wider audience with information about food, recipes, and solutions to both common and unusual cooking problems.

Writing the column has been a tremendously enjoyable and — thanks to the positive feedback I have received from readers — gratifying experience. Many people have asked for back copies of the column; in fact the demand has far outweighed the supply. Hence the production of this book, in which you will find information on food terms, advice on cooking and baking equipment and techniques, answers to everyday kitchen problems, and over 200 recipes.

Whether you are an experienced cook or just starting out, I hope this book will be a useful reference and constant companion in your culinary ventures.

Index of Subjects

List of Recipes

SOUPS AND PORRIDGE

MAIN COURSES:
MEAT, FISH, POULTRY AND VEGETABLE DISHES

BREAD, SCONES, MUFFINS AND PANCAKES

COOKIES, SQUARES, PASTRIES, PIES AND TARTS

CAKES

DESSERTS AND SWEETS

ICINGS, JAMS, DESSERT SAUCES AND SPREADS

CONDIMENTS AND SAUCES

BEVERAGES

Agar-Agar

Q: How do I mix egg whites with *agar-agar*? I find that when the *agar-agar* sets, all the egg white is on top.

A: *To ensure that the egg whites will mix well in the agar-agar solution, use a balloon whisk and beat egg whites until just stiff, but not dry.*

Q: I have been rather unsuccessful in making *agar-agar*. The texture is either too soft or too thick. Does using rock sugar instead of granulated sugar affect the texture? How long should the mixture boil?

A: *Agar-agar strands should first be soaked in water to soften and swell for 10-15 minutes so that they will dissolve easily when boiled. For a good textured jelly which is neither too diluted nor too thick, use 25 grams agar-agar strands to 4 cups water and 1¹/2 cups sugar. Simmer gently for 20 minutes or until agar-agar strands and sugar are dissolved. Using granulated sugar or rock sugar is a matter of preference and has no effect on texture.*

Q: Can you tell me how to make *agar-agar santan*? When I make it, there is always too much coconut milk at the bottom.

A: *Here's a recipe using agar-agar powder which dissolves more easily than agar-agar strands.*

Coconut Agar-Agar

30 g	*agar-agar* powder, dissolved in ¹/2 cup cold water
5¹/4 cups	boiling hot water
1¹/4 cups	sugar
4	pandan leaves, knotted
¹/4 teaspoon	green colouring
1 cup	thick coconut milk, from 1 grated white coconut

Put hot water, sugar and pandan leaves in a saucepan and stir over medium heat. Add dissolved *agar-agar* and boil for 12-15 minutes, stirring frequently.

Discard pandan leaves and pour out 3 cups of the *agar-agar* liquid. Stir in green colouring and pour into a tray or mould.

Boil remaining *agar-agar* liquid until it is reduced to approximately 1 cup. Stir in coconut milk. Bring to a boil and remove from heat.

When the green *agar-agar* is half set, gently pour coconut *agar-agar* mixture over green layer.

Leave to set at room temperature, then refrigerate.

Ajowan Seeds

Q: What are ajowan seeds?

A: Ajowan seeds are also known as omam. They are small, light brown, tear-shaped seeds from a shrub of the cumin family. They have a strong flavour which is similar to that of thyme. Ajowan seeds are used in Indian cuisine to flavour curries, chutneys and breads.

Apples

Q: I would like to share a cake recipe which I found in an American magazine many years ago. It is very easy to make and the result is a beautiful, moist, not-too-sweet apple cake. Hope you like it as much as I do.

American Grandma's Apple Cake

1 tin	(21 oz / 600 g) apple-pie filling (without additional flavouring)
2 cups	all-purpose flour
1 cup	sugar
1/2 cup	vegetable oil
2	eggs, beaten to blend
1 teaspoon	vanilla essence
1 teaspoon	cinnamon
1 teaspoon	baking powder
1 teaspoon	bicarbonate of soda
1/4 teaspoon	salt
1/2 cup	chopped walnuts
1/2 cup	raisins

Preheat oven to 170°C. Lightly grease a 23 cm round cake pan.

Combine all ingredients except walnuts and raisins in a large bowl and stir to blend. Mix in walnuts and raisins.

Pour into prepared cake pan and bake for about 1 hour and 10 minutes or until tester inserted in centre comes out clean. Cool in pan.

A: Your simple-to-follow recipe indeed makes a lovely moist apple cake. Thank you for sharing it with us. I encourage readers to try it out.

Q: My husband tells me of his student days in the UK and how he loved a particular dessert called Apple Crumble. I would like to surprise him on his next birthday by making it. Can you give me the recipe?

A: Apple Crumble makes a lovely dessert and I especially like to eat it warm with custard or a large scoop of vanilla ice-cream. I hope your husband will like this version.

Apple and Raisin Crumble

900 g   cooking apples, peeled, cored and sliced
75 g   raisins
1 teaspoon   ground cinnamon
30 g   brown sugar
1 tablespoon   water

225 g   plain flour, sifted
80 g   butter, diced
80 g   soft brown sugar
80 g   chopped mixed nuts

Place sliced apples, raisins, cinnamon, sugar, and water into a saucepan and cook gently until apples are just soft. Spoon mixture into a 1.75 litre ovenproof dish.

Put sifted flour into bowl of a food processor fitted with a cutting blade. Add butter and turn on processor for a few seconds until mixture is crumbly. Stir in sugar and nuts and mix well.

Spoon crumble topping over apple mixture. Use a fork to level it out but do not press it down.

Bake in preheated 175°C oven for 40-45 minutes until topping is dark golden brown.

Avocados

Q: What is the best way of removing an avocado seed? I always end up making a mess of the soft flesh.

A: Cut the avocado in half lengthwise with a sharp knife. Twist the two halves in opposite directions to separate them. Then plunge the tip of the knife into the avocado seed, twist and lift out the seed.

Baking Reagents

Q: What are bread improvers and dough conditioners? How much of each should I use for a recipe which uses 1 kg flour?

A: Bread improvers and dough conditioners are chemicals added to bread to soften it and improve its texture. Add one teaspoonful to 1 kg flour.

Q: What is the purpose of Quick 75?

A: Quick 75 is an imported brand of stabiliser used in the baking of sponge cakes to help the eggs rise rapidly and stiffly. It is acidic and this helps beaten eggs remain stable and not lose the airy, velvety and voluminous texture which is essential for light sponge cakes. Ovalette can be used instead.

Baking Utensils

WIDE CHOICE TO PAN OUT BAKING NEEDS

You want to take up baking and you are wondering how to start. Of course you will need some equipment: an oven, measuring spoons and cups, a scale, and some baking pans. The wide range of baking pans available can be confusing; knowing what they are and how they are used should make the selection easier.

As a general rule, invest in the best quality pans you can afford, as they will give better results and last much longer. Aluminium baking pans which conduct heat well are among the best all-round pans for everyday baking. They are easily available and can take hard scrubbing. Good quality non-stick pans are marvellous for certain cakes, muffins and breads, but take care not to scratch them.

Round and square aluminium tins of between 18 cm and 25 cm are essential for basic cake-baking. Two of each type are necessary for sandwich or layer cakes.

Springform cake pans, i.e. nonstick pans with a removable base or sides which unclip for easy unmoulding, are used for cheesecakes or sponge cakes with a jelly or mousse topping. Choose sturdy ones or they will warp and the batter will leak out during baking.

Pie or flan tins, available in stainless steel, nonstick material or porcelain, come in round, square and oval shapes. They are used for sweet and savoury pies. The metal ones with a removable base and fluted sloping sides are best. Useful sizes are between 18 and 25 cm.

Patty tins, which consist of a cluster of small cake tins, are useful for muffins, cupcakes and small pies. Choose the nonstick variety with a dozen sections.

Lamington tins are shallow rectangular pans; a typical size is 27 1/2 x 17 1/2 x 3 cm. They have slightly sloping sides and are made of tinned steel or aluminium. They are ideal for sliced or tray cakes and brownies.

Chiffon cake pans, also known as ring pans or tube pans, are deep pans with sloping sides and a ring in the centre. They are used for chiffon and angel food cakes. Aluminium ones are good enough.

Mangue cake pans are round, deep pans with sides that slope slightly. They are usually made of aluminium and are used to make the special French sponge cake.

16

Kugelhopf moulds or pans are deep ring moulds with heavy patterning. A nonstick variety is available. Kugelhopf is a popular Austrian raisin cake.

Savarin tins are shallow ring moulds with smooth rounded bases. They are made from tinned steel or aluminium and come in various sizes. Savarin moulds can be used for cakes, meat loaves, mousses and jellies.

Bread tins come in a great variety of sizes. A nonstick pan which holds a 2 lb (900 g) loaf is the most useful type. Its dimensions are approximately 22 x 12 x 7 cm. Other sizes are useful for tea breads and loaf cakes.

Biscuit or cookie trays should not fit the oven exactly. There should be a gap of at least 5 cm between the tray and the oven walls. The trays should be only 1 cm deep (deeper tins prevent even browning). Choose thick aluminium trays so that they will not warp.

As a start, I would recommend buying:

• One square aluminium cake baking tin

• One round aluminium cake baking tin

• One springform cake pan

• Two or three cookie trays

If you want to bake pies, muffins, cupcakes and bread, add a pie tin, a patty tin and a bread tin.

Q: I use stainless steel baking tins. The manufacturer's handbook suggests that for best results I should use baking temperatures 20-30°C lower than specified in recipes. Is this true?

A: Heavy coated steel pans hold heat very effectively and that is why manufacturers advise a reduction in baking temperature or cooking time to avoid over-baking. However, I find it most inconvenient to guess what the reduction should be for every recipe. Furthermore, these pans are not suitable for soft cakes and cookies. I recommend using normal, sturdy aluminium or nonstick bakeware which is well suited to everyday baking and is easy to clean.

ALL YOU NEED FOR GOOD BAKING

Besides various types of baking pans, there are many other basic kitchen gadgets required for baking.

A good quality **kitchen scale** is essential. There are two basic types: digital and spring. Digital scales are expensive but less prone to errors. Spring scales are cheaper, but make sure the scale is zeroed before use and read at centre level for accuracy. The container should be large enough to hold at least 1 kg of sugar or flour. Check the accuracy of your scales with a 250 g block of butter.

Measuring jugs are essential for measuring liquids. Clear ovenproof glass jugs of a reputable brand are value for money even though they may be expensive. Cheaper jugs should be checked for accuracy with a known measure of liquid. A useful size to buy is 500 ml. Measurements should be read at eye level for accuracy.

Measuring spoons are usually made of plastic and come in a set of different sizes. A tablespoon and teaspoon are equivalent to 15 ml and 5 ml respectively.

Mixing bowls are used for mixing small amounts of ingredients. Although plastic bowls are cheaper, ovenproof bowls are a better choice as they are more versatile (they can be used for melting butter and chocolate or for making custards, for example). A useful size is 16 cm. Reserve the large mixing bowl from your food processor or mixer for beating, creaming, whisking and rubbing in. Buy an extra bowl with your food processor because many recipes do call for whisking the egg whites separately.

The hand-held four-sided metal **grater** is extremely useful. Each side has different sized holes. The finest holes are ideal for grating rinds of citrus fruit. Use a clean toothbrush to clean the holes and dry the grater thoroughly before storing.

Pastry blenders consist of several curved wires or blades. They are indispensable for rubbing flour into fat. Make sure the wires or blades are strong.

For glazing breads, cookies and pastries, **pastry brushes** are essential. Buy good quality soft bristle brushes rather than nylon brushes which can melt if used on very hot surfaces. Flat brushes are more useful than rounded ones.

You'll need several **spatulas**. Metal ones are used for removing hot cookies and pastries from baking trays. A long metal spatula with a wooden handle and a wide blade (approx. 3 cm) is a good choice as it can also be used for spreading icing and frosting. Rubber spatulas are essential for scraping mixing bowls clean; choose ones with large flexible blades. The blade and handle should be in one piece; jointed spatulas are hard to clean and melted fat and butter can seep into the gaps.

Buy two **sieves**, as two ingredients may have to be sifted separately; if you only have one sieve you'll have to wash and dry it after each use. Metal sieves with a fine metal mesh are durable. A good size is 18 cm in diameter. Mechanical sieves are not only very expensive but are unsuitable for sifting large quantities.

You will also need some **skewers** for testing doneness of cakes. They can be wooden, plastic or metal.

Rolling pins are usually made of wood. The 26 cm barrel of a typical rolling pin is useful for biscuit dough. For pastries, a longer rolling pin, with a barrel of 30-38 cm, is more suitable. When buying rolling pins, make sure the barrel is very smooth and rolls easily. If available, buy rolling pins made of a nonstick material, as they are easier to handle and clean.

You'll need **wire racks** for cooling cakes, pastries and cookies. The racks prevent moisture from collecting on the base of the baked goods. Buy rustproof racks with a space of not more than 1 cm between the wires.

Nowadays, most ovens come with **oven timers**, but an extra one is useful if you have to be mobile around the house. It also helps when you have more than one thing in the oven at the same time.

An **oven thermometer** is useful for checking the accuracy of the oven's thermostat. An inaccurate baking temperature is one of the major causes of baking problems.

Bananas

Q: Which variety of bananas should I use to achieve a speckled effect in banana cake?

A: Many types of bananas can be used; the important thing is for them to be very ripe. (Making banana cake is a good way of using up overripe bananas.) If you want a highly speckled effect, use pisang rastali.

Q: I love banana cake, but a lot of past failures have discouraged me from making it again. It comes out looking good on the outside, but it is too wet inside. Where am I going wrong?

A: I would suggest using two well-ripened medium-sized pisang rastali; pisang emas *are too gooey for cakes. Make sure the oven is properly preheated to the correct temperature. Before removing the cake from the oven, test with a wooden skewer; if the cake is properly cooked the skewer will come out clean when inserted in the centre of the cake. Here is a recipe:*

Banana Cake

90 g	butter
90 g	castor sugar
1	egg
2	pisang rastali, mashed with 1 teaspoon lime juice
1 teaspoon	vanilla essence

SIFTED INGREDIENTS (COMBINED)

120 g	plain flour
1/2 teaspoon	baking powder
1/2 teaspoon	bicarbonate of soda
1 tablespoon	milk

Line and grease a 19 cm square cake tin with greased greaseproof paper.

Cream butter and castor sugar until light and fluffy, and beat in egg. Add mashed bananas and vanilla essence. Mix well. Fold in sifted dry ingredients and stir in milk.

Bake in preheated 175°C oven for 35-40 minutes.

Beancurd

THE TASTY AND VERSATILE BEANCURD

With increasing health awareness, more and more people are today turning to healthy foods. The simple, cheap, but highly nutritious beancurd, a by-product of the soya bean, fits beautifully into this category. Low in calories and free from cholesterol, it is rich in protein and is an excellent source of magnesium, calcium, phosphorus and iron. It has even been reported that a staple diet of soya beans, as adopted by the Japanese, can considerably reduce the risk of heart disease.

Beancurd may be bland, but it is a very versatile product which can be turned into great-tasting dishes. In fact, it is its blandness which makes beancurd the perfect ingredient because it can be led in any direction you choose. It can be deep-fried, stir-fried, boiled, braised, stewed or puréed. You can even make delectable desserts from it.

Several types of beancurd are available in our markets. Soft beancurd, sometimes called water beancurd, is generally made in large rectangular slabs which are then cut up and sold in squares. Japanese semi-soft beancurd

is sold in packed rolls. Soft and semi-soft beancurds are mainly used for steamed dishes and soups, and can also be puréed for salad dressings. Firm beancurd is normally available in small compressed squares; these are best for stir-frying, braising and stewing because they can be sliced or cubed.

Sometimes beancurd is cubed and then deep-fried until it is brown and crusty on the outside and almost dry on the inside. A popular use of this type of beancurd is in curries. Dried beancurd sheets are good for wrapping food. Beancurd sticks, which are thick, yellow strips of dried beancurd, are used for stir-frying, braising or in soups.

The best way to store soft, semi-soft or firm beancurd is to immerse it in water with a pinch of salt. It will keep in the refrigerator for 4-5 days if you change the water every day.

I have chosen some tempting recipes for you to try. I am sure you will enjoy them — I have yet to come across anybody who does not like beancurd.

Chicken and Beancurd Soup

150 g	chicken meat, shredded
Seasoning Ingredients	
$1/2$ teaspoon	salt
$1/2$ teaspoon	cornflour
$1/4$ teaspoon	pepper
6 cups	fresh chicken stock
3	dried black mushrooms, soaked and shredded
150 g	beancurd, cut into $1/2$ x 5 cm strips
100 g	carrots, shredded
4	fresh or canned button mushrooms, shredded
2 tablespoons	sweet potato flour, combined with 3 tablespoons water and strained
	Salt and pepper to taste
1	egg, lightly beaten with a fork
2 stalks	spring onions, chopped

Marinate chicken with seasoning ingredients and leave for 10 minutes.

Put chicken stock in a pot and bring to a boil. Add black mushrooms, beancurd, carrots, button mushrooms and spring onions. When soup begins to boil, lower heat and simmer for 5-8 minutes.

Increase heat, stir in sweet potato flour mixture gradually, stirring soup constantly. Add salt and pepper to taste.

Gradually add egg in a very slow, thin stream. Using a chopstick or fork, pull egg slowly into strands.

Ladle into individual bowls, garnish with spring onions and serve hot.

Steamed Spicy Stuffed Beancurd

1 roll	Japanese soft beancurd, cut into 10 slices
2 teaspoons	cornflour
100 g	chicken meat, minced

SEASONING INGREDIENTS

1/4 teaspoon	salt
1/4 teaspoon	pepper
1/2 teaspoon	sugar
1 teaspoon	sesame oil
1 teaspoon	cornflour
2 teaspoons	cooking oil, to be added last

CHOPPED INGREDIENTS (CHOPPED FINELY)

3	water chestnuts
2 slices	ginger
1	red chilli
1 stalk	spring onion

1 tablespoon	cooking oil
1 teaspoon	Chinese rice wine

SAUCE INGREDIENTS (COMBINED)

1/2 cup	fresh chicken stock
1/4 teaspoon	pepper
1/4 teaspoon	sugar
1/2 teaspoon	salt
1/2 teaspoon	Chinese rice wine
1/2 teaspoon	sesame oil
1 teaspoon	cornflour

Place beancurd slices on a heatproof dish and carefully scoop out a small hollow from the centre of each piece with a teaspoon or small knife. Dust hollows with a little cornflour.

Mix minced chicken with seasoning ingredients and stir in chopped ingredients.

Stuff and fill each beancurd slice with chicken mixture. Smooth tops with the back of a teaspoon.

Steam over rapidly boiling water for 10 minutes. Carefully drain liquid into sauce ingredients.

Heat wok with oil and sprinkle in wine. Pour in sauce ingredients and bring to a boil. Reduce heat and simmer for one minute or until sauce thickens. Pour over stuffed beancurd.

Fried Beancurd with Crab Meat Sauce

3 small squares	soft beancurd
1/4 teaspoon	salt
1/4 teaspoon	pepper
1/2 teaspoon	sesame oil

1 tablespoon	cooking oil
1	egg, beaten
1 tablespoon	plain flour
2 slices	ginger, finely shredded
1	shallot, finely sliced

SAUCE INGREDIENTS (COMBINED)

100 ml	fresh chicken stock
1/4 teaspoon	sugar
1/4 teaspoon	salt
1/4 teaspoon	pepper
1 teaspoon	light soya sauce

1 tablespoon	cooked crab meat
1 teaspoon	cornflour, combined with 1 tablespoon water
1/2 tablespoon	chopped spring onions
1/2 tablespoon	chopped coriander leaves

Mix beancurd pieces with salt, pepper and sesame oil, taking care not to break beancurd. Leave to marinate for 15 minutes. Drain well.

Heat oil for deep-frying. Carefully dip beancurd in beaten egg and coat with flour. Deep-fry until golden. Drain and place on serving dish.

Remove oil, leaving one tablespoon in wok. Lightly brown ginger and shallot and add sauce ingredients.

When sauce begins to boil, put in crab meat and thicken with cornflour mixture. Sprinkle spring onions and coriander leaves on top and serve.

Beancurd Biscuits

100 g	soft beancurd
250 g	plain flour
1 small	egg, beaten
6 tablespoons	sugar
	Sesame seeds

Put beancurd into a colander and allow to drip dry. Mash well with a fork.

Sift flour into a bowl. Add mashed beancurd, beaten egg and sugar. Knead well into a firm dough. Leave to rest for 20-25 minutes.

Take a small portion of the dough and coat with sesame seeds. Dust with flour and pass dough through a noodle roller several times. Adjust the regulating knob with each rolling until dough is paper-thin. If necessary, dust with a little flour to prevent sticking.

Cut into 2 1/2 cm strips, then cut again into rectangular pieces. Make a slit in the centre and tuck one side in to form a ribbon.

Deep-fry in hot oil over medium heat until golden brown.

Bread

THE JOY OF BAKING BREAD

Bread-making is no longer the tedious chore it once was. As long as you have a mixer with a dough hook or a robust food processor with a dough blade, you can whip up a batch of dough in 20 minutes.

There's nothing like the delicious aroma of freshly baked bread. One of the greatest joys of making bread at home is being able to savour warm crusty bread spread with butter and jam.

The basic ingredients are easy to find. Flour suitable for making bread is labelled under various names — strong flour, bread flour or high-protein flour. Strong white flour generally contains 72-74 per cent of the whole grain; buy unbleached if you want to avoid chemical whiteners. Wholewheat flour is darker and contains the whole grain. It is the healthiest flour as it contains all the vitamins and oils from the fibre (bran). Wholewheat bread has a slightly chewy and nutty flavour and is heavier than white bread.

Instant, easy-blend yeast is simple to use as it can be mixed directly with the flour, thus speeding up the process of proofing. Always use luke-warm liquid to mix the dough, as too hot a liquid can kill the yeast, thus preventing the dough from rising.

Here are two recipes for yeasted loaves — wholewheat bread and plain round loaf. These are the two easiest crusty loaves to make; each has a deliciously different flavour and a beautiful texture. They are good to eat simply with butter or margarine.

Once you become adept at churning out these basic loaves, let your imagination run loose and turn the dough into plaited loaves, small buns and rolls. Mix in currants, raisins, grated cheese and nuts. Or sprinkle with sesame seeds, black poppy seeds, chopped sunflower seeds, cheese or nuts.

Wholewheat Bread

500 g	wholewheat flour
1 teaspoon	salt
1 teaspoon	castor sugar
10 g	easy-blend dried yeast
30 g	butter or margarine
150 ml	lukewarm milk

Sift wholewheat flour into the bowl of an electric mixer. Return husks from sieve to bowl. Stir in salt, sugar and yeast. Blend in butter or margarine using a pastry cutter.

Pour in milk. Attach dough hook and beat for 4-5 minutes or until dough is smooth. Cover with a damp tea towel to prevent a skin forming on the surface. Leave to rise for 30 minutes or until doubled in bulk.

Punch dough down then knead again by hand for three minutes or until smooth. Shape the dough into either a ball (for a round loaf) or a rectangle, then place in a lightly greased 1 kg loaf tin. The dough should fill the pan three-quarters full. Lightly score the loaf to make patterns on the crust.

Cover dough with tea towel and leave to rise again for 15-20 minutes depending on room temperature. If desired, glaze with milk or water for a crunchy crust, or with beaten egg for a golden shiny finish.

Bake in preheated 220°C oven for 20 minutes. Reduce temperature to 180°C and bake for a further 15-20 minutes. Cool on a wire rack.

Plain Round Loaf

500 g	plain strong flour
1 teaspoon	salt
1 teaspoon	castor sugar
10 g	easy-blend yeast
30 g	butter or margarine
200 ml	lukewarm milk
75 ml	lukewarm water

Use same method as Wholewheat Bread.

Q: Can you give me some recipes for bread or buns which contain no yeast or eggs and which can be baked in a microwave convection oven?

A: Try this Brown Soda Bread which usually requires buttermilk but works just as well with milk or unsweetened soya bean milk. I have also given a Beer Bread recipe that makes a moist loaf.

Brown Soda Bread

675 g wholemeal flour
225 g plain flour
1 teaspoon bicarbonate of soda
4 teaspoons cream of tartar
2 teaspoons sugar
2 teaspoons salt
45 g margarine or butter
650-750 ml milk

Sift flour, bicarbonate of soda and cream of tartar together and stir in sugar and salt. Rub in the margarine or butter and mix in enough milk to form a soft dough.

Shape, with a minimum of kneading, into a large circle about 5 cm thick. With the handle of a wooden spoon, carve a 2-cm-deep cross on the top of the loaf.

Bake on a greased baking sheet in a preheated 190°C oven for 25-30 minutes. Allow to cool on a wire rack.

Beer Bread

60 g margarine or butter
1 dessertspoon soft brown sugar
290 ml beer
1 teaspoon salt
1 egg, beaten with a fork
225 g wholemeal flour
225 g strong white flour
12 g easy-blend yeast

Grease a 1 kg loaf pan with butter. Bring sugar, beer and remaining butter to boiling point, then allow to cool until lukewarm. Add salt and lightly beaten egg to beer mixture.

Sift flour into mixing bowl and stir in yeast. Make a well in the centre and pour in beer mixture. Mix with a knife and then beat in electric mixer fitted with a dough hook for 5-6 minutes until smooth and a little shiny. The dough should be very elastic.

Shape dough into a ball and put back in bowl. Cover with a piece of plastic wrap. Put in a warm place until it has doubled in bulk, about 30 minutes.

Take out, punch down and knead until smooth again. Shape into a loaf and put into prepared tin. Cover and leave to rise again until it doubles in bulk.

Bake in preheated 200°C oven for 35-40 minutes until it is brown on top and the bread sounds hollow when tapped on the underside. Cool on a wire rack.

Q: I have made white and wholemeal breads using ordinary dry yeast. Then I tried using instant yeast, but the bread came out dry and the top crust was very uneven and rough. Why did this happen?

A: *Yeast seems so mysterious because it is a living organism. It requires moisture, gentle warmth and sugar to activate its growth. As it grows, it produces carbon dioxide which makes the bread rise.*

Yeast is available in three forms — fresh, dried or granular, and powdered easy-blend or instant yeast.

Fresh yeast should be firm and moist and light cream-coloured. If it is crumbly and dark brown, it is stale and will not activate. To use it, dissolve the required amount into a little lukewarm liquid and mix into the dough. The amount of fresh yeast to use for 450-500 g flour is 30 g.

Dried yeast has to be reconstituted with warm water and sugar. Stir the yeast, sugar and lukewarm water together until the yeast dissolves. Leave to stand for 15 minutes until a frothy head appears. The yeast mixture is then ready for use. One word of caution, though. Dried yeast, like fresh yeast, does become stale. Check its expiry date and if it does not produce a frothy head, do not use it. For every 450 g flour, you'll need 2 teaspoons dried yeast.

Easy-blend yeast or instant yeast is my favourite, simply because it is the easiest to use. It can be mixed directly into the flour with the water added separately. No waiting time is required for the yeast to activate.

If your bread is crumbly and dry, then the loaf has been baked for too long or the oven temperature is too high. Also, too much flour may have been used in the dough.

Q: I do not have a dough mixer. Can I mix the dough by hand? Should it feel sticky?

A: *It is not necessary to use an electric mixer when making bread, although I like to use it because it saves time and effort. Hand-kneading the dough gives equally good results and I know many chefs who prefer to do it that way when making small amounts of bread, as they enjoy the yeasty smell of the dough as well as the good exercise from the kneading.*

When kneading bread dough by hand, mix the dry ingredients in a large bowl, then pour in warm liquid. Using one hand to hold the bowl, mix with a scooping and turning motion to form a lump of soft, smooth and elastic dough. It should not be sticky. Place the lump of dough on a smooth work surface dusted with a little flour to prevent sticking when kneading.

Q: *Could I have a recipe for garlic bread? My family loves it.*

A: *Here's how to make garlic bread:*

Garlic Bread

125 g butter
2 cloves garlic, crushed
1 French loaf

Cream butter with garlic until well blended.

Cut loaf of bread diagonally into thick slices; don't cut through the bread completely; the slices should still be attached at the bottom.

Spread garlic butter between each slice of bread. Wrap loaf loosely in kitchen foil and place in 220°C oven for 10 minutes.

Open foil and return to oven for a further 5-8 minutes to crisp.

Q: I would like to seek your advice on how to bake bread using rice flour, as my son has been found to be allergic to wheat.

A: Try this rice loaf. It has a dense but soft texture.

Rice Loaf

120 g butter
225 g castor sugar
  Finely grated rind of 1/2 lemon
4 eggs
225 g finely ground rice (rice flour), sifted

Preheat oven to 180°C. Line a 1 kg loaf tin with greased greaseproof paper.

Cream butter in a mixing bowl. Beat in sugar until light and fluffy. Add lemon rind and mix well.

Separate eggs. Add yolks to butter mixture one at a time, beating hard constantly.

Whisk egg white until fairly stiff but not dry. Take a spoonful of egg white and mix into butter mixture. Stir in half the ground rice and add another spoonful of egg white. Add the rest of the ground rice and then remaining egg white.

Pour into prepared tin. Make a slight hollow in the centre (to counteract tendency of bread to rise in the middle). Bake for 45 minutes or until firm to the touch and slightly shrunken at the edges.

Cool in tin for 5 minutes, then turn out to a wire rack to cool completely.

Breadcrumbs

Q: I would like to make my own breadcrumbs. Should I toast the bread or bake it in the oven?

A: Bake 2-day-old bread in a moderately hot oven until dry and crisp, but not brown. When cool, blend in a food processor (if you are making a large quantity) or in a mortar and pestle. Store breadcrumbs in a jar in a cool place.

Brownies

Q: I would very much appreciate it if you could give me a recipe for Brownies.

A: Try making these lovely brownies; they are extravagantly rich with loads of chocolate and are very quick to make. All you have to do is mix the ingredients together with a fork. Brownies make a special treat when served with a large scoop of vanilla ice-cream.

Rich Chocolate Brownies

125 g	butter
1 cup	castor sugar
1¹/₂ teaspoons	vanilla essence
¹/₂ cup	cocoa, sifted
4 large	eggs, beaten
¹/₃ cup	self-raising flour, sifted
200 g	good quality dark chocolate, chopped
75 g	chopped walnuts
	Vanilla ice-cream, optional

Line a lamington tin with greased baking paper.

Melt the butter and stir in castor sugar and vanilla essence. Mix in cocoa and stir in beaten eggs until well blended. Add self-raising flour, chopped chocolate and walnuts.

Pour into prepared pan and bake in preheated 175°C oven for 40 minutes. Cool and cut into squares.

Serve plain or topped with a scoop of vanilla ice-cream.

Butter

Q: I have cake and cookie recipes which call for softened or melted butter. How do I melt and soften butter? Can I use margarine instead?

A: Butter can be melted in a microwave or over a pan of hot water. Soften butter by simply leaving it at room temperature until it is soft. Yes, you can replace butter with margarine, but the flavour will not be as good.

Butter Cakes

SKILL IN MAKING A BUTTER CAKE FOR TEA

For tea time, nothing can beat the aroma of a well-baked butter cake. There are many recipes for butter cakes but they are all based on the half-pound or pound cake recipe. They are delightful eaten fresh from the oven.

A simple coating of butter cream turns the cake into a beautiful celebration cake. Butter cakes should have the delicious fragrance of butter coming through with every bite. They should not be overwhelmed with essence.

The fragrance and fine texture of butter cake come from using fresh, high quality pure butter. Creaming the butter with sugar until it is soft and smooth makes the cake light. Use fine castor sugar, as it creams easily.

It is important to add the ingredients gradually. Eggs should be added one at a time, allowing approximately one minute per egg for mixing. The dry ingredients should be sifted and added half at a time, preferably by gently folding in with a large spoon or spatula. To do this, gently plunge in the spoon or spatula into the bottom of the cake mixture, twist and bring it up and out along the sides of the bowl. Give the bowl a quarter turn every now and then until the dry ingredients are worked in. Pour the mixture into the prepared pan immediately.

Smooth the surface of the batter before baking. If a raising agent is used, spread out the batter a little from the centre to the sides, making a slight hollow in the centre.

Bake cakes in the centre of a preheated oven. To test if the cake is cooked, use a long satay stick or wooden skewer and insert it gently into the centre of the cake. If it comes out clean, the cake is cooked. If it is coated with gluey batter then it needs to bake at least 5 to 10 minutes longer. Another way to know when a cake is done is when the sides of the cake leave the sides of the pan. To further ensure that it is cooked, lightly touch the top of the cake. If no impression is left, the cake is ready to be taken out of the oven.

I am giving two of my own butter cake recipes. The Rich Butter Cake is deliciously buttery and moist, and keeps well if stored in an airtight container in the refrigerator. Leave at room temperature for 15-20 minutes before serving. The Butter Walnut Cake has a beautifully soft texture and a rich aroma of butter and walnuts. This cake is best eaten the same day, fresh from the oven.

Rich Butter Cake

250 g   cold butter cut into small cubes
135 g   castor sugar
5 large   eggs, separated

SIFTED INGREDIENTS (COMBINED)
135 g   high-ratio flour
2 teaspoons   baking powder

Line a 20-23 cm cake pan with greased greaseproof paper.

In a mixing bowl, cream butter with half the castor sugar until light and creamy. Add egg yolks one at a time and beat well until light and fluffy.

Sift in flour and baking powder half at a time and mix well on lowest speed in an electric mixer.

In a separate clean bowl, whisk egg whites until just turning frothy. Add remaining sugar and continue whisking until mixture is glossy and just stiff. Do not over-beat. Fold into flour mixture using a large metal spoon.

Turn mixture into prepared pan. Make a shallow well in the centre so that cake will have a level surface when baked. Bake in the centre of preheated 175°C oven for 50-60 minutes or until done when tested with a wooden skewer.

Walnut Butter Cake

250 g	cold butter, diced
225 g	castor sugar
1 teaspoon	vanilla essence
5	large eggs

SIFTED INGREDIENTS (COMBINED)

240 g	high-ratio flour, sifted with
2 teaspoons	baking powder
2 tablespoons	milk
120 g	coarsely chopped walnuts
	Apricot jam
	Icing sugar

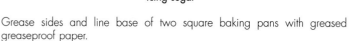

Grease sides and line base of two square baking pans with greased greaseproof paper.

Cream butter for 1 minute and add castor sugar and vanilla essence. Beat until light and creamy. Add eggs one at a time, beating well after each addition. (If mixture begins to curdle, beat in 90 g of the flour before adding remaining eggs.)

Fold in remaining flour and beat in milk. Stir in walnuts. Divide mixture evenly between the pans. Level the surface with a spatula.

Bake in moderate oven for 15-20 minutes until cooked through when tested with a skewer.

Cool in the tin and sandwich with jam. Dust surface with icing sugar or decorate with butter cream.

Q: I have just bought a microwave convection oven. My cakes end up either uncooked in the centre or too dry. I bake them at 160°C for one hour. What am I doing wrong?

A: If the centre of the cake is always uncooked, try baking at 180°C. Before removing the cake from the oven, test the cake with a skewer, slightly away from the centre. If it comes out clean then the cake is cooked through. However, if the cake always comes out dry, reduce cooking time. Here is a recipe for Chocolate Orange Cake using the microwave convection oven method.

Chocolate Orange Cake

60 g	dark cooking chocolate, chopped
60 g	butter at room temperature
1/4 cup	milk
180 g	self-raising flour, sifted
20 g	cocoa, sifted
1	egg
250 g	castor sugar
	Grated rind of 1 orange
1/4 cup	orange juice
1/4 cup	milk

CHOCOLATE ICING

180 g	icing sugar, sifted
20 g	cocoa, sifted
2 teaspoons	soft butter
1 teaspoon	vanilla essence
2 teaspoons	hot milk

Put chocolate, butter and milk in a bowl, and cook on High for one minute. Stir until melted. Stir in flour, cocoa, egg, sugar, orange rind, juice and milk. Mix until smooth.

Grease and line base of a 20 cm round cake pan. Pour cake batter into pan. Cook on convection microwave at 180°C for 20 minutes or until just cooked when tested with a skewer. Cool and spread with chocolate icing.

To make chocolate icing
Put icing sugar and cocoa into a heatproof bowl and stir in butter and milk. Place bowl over hot water and stir until mixture is smooth and spreadable.

Q: Recently, I tasted a delicious durian cake containing real durians. I would appreciate it very much if you could provide me with a recipe for this.

A: *Here is a rich butter cake recipe with durian pulp added.*

Butter Durian Cake

240 g	butter
225 g	castor sugar
4	large eggs
100 g	mashed durian pulp

SIFTED INGREDIENTS (COMBINED)

240 g	self-raising flour
1 teaspoon	bicarbonate of soda

2-3 tablespoons milk

Line a 23 cm round cake tin with greased greaseproof paper.

Cream butter and castor sugar until light and fluffy. Beat in eggs, one at a time, beating well after each addition. Beat in durian pulp until well blended.

Fold in sifted ingredients and enough milk to give a soft dropping consistency. Pour into prepared pan and spread out batter, making a slight hollow in the centre.

Bake in preheated 175°C oven for 50-60 minutes or until cake is cooked when tested with a skewer.

Buttermilk

Q: What is buttermilk? Is this in liquid or powdered form? What can be used as a substitute and where can I get it?

A: *Buttermilk is the product that remains after milk has been churned to make butter. Nowadays buttermilk is made by adding special cultures to skim milk, and is usually sold as cultured buttermilk.*

It is available in leading supermarkets in powdered form. Mix with water and use as required.

Fresh buttermilk has a very short shelf life and is seldom available in our supermarkets. You can use skim milk as a substitute, although the fat content in buttermilk is higher.

Cake-Making

Q: Can you please explain what is meant by blending, beating and folding?

A: *"To blend" is to combine two or more ingredients well. You can blend by hand or with a mixer.*

"To beat" is to mix rapidly in order to make a mixture smooth and light. You can beat by hand using a rotary whisk, a fork or a wooden spoon in a circular motion, lifting and dropping the mixture as you work. You can use an electric mixer fitted with a beater (for fat and sugar) or a balloon whisk (for eggs and sugar).

"To fold" is to incorporate a lighter aerated ingredient, such as beaten eggs, egg whites or cream, into a stiffer, heavier mixture. What you have to do is blend the ingredients without bursting the air bubbles. Folding beaten egg whites into a cake mixture is best done by hand with either a spatula or metal spoon. Always fold the light egg whites into the heavier mixture. Combine the ingredients by plunging the rubber spatula or metal spoon down through the centre to the bottom of the bowl; lift mixture and deposit on top.

Q: I tried making a mocha cake, but the base came out hard. Why was that? If I want to bake the cake in one tin instead of in layers, do I need to adjust the temperature and time?

A: One of the ingredients for the Mocha Cake is Ovalette, a stabiliser. When Ovalette is used, all liquid ingredients, in this case eggs and coconut milk, have to be well-chilled so that the cake will turn out light, moist and spongy. Use the eggs straight from the refrigerator. You can bake the mixture in a single layer and double the baking time.

Q: Why is it that when I bake a cake, it cracks in the centre?

A: When the top of a cake splits or cracks, it's usually because the oven was too hot or the cake was baked in too small a tin.

Q: When I fold in flour, should I use a spatula or a mixer?

A: Flour and other dry ingredients need to be thoroughly mixed into the cake batter so that they are evenly distributed. You can use either a thin plastic spatula or metal spoon. Cut through mixture and fold lightly to keep in as much air as possible. An electric mixer will give equally good results. Turn the mixer to its lowest speed and mix until there are no visible drifts of flour. Stop and scrape all around the bowl with a rubber spatula and turn on the mixer again until just blended.

Q: Why is the surface of my cake sticky? Is it because of too much sugar or because my oven is not hot enough?

A: A sticky cake surface is the result of baking at too low a temperature. Check the oven temperature with an oven thermometer and raise the oven thermostat setting to make up the difference.

Q: What is the simplest way to slice a cake into layers?

A: To cut a cake into layers, you will need a 25-30 cm serrated bread knife. If you cannot keep your hand steady enough to cut the cake into even layers, place the cake between two parallel pieces of wood taped to the tabletop. (The pieces of wood should be of equal thickness and longer than the diameter of the cake.) Rest the serrated knife on the two pieces of wood and slide it across the cake using a sawing motion.

Q: What do I do if a power failure occurs when I am in the middle of baking a cake? The last time it happened, I just left the cake in the oven until the power came back. The cake got burnt on one side and was a bit uncooked in the centre.

A: If the power supply is cut off, leave the cake in the oven and hope for the best. If the power returns within 5-10 minutes, you can continue baking. If it is longer than that, you will have to discard the cake.

Q: Whenever I bake a cake, it rises nicely but sinks back down when it cools. How can I stop this from happening?

A: *Either reduce the amount of leavening agents in the batter or allow the cake to bake longer (approximately five minutes or more) until thoroughly set and cooked through when tested with a wooden skewer.*

Q: I tried to make a rich butter cake and although it was tasty, it sank. What did I do wrong?

A: *A cake can sink in the middle for several reasons. Paying attention to the following details should prevent your cake from sinking.*

Oven heat should be accurate; a variance of 25°C can affect the success of the baking. Use an oven thermometer, which will quickly tell you whether the temperature in your oven agrees with the setting. If it doesn't, adjust your oven accordingly.

Bake cakes on the centre shelf of the oven, as this is generally the best position with the most stable temperature. Too hot an oven browns the cake too quickly on the outside leaving the centre uncooked.

Do not be tempted to open the oven door until at least half way through baking. The sudden cold draft can make the cake sink right before your eyes.

Cakes should be tested a couple of minutes before the end of the baking time to ensure that they are cooked. Use a long wooden cocktail stick or skewer and stick it gently into the centre of the cake. If it comes out clean, the cake is cooked. If it is coated with a gluey batter, it needs to bake for at least five or 10 minutes longer. Another sign that a cake is done is when the sides of the cake leave the sides of the pan. To further ensure that it is cooked, lightly touch the top of the cake. If it springs back leaving no imprint, the cake is ready.

Q: A favourite of mine is *kek lapis*. I have been quite successful making it but the only disappointment is the layers don't bake evenly; they come out dark in the centre and light at the edges. What could be the problem?

A: *The uneven colour of your* kek lapis *is due to uneven heat in your oven. You can try turning the cake pan every now and then to get a more even colour. You may have to begin baking the cake on the middle shelf and then, as the layers get higher, lower the cake tin to the bottom shelf to get it to cook through without burning. I am sure you will get it right after a few tries.*

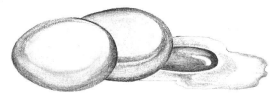

Canned Fruit

Q: How long can I keep canned fruit after opening the tin?

A: If you have to store canned fruit after opening it, remove the fruit from the can and keep it in a clean, airtight container in the refrigerator for up to three days.

Caraway Seeds

Q: What are caraway seeds?

A: Caraway seeds are tiny, crescent-shaped, brownish-black seeds with a strong aromatic flavour. They come from the caraway plant, which has feathery green leaves and pink-tinged white flowers and grows profusely in the Mediterranean region and in North Africa. The seeds are used in cakes, breads and cheeses.

Carob

Q: I recently came across some recipes using carob as a healthy alternative to chocolate, but I have not been able to find it at any of our supermarkets. Can I use chocolate instead?

A: You should be able to get carob powder at health food stores. If not, you can use cocoa powder as a substitute in most cake, cookie, dessert and confectionery recipes.

Cheesecakes

THE ALLURE OF CHEESECAKES

Cheesecakes, whether rich and creamy or light and smooth, are high on most people's list of favourite desserts. A well-made cheesecake can be the perfect ending to either a simple lunch or a grand dinner.

There are two basic types of cheesecakes: baked and unbaked. Baked cheesecakes are rich and creamy, while unbaked cheesecakes are light and smooth.

Making a cheesecake is quick and easy, but an accurate oven temperature is crucial for baked cheesecakes. They need low temperatures and, after baking, are best left to cool and settle undisturbed with the oven door open. Use a good rustproof fluted metal flan tin or a nonstick springform baking pan, so that the cheesecake can be easily slipped out onto a serving dish when cool.

For cheesecakes to be smooth, the cream cheese must be thoroughly blended. To achieve this, bring the cheese to room temperature and then beat it in an electric blender or food processor.

Using biscuit crumbs is a delightful short cut to making a crust for cheesecakes. Digestive biscuits or graham crackers can be crushed quickly in a food processor.

Both baked and unbaked cheesecakes should be covered and chilled for a couple of hours, preferably overnight, before eating. Serve topped with fresh whipped cream and fresh fruit or chocolate shavings or finished with a fruit glaze.

Leftover cheesecake should be tightly wrapped in plastic wrap, and kept in the refrigerator. Cheesecakes freeze well whether baked or unbaked. Freeze in airtight plastic containers.

Here are three recipes for baked cheesecakes, including a decadent chocolate cheesecake, and two recipes for unbaked cheesecakes.

Baked Cheesecake

CRUST

150 g	digestive biscuit crumbs
90 g	butter, melted

FILLING

500 g	cream cheese, at room temperature
60 g	castor sugar
3	eggs, separated
75 g	cream
30 g	plain flour, sifted
1 teaspoon	vanilla essence
	Pinch of salt

Grease well a 22 cm springform cake pan. Mix biscuit crumbs with melted butter and spread on base of cake pan, pressing mixture down with the back of a wooden spoon. Refrigerate while you prepare the filling.

Put cream cheese, half the sugar, egg yolks, cream, flour and vanilla essence into an electric blender or food processor and blend until smooth and creamy.

In a clean bowl, whisk egg whites with salt for two minutes until fluffy, then add remaining sugar gradually and beat just until stiff.

Carefully mix cream cheese mixture with beaten egg whites and pour onto chilled crust.

Bake in preheated 160°C oven for 50 minutes or until centre is quite firm. Turn off oven and leave cheesecake to cool inside oven with door ajar. Chill in refrigerator for two hours or overnight.

Baked Chocolate Cheesecake

CRUST

150 g	digestive biscuit crumbs
90 g	butter, melted

FILLING

120 g	dark chocolate, at room temperature
125 ml	cream
500 g	cream cheese, at room temperature
180 g	castor sugar
2 teaspoons	grated orange rind
	Pinch of salt
3	eggs
1 tablespoon	orange juice

TOPPING

Whipped cream
Chocolate shavings or chocolate curls

Grease well a 22 cm springform cake pan. Mix biscuit crumbs with melted butter and spread on base of cake pan, pressing mixture down with the back of a wooden spoon. Refrigerate while you prepare filling.

Put chocolate in double boiler and melt over gentle heat. Remove from heat and stir in cream until well blended. Set aside to cool.

Beat cream cheese until soft and fluffy. Add sugar, orange rind and salt and beat until well blended. Gradually beat in chocolate mixture until thoroughly combined. Beat in eggs one at a time, then orange juice.

Pour filling onto chilled crust. Bake in preheated 160°C oven for 50-60 minutes until centre is quite firm.

Turn off oven and leave cheesecake to cool inside oven with door ajar. Chill in refrigerator for two hours or overnight.

Decorate cake with whipped cream and chocolate shavings or curls.

Q: Recently I tasted a really great yoghurt cheesecake. It was light and creamy and had a thin layer of sponge cake on the bottom. Do you have the recipe?

A: Here is a recipe for a sponge-based cheesecake with a light and tangy filling. Remember to serve well-chilled straight from the refrigerator.

Lemon Yoghurt Cheesecake

SPONGE BASE

1	large egg, separated
30 g	castor sugar
30 g	self-raising flour, sifted,
	Pinch of salt
1 teaspoon	butter, combined with 1 tablespoon water

FILLING

500 g	cream cheese, at room temperature
2	eggs
125 g	castor sugar
1 cup	thick yoghurt
1¹/₂ tablespoons	lemon juice
1 teaspoon	grated lemon rind
1¹/₂ teaspoons	vanilla essence
1 tablespoon	sherry or fruit juice (pineapple or orange)
1 tablespoon	gelatine
¹/₂ cup	hot water

TOPPING

30-50 g	dark chocolate, melted

To Make Sponge Base
Whisk egg white until stiff. Gradually beat in sugar and then egg yolk. Fold in flour and salt. Stir in water and butter and mix well.

Pour batter into a 20 cm springform cake pan lined with greased greaseproof paper. Bake in preheated 175°C oven for 12-15 minutes. Cool on wire rack. Peel off paper lining.

Grease and line pan again and place cake in tin.

To Make Filling
Beat cream cheese until smooth.

In a separate bowl, whisk eggs and sugar until light and fluffy. Blend with softened cream cheese. Beat in yoghurt, lemon juice and rind, vanilla and sherry or fruit juice.

Sprinkle gelatine over hot water and stir until dissolved. Cool a little, then add to cream cheese mixture and mix well.

To Assemble Cake
Pour filling on top of sponge layer and refrigerate overnight. If desired, drizzle melted chocolate on top.

Q: I tasted a one-layer cheesecake at a hotel last year and have been looking out for the recipe without success. Most of the recipes I have come across are for two-layer cheesecakes. Can you help?

A: Here is the recipe for Baked Whole Cheesecake.

Baked Whole Cheesecake

650 g	cream cheese, at room temperature
150 g	butter, at room temperature
1¹/₃ cups	castor sugar
8 large	eggs, separated
1 teaspoon	freshly grated lemon rind
1 teaspoon	vanilla essence
1 teaspoon	almond essence
1 teaspoon	lemon essence
¹/₄ cup	cornflour, sifted
	Icing sugar for dusting

In an electric mixer, blend cream cheese and butter until light and fluffy. Add half the castor sugar, egg yolks, lemon rind and all essences.

Beat mixture on lowest speed for 2-3 minutes or until well combined. Add cornflour and beat mixture until just combined.

In a bowl with a cleaned beater, beat egg whites until they hold soft peaks. Beat in remaining castor sugar a little at a time until the egg whites hold stiff peaks. Fold into cream cheese mixture gently but thoroughly.

Pour batter into a greased 30 x 30 x 6 cm cake pan and put pan into larger baking pan. Add enough hot water to the baking pan to reach halfway up sides of cake pan.

Bake cake in middle of a preheated 175°C oven for 40-50 minutes or until top is golden brown and cake is set. Remove cake pan from water bath and let it cool completely in pan or on a rack. Chill for 10-12 hours or overnight.

To remove cheesecake from mould, dip cake pan in a large pan of hot water for 5 seconds. Invert a platter over it and invert cheesecake onto the platter. Dust top of cake with icing sugar.

Q: Recently I tried making a strawberry cheesecake, but it didn't set and had chewy bits of gelatine in it. What happened?

A: *Your problem was that the gelatine wasn't properly dissolved. Try putting the bowl of gelatine and water in a small pan over simmering water. Stir until gelatine dissolves completely into a clear gel.*

Q: When I baked a cheesecake, the top came out brown. Is it supposed to be like that or did the cake burn?

A: *Baked cheesecakes can have a light brown surface but shouldn't be burnt. If the top of the cheesecake browns too quickly, slide a tray on the top shelf halfway through baking time.*

Q: I love cheesecake and have tried out lots of recipes. Do you have a recipe for a strawberry cheesecake?

A: *This Fresh Strawberry Cheesecake is deliciously light, creamy and fruity. Strawberries can be quite expensive but they are low in calories and high in vitamins and minerals.*

Fresh Strawberry Cheesecake

CRUST

125 g	butter, melted
300 g	digestive biscuits, crushed
125 g	plain chocolate, melted (optional)

FILLING

250-300 g	fresh strawberries
250 g	cream cheese
60 g	castor sugar
200 g	thick strawberry yoghurt
15 g	powdered gelatine, combined with
	3 tablespoons boiling water
200 ml	whipping cream

Chocolate, melted
Strawberries for decoration

To Make the Crust
Mix the butter with the crushed biscuits and chocolate until well blended.

Lightly grease a 24 cm flan tin (preferably one with a detachable bottom). Press crumbs firmly and evenly onto bottom and sides of tin with the back of a metal spoon.

Chill while you are preparing filling.

To Make the Filling
In food processor, blend strawberries until puréed. Add cream cheese, sugar and yoghurt and blend well. Dissolve gelatine in hot water and add to strawberry mixture with processor switched on.

Whip the cream until soft peaks form. Pour strawberry mixture into cream and mix either by hand or on low speed.

To Assemble Cake
Pour filling into crust and smooth top with spatula. Chill for at least four hours or overnight.

Meanwhile, half dip the extra strawberries into the melted chocolate. Leave to set on greaseproof paper. When ready to serve, arrange strawberries around edge of cake.

Chicken

Q: I am only 17 but like to watch your TV programmes. I love to eat "Hot and Spicy" Kentucky Fried Chicken. Do you know how to make it?

A: Try this version of Spicy Fried Chicken, which is my own concoction. I'll let you be the judge of whether it is as good as KFC.

Spicy Fried Chicken

1 kg	chicken, cut into fairly large pieces, or 4 whole chicken thighs

SEASONING INGREDIENTS

1/2 tablespoon	sugar
1 teaspoon	salt
1 teaspoon	pepper
1 teaspoon	curry powder
1	egg, lightly beaten
2 tablespoons	water
2 tablespoons	self-raising flour

FLOUR COATING (COMBINED)

60 g	cornflakes, finely ground
240 g	self-raising flour
1/2 teaspoon	salt
1/2 teaspoon	pepper
1/4 teaspoon	bicarbonate of soda

BATTER (MIXED UNTIL SMOOTH)

1/2 tablespoon	curry powder
60 g	self-raising flour
3/4 cup	water or milk
1/4 teaspoon	pepper
1/4 teaspoon	salt

Oil for deep-frying

Marinate chicken pieces in seasoning ingredients for one to two hours.

Just before frying, coat chicken with flour mixture. Dip into batter and drop into hot oil.

Fry over high heat for one minute then reduce heat to moderate and cook until chicken is golden in colour. Drain well.

Q: I'd like to know how to roast a chicken. Should I wrap the chicken in tin foil to prevent splattering in the oven?

A: Try this recipe for Roast Chicken with Herbs. The chicken won't brown nicely if you cover it with foil; use foil only if the chicken starts to get too brown.

Roast Chicken with Herbs

1.6-1.8 kg	whole cleaned chicken
60 g	butter
2 teaspoons	salt, or to taste
1 teaspoon	pepper
1 teaspoon	prepared mustard
5 stalks	chives
2	leeks (green part only)
2	spring onions
3	coriander leaves
2-3 sprigs	parsley
1/2 teaspoon	dried tarragon
300 ml	fresh chicken stock or 150 ml each fresh chicken stock and white wine

Wash chicken thoroughly and dry well with paper towels. Using a butter knife, loosen the breast skin of the chicken, taking care not to puncture the skin. Spread some butter underneath it.

Rub outside of chicken with remaining butter and half of the salt and pepper. Rub remaining salt and pepper and mustard inside chicken. Push leeks and herbs into cavity of chicken. Tie drumstick ends together with a piece of string.

Place chicken in a roasting tin just big enough to hold the chicken. Pour in chicken stock to a depth of 1 cm.

Roast in preheated 200°C oven for 80-90 minutes, basting chicken every 20 minutes. Cover with foil once chicken is well browned. Test thickest part of thigh with a skewer; the chicken is cooked when juices run clear.

Skim fat off juices and make gravy. Season and thicken with a little cornflour mixture.

Serve with buttered new potatoes, broccoli and asparagus.

Q: I like chicken cooked with *kicap* (soya sauce), as served in Chinese restaurants. Could you provide the recipe?

A: I hope you like this recipe.

Soya Sauce Chicken

600 g	chicken, cut into bite-size pieces

SEASONING INGREDIENTS

2 teaspoons	light soya sauce
2 teaspoons	thick soya sauce
2 teaspoons	oyster sauce
1^1/2 teaspoons	sugar
^{1}/2 teaspoon	salt
^{1}/2 teaspoon	pepper
2 tablespoons	cooking oil
5 cm piece	young ginger, sliced
8	Chinese black mushrooms, soaked to soften
1 tablespoon	Chinese rice wine
1 cup	fresh chicken stock
2-3 stalks	spring onions, cut into 2^1/2 cm lengths
3 stalks	fresh coriander, cut into 2^1/2 cm lengths
2 teaspoons	cornflour, combined with 2 tablespoons water

Coriander leaves, for garnish

Marinate chicken in seasoning ingredients for at least 30 minutes.

Heat oil in a deep saucepan and put in ginger and Chinese mushrooms. Stir-fry for two minutes, then add marinated chicken. Cook, stirring frequently for five minutes or until chicken changes colour. Stir in Chinese rice wine and toss for two minutes.

Add stock and bring to a boil. On medium heat, simmer until chicken is cooked through and tender.

Add spring onions and coriander and stir in cornflour mixture until sauce thickens. Serve garnished with coriander leaves.

Q: I have tried many recipes from your books and they are terrific. May I have the recipe for Tandoori Chicken?

A: *Here is my version of Tandoori Chicken that I often make. I use a turbo broiler and the chicken turns out deliciously succulent. If you do not have a turbo broiler, you can bake the chicken in a very hot oven; use a wire rack over a tray to catch drips.*

Tandoori Chicken

5	whole chicken thighs

TANDOORI MIX

2 teaspoons	chilli powder
2 teaspoons	coriander (*ketumbar*) powder
2 teaspoons	*garam masala*, see recipe below
1/2 teaspoon	turmeric (*kunyit*) powder
4 cloves	garlic, ground for juice
2 1/2 cm piece	ginger, ground for juice
1	onion, ground for juice
2 tablespoons	yoghurt
3/4 tablespoon	lemon juice
1 teaspoon	salt
	A dash of red colouring, optional

Shallot oil

Skin chicken and make crisscross slashes all over both sides. Marinate in tandoori mix overnight in the refrigerator.

Brush chicken with shallot oil and pour half of the marinade over it. Roast in preheated turbo broiler at 190°C for 15 minutes on one side. Turn over, brush with shallot oil and cover with remaining marinade. Roast for another 15-20 minutes.

Serve with cucumber and tomato slices.

To Make Garam Masala

3 tablespoons	coriander powder
1 teaspoon	cumin (*jintan putih*) powder
1/2 teaspoon	black peppercorns
1/2 teaspoon	black fine cumin seeds
1/2 teaspoon	cinnamon powder
5	cardamoms, podded
5	cloves

Blend spices in electric grinder until very fine. Store in an airtight container.

Q: My children love chicken chops. I would be very grateful if you could provide me with a recipe.

A: *Here is a recipe which your children may find much to their taste.*

Chicken Chops with Onion and Mushroom Sauce

2 large whole chicken thighs, deboned

SEASONING INGREDIENTS 'A'
1/4 teaspoon salt
1/4 teaspoon pepper
1/2 teaspoon sugar
1 egg, lightly beaten

8-10 dried Chinese mushrooms, softened in water

SEASONING INGREDIENTS 'B'
1/4 teaspoon salt
1/4 teaspoon pepper
1/4 teaspoon sugar
1/2 teaspoon light soya sauce

150 g cream crackers, finely ground
4 tablespoons cooking oil
1 onion, sliced
1/2 tablespoon plain flour

SAUCE INGREDIENTS (COMBINED)
1 cup fresh chicken stock
1/2 teaspoon sugar
1/2 teaspoon salt
1 teaspoon light soya sauce
1 teaspoon thick soya sauce

60 g green peas
1 tomato, sliced
Lettuce leaves

Rinse and dry chicken with paper towels. Using blunt edge of a cleaver, bash underside of chicken to tenderise meat. Marinate in seasoning ingredients 'A' for 30 minutes.

Season mushrooms with seasoning ingredients 'B' for 15 minutes.

Just before frying, coat chops thoroughly with cream cracker crumbs. Heat oil in pan or wok until hot. Cook chops on both sides over low heat until golden-brown. Transfer chops onto a serving dish and keep warm. Strain the oil.

Reheat a clean pan with 1 1/2 tablespoons of the oil and stir-fry the onion over high heat until onion is transparent. Add mushrooms and stir-fry for 2 minutes.

Add flour and fry for 30 seconds. Pour in combined sauce ingredients and simmer until sauce is thick. Stir in peas.

Pour sauce over the chops. Garnish with tomato slices and lettuce leaves, and serve.

Children's Lunch Box

What can I give them today? It is a question I often have to answer. "My children prefer the deluge of junk food that's easily available in and out of school and I am at my wits' end," laments a mother of two primary schoolchildren. Coming up with nutritious alternatives can be quite a brain-racking task for mothers, especially when junk food is so attractively packaged for children.

Children can be fussy eaters. Like adults, they like variety. So put a little more effort into lunch box menus; plan unexpected little surprises and make lunch boxes a treat.

A plain cheese sandwich can be made more interesting with the addition of chopped raisins and sultanas. Instead of a ham sandwich, try shredded chicken with chopped asparagus, sweet corn with mayonnaise or chicken floss with cucumber slices. Break the boredom of sandwiches with potato cakes, cheese scones sandwiched with cucumber slices, chicken pies and sausage rolls.

Add a little temptation to lunch boxes, like muesli fruit bars or homemade cookies. You can also pack in fruit such as bananas, apples, slices of guava dipped in a little salt to prevent discoloration, or papaya chunks sprinkled with lime juice.

Pack an extra portion for your child to share with a friend. It makes snacking so much more fun, and will help your child learn how to share.

Here are a few recipes for snacks to tempt your children.

Cheese and Cornflake Crispies

240 g	butter
180 g	grated cheddar cheese
1/4 teaspoon	salt
1/2 teaspoon	pepper

SIFTED INGREDIENTS (COMBINED)

250 g	self-raising flour
1 teaspoon	baking powder

2 cups	crushed cornflakes
1	egg plus 1 egg yolk, beaten together with 1 tablespoon milk

Cream butter until soft. Add cheese, salt and pepper together with sifted dry ingredients and cornflakes.

Pour in beaten egg mixture and mix well.

Take small portions of the dough and roll out between two sheets of plastic wrap.

Cut with cookie cutters and place on greased baking sheets. Bake in moderate oven (175°C) for 15-20 minutes until golden.

Fruity Finger Buns

45 g	fresh yeast
1 teaspoon	sugar
1¹/₂ cups	warm milk
480 g	plain flour
¹/₂ teaspoon	nutmeg, optional
¹/₂ teaspoon	allspice, optional
¹/₂ teaspoon	salt, optional
90 g	castor sugar
60 g	butter, at room temperature
1	egg, beaten
150 g	mixed fruit

GLAZE

¹/₂	egg white, beaten
1 tablespoon	water

GLACÉ ICING (COMBINED)

60 g	icing sugar
1 teaspoon	hot water
¹/₄ teaspoon	vanilla essence

Lightly grease two 18 x 27 cm lamington tins.

Cream yeast with sugar, stir in milk, and allow to stand for 10 minutes until mixture turns frothy.

Sift flour and spices into a bowl, add salt and castor sugar. Rub in butter, add beaten egg, mixed fruit and yeast mixture. Beat well in electric mixer for two minutes.

Cover bowl with a cloth and allow to stand for 45 minutes or until it doubles in bulk.

Punch the dough down, turn onto floured board and knead until smooth. Cut into 16 equal pieces. Roll each piece into a finger shape and place in rows of four in prepared tins.

Leave to rise for 15-20 minutes. Bake in hot oven (210°C) for 20 minutes. Five minutes before removing rolls from the oven, brush tops of buns with egg glaze.

Remove from oven and cool on wire racks. Decorate with piped glacé icing.

Cheese Scones

240 g	self-raising flour
1 teaspoon	baking powder
1/2 teaspoon	pepper
1 teaspoon	salt
1	medium onion, finely chopped
60 g	grated cheddar cheese
45 g	butter, melted
3/4	cup milk

EGG GLAZE (BEATEN TOGETHER)

1	egg yolk
1 teaspoon	evaporated milk, or 1/2 teaspoon fresh milk

Sift flour, baking powder and pepper into a bowl. Add salt, onion and cheese and mix well. Add butter to milk and pour into dry ingredients. Mix to a soft dough with a spoon.

Turn out onto a lightly floured board and roll out dough on a sheet of plastic wrap until 2 cm thick. Cut into 5 cm rounds.

Place on lightly greased baking trays and bake in 205°C oven for 20 minutes until golden. Remove from oven and brush scones immediately with egg glaze.

Potato Chicken Scones

270 g	plain flour
3 teaspoons	baking powder
1 teaspoon	salt
90 g	butter
90 g	cooked chicken, chopped
2 sprigs	coriander leaves, chopped
180 g	mashed potatoes
1/4 cup	milk

EGG GLAZE (BEATEN TOGETHER):

1	egg yolk
1 teaspoon	evaporated milk, or 1/2 teaspoon fresh milk

Sift flour and baking powder and add salt. Rub in butter with a pastry knife or cutter until mixture resembles fine bread crumbs. Stir in chicken and coriander. Add potatoes and mix well. Stir in milk to make a soft dough.

Turn onto a lightly floured board and roll out on a sheet of plastic wrap until 11/2 cm thick. Cut into 5 cm triangles with a knife dipped in flour.

Place on tray lined with greased greaseproof paper. Bake in 200°C oven for 20-25 minutes until golden brown. Remove from oven and brush scones immediately with egg glaze.

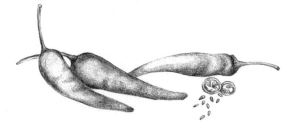

Chillies

Q: How much less chilli do I have to use to make a dish milder in flavour?

A: To reduce the pungency of chillies, it is better to remove the seeds rather than reducing the quantity of chillies. In curries, especially, it is the chillies that give a dish its appetising bright colour.

Q: We enjoy eating pickled green chillies with noodles. Could you please tell me how to pickle chillies?

A: The recipe for Pickled Green Chillies is as follows:

Pickled Green Chillies

1.15 litres	water
1 tablespoon	sugar
1 teaspoon	salt
300 g	green chillies, sliced thickly

VINEGAR SYRUP

250 ml	water
4 tablespoons	sugar
1¹/₂ teaspoons	salt
120 ml	vinegar

In a saucepan, bring water, sugar and salt to the boil. Put in sliced chillies and boil for 30 seconds over high heat.

Pour into colander to drain. Spread chillies out onto a tray to cool quickly and to prevent overcooking.

Put vinegar syrup ingredients into an enamel saucepan and boil for 3-4 minutes. Cool completely.

Put cooled chillies into a glass jar or container and pour in vinegar syrup to cover. Allow chillies to soak for at least one day.

Store in refrigerator.

Q: Where can I get chilli oil?

A: You can buy chilli oil at Chinese sundry shops or you can make your own. Soak about 20 dried chillies in hot water until soft. Drain and remove the stems. Place chillies in a blender with 8-10 tablespoons of cooking oil. Blend mixture until grainy and pour into a saucepan. Cook over low heat, stirring frequently for about 3 minutes. Strain the oil and keep in an airtight jar.

Chinese Steamed Cakes

Q: I am having trouble finding recipes in English for steamed cakes. Can you help?

A: Here is a recipe for the steamed white sugar cake called pak tong koh *in Cantonese. It is sweet, soft and spongy.*

White Sugar Cake (Pak Tong Koh)

300 g	rice flour, sifted
1¹/₂ cups	water
1 tablespoon	sugar
¹/₂ tablespoon	dry or easy-blend yeast
¹/₂ cup	warm water
1¹/₂ cups	water
300 g	sugar

Grease a 22 cm round cake pan with corn oil and set aside.

Put sifted rice flour into a mixing bowl together with 1 cup of water and knead into a soft dough. Remove 50 g of the dough and place in a small saucepan together with ¹/₂ cup water.

Stir with a wooden spoon until paste dissolves. Then cook over low heat, stirring constantly until a thick sticky paste forms. Let it cool, then add to uncooked dough. Mix well.

Stir sugar and yeast into warm water and add to flour mixture. Cover and proof for 1¹/₂ hours until foamy.

Meanwhile, put water and sugar in a saucepan and cook over low heat until sugar dissolves and liquid boils. Let syrup cool, then mix with rice flour mixture. Blend well. Let stand for 12 minutes.

Pour mixture into prepared pan. Steam over rapidly boiling water for 20 minutes. To prevent water vapour from dripping onto the cake, wipe cover and wrap with a large tea towel. (Make sure ends of towel don't hang down and catch fire.)

Cool and serve cut into diamond-shaped pieces.

Q: I tried making *fatt koh* and it turned out quite well except for its rough texture. Is it due to the brand of rice flour I used? I would also appreciate a recipe for *fatt koh* using yeast instead of Eno fruit salt.

A: The texture of the fatt koh *will be fine if you use finely ground pure rice flour. Here's a recipe using sweet potato and yeast. It is spongy and fine-textured. I like to eat it topped with grated young coconut mixed with a little salt.*

Sweet Potato Fatt Koh

50 g plain flour, sifted
2 teaspoons instant yeast
60 ml warm water

225 g steamed sweet potatoes
175 ml water

1 large egg
200 g castor sugar

SIFTED INGREDIENTS (COMBINED)
200 g plain flour
1 teaspoon baking powder

To make dough, put flour in a small bowl with yeast. Add water and mix thoroughly with a spoon. Cover bowl with tea towel and leave to rise for 10 minutes.

Liquidise steamed sweet potatoes with water until finely blended. Set aside.

In the bowl of an electric mixer, whisk egg together with sugar until light and fluffy. Add flour, baking powder and sweet potatoes and beat until well blended. Add dough and beat again to mix well. Cover and leave to rise for approximately one hour.

Spoon into 18 lightly greased *fatt koh* cups (7 cm diameter) and allow to rise again for 10 minutes. Steam over rapid boiling water for 20 minutes.

Q: Could you please share with me your *mah lai koh* recipe?

A: Here is a recipe for a springy, moist, steamed sponge cake. If you like, you can sprinkle on some dried melon seeds before steaming. Make sure there is enough water in the steamer to steam the cake for 40 minutes.

Steamed Sponge Cake (Mah Lai Koh)

150 g plain flour, sifted
35 g sugar
1 teaspoon easy-blend yeast
75 ml lukewarm water
230 g castor sugar

SIFTED INGREDIENTS (COMBINED)
35 g strong flour
20 g milk powder
35 g custard powder

5 large eggs, beaten with a fork
150 ml corn oil
2 teaspoons alkaline water
1 1/2 teaspoons baking powder, sifted with 3/4 teaspoon bicarbonate of soda

Sift flour into a bowl and stir in sugar and yeast. Add water and knead to form a smooth dough. Place dough in a covered plastic container and leave to proof for 12 hours or overnight.

Line a 20 cm diameter deep bamboo basket with greased greaseproof paper. Place dough in bowl of a food processor fitted with a dough blade. Put in sugar and turn on food processor to blend. Add sifted ingredients and continue to mix until blended.

Remove dough blade and attach a balloon whisk. Add beaten eggs and beat until well combined. Beat in oil, alkaline water and sifted baking powder and bicarbonate of soda. Leave batter to rise, covered, for 2 hours.

Pour into prepared basket. Steam over rapidly boiling water for 40-45 minutes.

Chinese New Year

SWEET DELIGHTS FOR THE NEW YEAR

Every festival has its traditional sweet delights which form an essential part of the celebration. Without them, the festivals would not be the same. For Chinese New Year, we have *nien koh, kuih kapit, kuih bangkit*, peanut cookies and many more.

One of my great favourites is *nien koh* or Sweet New Year Cake. It is a sweet, sticky, glutinous rice cake made as an offering to the Kitchen God (*Chow Kong*) to ensure that he will make "sweet" reports of the family's past year's conduct when he makes his annual trip to heaven.

Even if you do not follow this practice, you will enjoy eating *nien koh*, especially when it's homemade. Even though it is time consuming to pre-pare, it is worth the effort. The cake can be steamed and served in small lumps rolled in grated white coconut mixed with a pinch of salt. Or it can be cut into slices (plain or sandwiched with slices of yam or sweet potato), dipped in batter and fried in butter.

In addition to the recipe for *nien koh*, I am providing the recipe for the ever-popular peanut cookie (*fah sang peang*). The Chinese word *sang* means "alive" and eating peanut cookies is symbolic of making one alive and healthy.

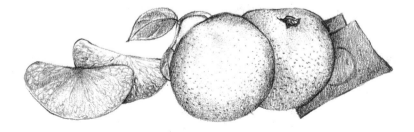

For health and wealth, I have also concocted two special biscuits: an eggless "good health" cookie (*kien hong peang*) and a "prosperity" cookie (*fatt choy peang*) made with *fatt choy*, which literally means "prosperity" in Chinese. It is a seaweed resembling a mass of fine black hair and is also known as hair vegetable or black moss.

Sweet New Year Cake (Nien Koh)

300 g   glutinous rice flour
1 cup   water
300 g   sugar
      Banana leaves, cut into 6 cm strips and scalded

Line two 9 cm round cake tins (pineapple ring or desiccated coconut tins make excellent substitutes) with banana leaves. The banana leaves should be 5 cm higher than the cake tins. Fold leaves over edge of cake tin and tie with a piece of string or a rubber band.

Sift glutinous rice flour into a mixing bowl. Pour in water and mix well. Add sugar and mix with a wooden spoon until sugar completely dissolves.

Pour batter into prepared tins and place in a steamer. Steam over rapidly boiling water for 1 hour.

Remove cover. Dip a spoon into some cooking oil and lightly oil and smooth cake surface with back of spoon. Cover tins with a layer of greaseproof paper and foil. Reduce heat to moderate and steam for 9 hours. Maintain water level in the steamer by regularly adding boiling water.

When done, cake will turn a caramel brown. Leave in tin to cool for 24 hours before removing.

Peanut Cookies (Fah Sang Peang)

350 g   shelled roasted peanuts
270 g   castor sugar
1 teaspoon   vanilla essence
350 g   plain flour, sifted
1 cup   good quality groundnut oil
      Glacé cherries, cut into 1/4 cm pieces, for decoration

EGG GLAZE *(COMBINED AND BEATEN TOGETHER)*
2 egg yolks
2 teaspoons milk

Blend peanuts in an electric blender until fine and crumbly.

In a large mixing bowl, combine peanuts, sugar, vanilla and flour. Make a well in the centre and pour in groundnut oil. Mix well with a wooden spoon. Lightly run through the mixture with fingers to bind into a crumbly dough.

Shape into balls about the size of a cherry. Make a shallow dent in each ball with the pointed end of a chopstick. Press a piece of cherry into each dent and brush cookies well with egg glaze.

Bake in preheated 175°C oven for 20-25 minutes or until golden.

Prosperity Cookies (Fatt Choy Peang)

10 g *fatt choy* (black moss)

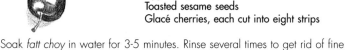

SIFTED INGREDIENTS *(COMBINED)*
180 g self-raising flour
1 teaspoon baking powder
60 g custard powder

125 g ground almonds
125 g desiccated coconut
200 g castor sugar
240 g butter, cold and cut into cubes
1 small egg, beaten

1 egg white, beaten
Toasted sesame seeds
Glacé cherries, each cut into eight strips

Soak *fatt choy* in water for 3-5 minutes. Rinse several times to get rid of fine sand particles. Strain and press out water, and dry in the sun or in an oven for about 30 minutes. Chop and set aside.

Tip sifted ingredients into a food processor. Add *fatt choy*, ground almonds, desiccated coconut and castor sugar. Turn on food processor for 5 seconds. Put in butter and beaten egg and turn on processor again for 10-12 seconds until mixture clings together. Turn out onto a plastic bag or bowl. Cover with plastic wrap and chill for 30 minutes to one hour.

Roll out dough, one-third at a time, between two sheets of plastic wrap to a thickness of 5 mm. Cut into rounds with a 5 cm petal-shape cookie cutter. Place rounds on baking trays lined with nonstick baking paper. Brush cookies with beaten egg white, sprinkle surface generously with sesame seeds and press a cherry strip into the centre of each cookie.

Bake in preheated 175°C oven for 20 minutes or until golden brown. Cool on wire racks before storing in airtight containers.

Makes approximately 95 cookies.

Good Health Cookies (Kien Hong Peang)

120 g	soft margarine
110 g	castor sugar
	Grated rind of 1 orange or lemon
50 g	thick yoghurt
1/2 teaspoon	lemon essence

SIFTED INGREDIENTS (COMBINED)

150 g	self-raising flour
1/2 teaspoon	baking powder
1/4 teaspoon	bicarbonate of soda

	Pinch of salt
100 g	soft dried longans, chopped finely, or sultanas
60 g	roasted cashew nuts, chopped

Line baking trays with nonstick baking paper.

In the bowl of an electric mixer, using a beater on medium speed, cream margarine and sugar until light and creamy. Beat in orange or lemon rind, yoghurt and lemon essence until well combined.

Stir in sifted ingredients and salt, and mix until well blended. Add dried longans (or sultanas) and cashew nuts and mix well.

Using 2 teaspoons, shape and drop rounded teaspoonfuls of the mixture onto prepared trays.

Bake in preheated 190°C oven for 15 minutes or until golden brown. Cool on tray for one minute before transferring onto wire racks to cool completely.

Makes approximately 50 cookies.

COOKING UP A FUN REUNION DINNER

On New Year's Eve, most Chinese families get together for a reunion dinner to usher in the new year. Often, no effort is spared to lay out an elaborate feast of traditional specialities. But considerable time and work are required in the preparation of such a meal.

With the hustle and bustle of modern living, this can be tiring, so I am sure there are many out there just dreading the thought of preparing the meal. I would like to suggest an interesting change: tabletop cooking. It is simple, fast and requires little effort. The food, eaten hot off the pan, is very tasty. All you need is an electric tabletop griddle which you can buy in any big department store. No extensive washing is required as the griddle can just be wiped clean with paper towels after each course is cooked and served.

Preparation is easy and there is no need for anyone to toil frantically in a hot kitchen and end up exhausted before the meal begins. The food can even be prepared and frozen days ahead and then thawed on the day of the dinner.

Fried Garlic Pork

500 g   lean pork fillet, sliced

SEASONING INGREDIENTS
1 1/2 tablespoons   light soya sauce
1/2 teaspoon   five-spice powder
1/2 teaspoon   black pepper powder
1/2 teaspoon   sugar
1 teaspoon   black peppercorns, lightly crushed
1 tablespoon   chilli oil

FOR THE GRIDDLE:
1 tablespoon   shallot oil
12 cloves   garlic, sliced

Season pork with seasoning ingredients. Heat shallot oil and fry garlic until lightly browned. Add seasoned pork and stir-fry over high heat for 8-10 minutes or until pork is cooked.

Lettuce in Oyster Sauce

300 g   lettuce, washed and drained well

SAUCE INGREDIENTS (COMBINED)
1 dessertspoon   light soya sauce
1 dessertspoon   oyster sauce
1/4 teaspoon   pepper
1/2 teaspoon   salt

FOR THE GRIDDLE:
1 1/2 tablespoons   vegetable cooking oil
3   shallots, sliced

Heat oil and fry shallots until light and golden brown. Put in lettuce and cover pan for 30 seconds. Remove cover and pour in sauce ingredients. Toss well.

Snow Pea Shoots with Garlic

300 g   snow pea shoots, rinsed and drained

FOR THE GRIDDLE:
2 tablespoons   shallot oil
5-6 cloves   garlic, minced
1/2 tablespoon   light soya sauce
1/2 teaspoon   sesame oil

Heat shallot oil and lightly brown garlic. Put in snow pea shoots, soya sauce and sesame oil and stir-fry over high heat for 1 minute.

Variation: other quick-frying vegetables that can be used are sweet pea pods, water convolvulus (*kangkung*), spinach and bean sprouts.

Beef

500 g beef, thinly sliced

SEASONING INGREDIENTS
1 teaspoon sugar
1 teaspoon pepper
1/2 teaspoon salt
2 teaspoons Worcestershire sauce
2 teaspoons French mustard
1 teaspoon Dijon mustard
2 teaspoons lemon juice
1 tablespoon brandy or sherry
1 tablespoon chopped parsley, spring onions or coriander leaves

FOR THE GRIDDLE:
1 1/2 tablespoons oil or 50 g butter
3 cloves garlic, minced

Season beef with seasoning ingredients.

Heat oil or butter and lightly brown garlic. Put in beef and stir-fry on high heat for 6-8 minutes or until cooked.

Chicken

500 g boneless chicken meat, cut into 2 cm pieces

SEASONING INGREDIENTS
2 teaspoons *sar char* sauce (Taiwanese barbecue sauce)
1 teaspoon ginger juice
1 teaspoon sugar
1/2 teaspoon pepper
1/2 teaspoon salt
1 teaspoon chilli powder

FOR THE GRIDDLE:
1 tablespoon oil
1/2 onion, sliced
6 cloves garlic, chopped
2 stalks spring onion, chopped

Season chicken with seasoning ingredients.

Heat oil and cook onion until soft. Add garlic and then the chicken. Stir-fry for 8-10 minutes or until cooked, and sprinkle spring onions on top.

Prawns

600 g medium-large prawns, eyes and feelers trimmed

2 teaspoons	light soya sauce
1/2 teaspoon	black pepper
1/2 teaspoon	salt
1 teaspoon	sugar
	Juice of 1 large lime
10	chilli padi, finely chopped
1 clove	garlic, finely chopped
1	shallot, finely chopped
2 cm piece	ginger, finely chopped
8	mint leaves, finely sliced
12	basil leaves (*selasih*), finely sliced
8	*daun limau perut*, finely sliced

FOR THE GRIDDLE:

1 1/2 tablespoons	shallot oil
4 cloves	garlic, finely minced

Marinate prawns in seasoning ingredients.

Heat oil and lightly brown garlic. Put in marinated prawns and stir-fry on high heat until prawns are cooked through.

Chilli Chicken

500-600 g	boneless chicken, sliced

SEASONING INGREDIENTS

1 dessertspoon	light soya sauce
1 dessertspoon	oyster sauce
1 teaspoon	ginger juice
1/4 teaspoon	salt
1 tablespoon	water
3 level teaspoons	cornflour

FOR THE GRIDDLE:

1 1/2 tablespoons	shallot oil
3 cloves	garlic
5	dried chillies, rinsed and cut into 3 pieces each

Season chicken with seasoning ingredients.

Heat shallot oil and lightly brown garlic. Put in chillies and toss for 30 seconds. Add chicken and stir-fry for 8 minutes or until cooked.

Cuttlefish

300 g	medium-small cuttlefish, cut into 2 1/2 cm pieces

SEASONING INGREDIENTS

1/2 teaspoon	salt
1/2 teaspoon	sugar
1/4 teaspoon	pepper

1 teaspoon	ginger juice
2 teaspoons	curry powder
	Juice of half a big lime
1 sprig	curry leaves

FOR THE GRIDDLE:

1 tablespoon	shallot oil
2 cloves	garlic

Season cuttlefish with seasoning ingredients.

Heat oil and lightly brown garlic. Stir-fry cuttlefish over high heat for 5 minutes or until cooked.

Chinese Wine

Q: What is Chinese cooking wine and where can I obtain it?

A: *Chinese cooking wine is rice wine and is easily available at most provision stores. A fine quality Chinese rice wine is Shao Hsing Hua Tiau Wine. It is light brown, and just a small amount will enhance the flavour of any dish.*

Chocolate

Q: Recently I bought a tin of cocoa thinking that I could make a nice cup of hot chocolate, but it was horribly bitter, not creamy and smooth. Can you give me a recipe?

A: *Here's a recipe for a lovely hot chocolate drink.*

Frothy Hot Chocolate

1 tablespoon	cocoa powder
500 ml	hot milk
2 tablespoons	castor sugar
1/4 teaspoon	vanilla essence
500 ml	cold milk

Blend cocoa powder with hot milk and bring to a gentle boil. Add castor sugar and vanilla essence. Stir well to dissolve sugar.

Pour into a blender, add cold milk and whisk until frothy. Serve hot or cold.

Q: How do I make a chocolate cake that is very moist but not soggy in the middle?

A: *Here is a recipe for a light and moist chocolate cake. It is absolutely delightful served plain with coffee. You can also turn it into a scrumptious dessert cake by sandwiching and topping it with chocolate icing.*

Moist Chocolate Cake

180 g   butter
360 g   castor sugar
3   large eggs
1 teaspoon   instant coffee granules
1 tablespoon   hot water
1 tablespoon   brandy
1 teaspoon   vanilla essence
1   cup water

SIFTED INGREDIENTS (COMBINED)
240 g   plain flour
75 g   cocoa powder
1 teaspoon   baking powder
1 teaspoon   bicarbonate of soda
1/2 teaspoon   salt

Grease sides and line base of a 35 x 11 cm loaf pan or a 20 cm square cake tin with greased greaseproof paper.

Cream butter and castor sugar together until light and fluffy. Add eggs, one at a time, beating well.

Dissolve coffee granules in hot water. Stir in brandy and vanilla. Add to remaining water and stir.

Stir coffee mixture alternately with sifted dry ingredients, a third at a time, into the butter mixture. Blend well and turn into prepared tin.

Bake in preheated 175°C oven for 55-60 minutes. Leave cake to cool in the tin for 20-30 minutes, then turn out onto a wire rack to cool completely.

Q: How do you make chocolate cake look really dark? Is it by putting in more chocolate or by using colouring?

A: To make a really dark chocolate cake, use good quality plain chocolate, which is darker than milk chocolate. You can also use commercial chocolate paste or chocolate emulco, but I always prefer natural ingredients for home baking.

Q: When I make chocolate cakes, they tend to crumble when I cut them. How can I overcome this?

A: A crumbly cake can be the result of many things: there might have been too much flour or too little liquid in the batter; the butter might not have been properly creamed with the sugar; too much raising agent might have been added; and the cake might have been baked for too long or at too high a temperature.

Q: Will pouring hot cocoa into batter for chocolate cake affect the baking process?

A: Yes, if you pour hot cocoa, or any hot liquid, into cake batter you will partially cook the eggs and make the cake very dense.

Q: Can you give me a recipe for Black Forest Cake?

A: Black Forest Cake has enjoyed great popularity and there are many versions of it. This recipe is a sponge-cake version held together with lots of cream and black cherries.

Black Forest Gateau

4	eggs
110 g	castor sugar
60 g	melted butter, cooled
85 g	plain flour, sifted
30 g	cocoa, sifted
275 ml	double or whipping cream
1 tablespoon	castor sugar
1 can	dark black cherries
1-2 tablespoons	Kirsch or rum
50 g	plain chocolate

Line base of a 20 cm cake tin with greased greaseproof paper. Grease the sides with margarine, and dust with a little flour. Tip out any excess.

In the bowl of an electric mixer, whisk eggs and sugar until very light and fluffy, about 5 minutes. The mixture is ready when it leaves a ribbon trail when the whisk is lifted. Whisk in butter quickly. If you do this too slowly, the cake will collapse.

Fold in sifted flour and cocoa powder with a large metal spoon. Pour into prepared pan. Tap pan lightly on table top to break large air bubbles.

Bake in preheated 190°C oven for 30-35 minutes. Leave to cool in tin for 10 minutes before turning out onto a wire rack to cool completely. Split cake into thin rounds.

Whip cream in a chilled bowl with castor sugar until it stands in soft peaks and has a spreadable consistency.

Drain can of cherries and combine two tablespoons of syrup with Kirsch or rum. Sprinkle syrup over cake layers and sandwich layers with cream and cherries. Spread with cream.

Cover entire cake with remaining cream using a palette knife. Finish off by piping large star rosettes decoratively on top and arranging whole cherries around the edge. Grate chocolate and sprinkle all over cake. Keep cake refrigerated.

Q: I would like to know why I can never get my chocolate curls right for my Black Forest Cake. They either collapse or crack. I melt cooking chocolate in a double boiler, pour it out onto a glass tray and scrape it with a knife. The chocolate doesn't set, even after an hour. I try leaving it in the fridge for a while, but it stays soft.

A: Melting chocolate for cooking or for decoration requires much care and patience. Use good quality cooking or dark chocolate rather than milk chocolate which has a higher fat content and tends to burn more easily.

When melting chocolate either for spreading, piping or making chocolate curls, the golden rule to remember is never to overheat the chocolate. It should never be melted over direct heat. Break the chocolate into small pieces into a heatproof bowl. Place bowl over a pan of hot water. The base of the bowl should not touch the hot water. Leave chocolate to stand, stirring occasionally, until it turns soft and smooth.

To make curls, spread melted chocolate over a cold smooth surface, such as ceramic tile, granite or marble. Leave until cold and set, but do not chill. Holding a large sharp knife flat against the chocolate, scrape gently over the surface to form curls. Refrigerate until firm enough to handle.

Q: I am in my late 70s and love baking cakes for my children and grandchildren. My son has asked me to bake a chocolate fudge cake for my grandson's birthday. Could you please give me a recipe?

A: Few children can resist the temptation of a rich chocolate fudge cake. This recipe makes a great birthday cake.

Rich Chocolate Fudge Cake with Chocolate Cream

125 g	plain dark chocolate
5 tablespoons	boiling water
180 g	butter, at room temperature
175 g	light brown sugar
3	eggs
1 tablespoon	vanilla essence
200 g	self-raising flour, sifted together with
30 g	cocoa powder

FILLING

180 g	butter, at room temperature
300 g	icing sugar, sifted
1 level teaspoon	cocoa powder
3 tablespoons	hot water
2 teaspoons	instant coffee

ICING

180 g	plain chocolate, broken into pieces
150 ml	whipping cream or double cream

Grease sides and line base of two 20 cm round cake tins with greased greaseproof paper.

Break chocolate into a deep bowl, add boiling water and leave to melt.

Cream butter and sugar together until light and fluffy. Add eggs, one at a time, beating well. Mix vanilla essence with melted chocolate to make a smooth paste, then stir into butter mixture. Fold in sifted flour and cocoa. Divide mixture equally between tins and smooth tops.

Bake in the centre of a preheated 175°C oven for 25 minutes or until firm and springy to the touch. Leave in tins to cool for 15 minutes before turning out onto wire racks to cool completely. When cold, slice each cake in half horizontally to make four layers.

To Make Filling
Cream butter and icing sugar together. For chocolate filling, place $1/3$ of the mixture into a small bowl. Beat in cocoa powder mixed with 1 tablespoon of hot water. For coffee filling, mix coffee with remaining hot water, then blend with remaining butter and sugar mixture.

Sandwich cakes together with alternating layers of coffee and chocolate filling.

To Make Icing
Melt chocolate and cream in a bowl over simmering water. Stir until chocolate melts. Let mixture cool and thicken a little, then pour over cake, spreading with a palette knife to cover the cake. Leave to set.

Decorate and pipe with plain butter cream, if desired.

Christmas

BAKING CHRISTMAS TREATS

Like any other festivity, Christmas would not be Christmas without the sweet treats and special dinner for family and friends. If you have to do all this, don't leave the planning and preparations till the last minute. Start collecting ideas and getting organised early.

Many things can be prepared far in advance. Cookies keep well in airtight containers. Mince pies can be made three weeks ahead and simply require a few minutes for final assembly before serving. You can make the Christmas cake and pudding two weeks before Christmas; this will give them time to mature and develop their flavour. The cake is then ready for coating with marzipan and icing a week before Christmas. Wrap the pudding well in foil and freeze; steam again for two to three hours on the day of the dinner.

Christmas Spice Cookies

120 g butter
75 g white vegetable shortening
120 g castor sugar
1 egg

SIFTED INGREDIENTS (COMBINED)
240 g plain flour
1/2 teaspoon ground cinnamon
1/2 teaspoon allspice

90 g chopped walnuts

1/2 egg white, beaten, for glazing
Coarsely chopped walnuts or almond halves for decoration

Line cookie trays with greased greaseproof paper. Cream butter and shortening with castor sugar until light and fluffy and beat in egg until combined. Stir in sifted ingredients and mix in walnuts. Refrigerate mixture for one hour or until it no longer feels sticky.

Shape into 2 cm balls. Flatten lightly with the bottom of a glass wrapped in a cloth.

Brush each cookie with beaten egg white and top with a piece of nut. Bake in 190°C oven for 15 minutes or until light golden. Cool on wire racks and store in airtight containers.

Starry Biscuits

225 g self-raising flour
1 1/2 teaspoons ground mixed spice
1 teaspoon baking powder
125 g butter
125 g brown sugar
1 small egg, lightly beaten
A little milk

225 g icing sugar, sifted
2-3 tablespoons orange juice
Silver balls

Sift flour, mixed spice and baking powder into a bowl. Rub in butter with a pastry cutter until mixture resembles fine breadcrumbs. Stir in sugar. Add egg and enough milk to make a stiff dough. Knead until smooth. Wrap in polythene bag and chill for one hour.

Roll out dough, a little at a time, to a thickness of 6 mm. Stamp out large star shapes with a star cookie cutter.

Place on greased baking trays and bake in preheated 190°C oven for 15 minutes or until golden. Allow to cool a little.

Put icing sugar into a bowl and beat in orange juice until smooth. Put into a piping bag fitted with a plain writing nozzle. Decorate cookies as desired and top with silver balls. Leave to dry.

Fruity Christmas Cake

450 g	raisins
450 g	sultanas
60 g	mixed peel, finely chopped
45 g	preserved stem ginger, chopped
225 g	glacé cherries, quartered
180 g	blanched almonds, chopped
8 tablespoons	brandy

420 g	butter or margarine
390 g	dark brown sugar
8	eggs

SIFTED INGREDIENTS (COMBINED)

450 g	plain flour, sifted
1 teaspoon	ground cinnamon
1/2 teaspoon	grated nutmeg
1 teaspoon	ground mixed spice

	Sieved apricot jam, for glazing cake
1.2 kg	marzipan

ROYAL ICING

3	egg whites
625 g	icing sugar, sifted
3-4 teaspoons	lemon juice
1 1/2 teaspoons	glycerine

Wash fruit well, drain thoroughly and dry on a tea-towel or in the sun for a couple of hours. Stir in chopped almonds and 3 tablespoons of brandy. Leave for 4 hours or overnight.

Line a 23-25 cm square cake tin with greased greaseproof paper and wrap outside of tin with brown paper.

Cream butter and sugar until pale and light. Add eggs, one at a time, beating well after each addition. Fold in sifted ingredients, followed by fruit and remaining brandy. Mix well and turn into prepared tin.

Bake in preheated 150°C oven for 3-4 hours or until a skewer inserted in centre of cake comes out clean.

Leave cake to cool in tin, then turn out, remove lining paper and wrap in fresh greaseproof paper and foil.

Store in refrigerator for at least 7-10 days to allow cake to mature.

To Cover Cake with Marzipan
Heat a little apricot jam in a saucepan until it starts to boil. Pass through a sieve.

Remove lining paper from cake and place upside down on cake board (the base of the cake is flat and smoother for icing). Brush top and sides of cake with sieved apricot jam.

Roll out marzipan between two sheets of plastic wrap until 40 cm square or large enough to cover cake. (Check for size by measuring length up one side of cake, across top and down other side.)

Peel off bottom sheet of plastic wrap and centre marzipan over cake, allowing edge furthest away to just touch board. Carefully peel off top sheet of plastic. Press down top, sides and corners of marzipan. Trim off excess.

To Make Royal Icing

Whisk egg whites until slightly frothy. Beat in a quarter of the icing sugar, then continue adding sugar gradually, beating well after each addition, until about a quarter is left.

Add lemon juice and continue beating for about 10 minutes or until icing is smooth, glossy and white. Add remaining sugar and glycerine and beat until icing reaches required consistency. Do not over-beat. Cover the bowl with a damp cloth while decorating the cake.

Spread icing over top and sides of cake and spread roughly with a palette knife. Draw the icing up in peaks.

Arrange Christmas decorations on top, if desired. Colour remaining icing with a few drops of red colouring and fill a piping bag fitted with a writing nozzle. Pipe "Merry Christmas" greeting across surface. Attach small, red bows on sides, if desired.

SERVING UP A CHRISTMAS TRADITION

Christmas would not be the same without a deliciously rich and moist pudding. The traditional Christmas pudding is dark and rich with dried fruit and nuts, but I am also giving a recipe for a pudding made with sago, which gives it a springy bite.

Puddings are not as difficult to put together as most people imagine. Once all the ingredients are assembled, it takes only a few minutes to mix the pudding. The steaming takes five or six hours, but the only attention required during this time is to occasionally top up the steamer with boiling water.

For a successful pudding, take note of the following:

If using liquor to plump up the fruits, make sure the pudding mixture is left to stand overnight.

Before steaming, cover the pudding dish with either greaseproof paper or foil and tie it securely to the pudding bowl to prevent water from seeping in.

If using a saucepan, place a trivet or wire rack in the pan so that the bowl doesn't touch the heat and crack.

Always top up the steamer with boiling water; adding cold water will cause a sudden drop in temperature, resulting in a heavy pudding.

The lid of the steamer must fit well to prevent too much steam from escaping and drying out the pudding too quickly.

Cooked puddings should be kept in the fridge. To serve, reheat by steaming for an hour.

You can make your pudding ahead of time to mature, but even if you make it at the last minute, it will still taste great.

Christmas Pudding

180 g	large seedless raisins
125 g	currants
125 g	sultanas
125 g	grated carrots
125 g	fresh breadcrumbs
50 g	plain flour, sifted
125 g	chilled or frozen butter, grated
125 g	soft dark brown sugar
30 g	toasted flaked almonds
1/2 teaspoon	ground mixed spice
	Grated rind of 1 lemon
3 tablespoons	thick-cut marmalade
3	eggs, beaten
50 ml	brandy or whisky

Butter a 1.1 litre pudding dish and set aside.

Mix all ingredients until thoroughly combined. Spoon into pudding dish and level the top.

Cut a piece of greaseproof paper and foil and place on pudding dish, paper side down. Tie a string around the rim of the dish to secure the paper and foil.

Steam over gentle boiling water for 4-5 hours.

To serve, turn pudding into a serving dish. Warm a few tablespoons of brandy and pour over pudding. Light with a match.

Serve with whipped cream or custard sauce.

Custard Sauce

600 ml	milk
1 heaped tablespoon	custard powder
3	egg yolks
	Castor sugar to taste
1 tablespoon	brandy

Reserve 2 tablespoons of the milk and bring the remainder to the boil.

Mix custard powder and egg yolks into the 2 tablespoons of cold milk and combine into a smooth paste.

Stir in boiling milk and return custard to saucepan. Stir in sugar and brandy to taste and simmer, stirring, for no longer than 30 seconds to thicken.

Serve sauce alongside Christmas pudding.

Advance Preparation
Make a day ahead. Before serving, warm through in a microwave oven, or reheat over a saucepan of simmering water.

Steamed Sago Pudding

130 g	sago, rinsed and drained
500 ml	milk
320 g	sultanas, chopped
170 g	raisins, chopped
175 g	stale breadcrumbs
300 g	brown sugar

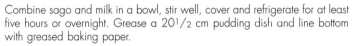

SIFTED INGREDIENTS (COMBINED)

2 tablespoons (30 g)	plain flour
2 teaspoons	bicarbonate of soda

1 teaspoon	vanilla essence
2	large eggs, beaten
60 g	melted butter

Combine sago and milk in a bowl, stir well, cover and refrigerate for at least five hours or overnight. Grease a 20½ cm pudding dish and line bottom with greased baking paper.

Place sago mixture in a nonstick pan and stir constantly over low heat for about 10-15 minutes or until sago is clear.

Combine sago mixture with remaining ingredients in a large bowl and mix well. Spoon into prepared pudding dish. Cover with baking paper and then foil, and cover with lid or secure with a piece of string. Fold surplus foil around dish to form a good seal.

Place pudding dish onto a 2 cm high rack in a large pan or steamer. Pour enough boiling water to come halfway up side of steamer. Cover steamer and steam pudding for three hours. Replenish steamer with boiling water every hour or as necessary.

Stand for 15-20 minutes before turning pudding out. Serve hot or cold, either plain or with cream.

MINCE PIES

Mince pies, a must for Christmas, are made with rich shortcrust or almond pastry. Despite the name, there is no meat in mincemeat. A typical recipe is a fruity mix of dried and candied fruit, apples and nuts steeped in rum, brandy or Madeira.

For best results, the mincemeat filling should be made about a month before making the pies. This will allow the flavours to mature. Store mince-meat in sterilised jam jars in the refrigerator. (To sterilise jars, wash them in hot, soapy water, then rinse well and dry in the oven.)

If you cannot find the time to make mincemeat, buy jars of it from the supermarket. You can improve the flavour by adding the grated rind of half an orange or lemon, one peeled and chopped cooking apple and two tablespoons of brandy or rum to each 450 g jar.

Mince Tarts

275 g	plain flour
30 g	ground almonds
175 g	unsalted butter
	Grated rind of 1 orange
4-5 tablespoons	orange juice
500 g	homemade mincemeat (see below)
1	egg white, beaten, for glaze
300 ml	whipping cream
50 g	icing sugar plus extra for dusting

FRUITY MINCEMEAT

180 g	green apples, peeled, cored and finely chopped
	Juice and grated rind of half a lemon
75 g	dates, finely chopped
120 g	seedless raisins, chopped
150 g	dried apricots, finely chopped
180 g	sultanas, finely chopped
40 g	glacé cherries, rinsed and chopped
30 g	stem ginger, drained and chopped
60 g	cashew nuts, roasted and finely chopped
90 g	shredded vegetable suet
150 g	soft dark brown sugar
$1/2$ teaspoon	ground cinnamon
$1/2$ teaspoon	mixed spice
$1/4$ teaspoon	ground mace
$1 1/2$ tablespoons	dark rum

To Make Fruity Mincemeat

Put apples and lemon juice in a large bowl and mix thoroughly to prevent apples from browning. Stir in dried fruit, ginger and cashew nuts and mix well. Add suet, sugar, spices and rum and mix well. Cover bowl tightly with plastic wrap and refrigerate overnight.

To Make Tarts

Heat oven to 200°C and grease two 12-cup patty tins.

Sift flour into a mixing bowl and stir in ground almonds. Rub in butter until mixture resembles breadcrumbs. Stir in orange rind. Add enough of the orange juice to mix to a soft but not-too-sticky dough. Place dough in a polythene bag and chill in the refrigerator for 30 minutes.

Roll out two-thirds of the dough on a lightly floured surface until 3 mm thick. Using a 9 cm fluted cutter, stamp out 24 circles and line prepared tins. Place a tablespoon of the mincemeat into each pastry case.

Bake for 20-25 minutes until pastry is golden brown.

Meanwhile, roll out remaining pastry as before and, using a 5 cm star-shaped cutter, stamp out 24 pieces. Brush with beaten egg white and bake for 8-10 minutes or until golden brown. Remove pies from tins. Cool pies and stars on wire racks.

Whip cream until soft peaks form. Fill piping bag attached with a star nozzle and pipe a rosette of cream onto each cooled tartlet. Top with a pastry star. Dust with icing sugar and serve.

To Store Mince Tarts
Open-freeze cooked pastry stars and tarts separately. When frozen solid, pack into airtight containers.

To thaw, leave in the refrigerator for 3 hours. Heat oven to 200°C and bake tarts and stars between two baking sheets until they are warmed through (about 8-10 minutes for tarts and 2 minutes for stars). When cool, assemble tarts.

Mince Pies

PASTRY

240 g	plain flour
	Pinch of salt
150 g	butter, cut into small pieces
15 g	castor sugar
15 g	ground almonds
1 to 2 tablespoons	cold water

400 g	mincemeat
	Milk or beaten egg to glaze
	Brown sugar to decorate
	Single or double cream

Sift flour and salt into a bowl. Rub in butter with fingertips until mixture looks like fine breadcrumbs. Stir in sugar and almonds. Add 1 tablespoon water and, using a knife, mix to a stiff, crumbly dough, adding more water if necessary.

Draw dough together with fingertips and turn out onto a floured working surface. Knead lightly for one minute, then wrap in foil and chill in refrigerator for 30 minutes.

Roll out pastry thinly and cut 12 circles using a 7^1/$_2$ cm plain cutter and 12 circles using a 6 cm cutter.

Line deep 12-cup patty tin with decorated paper cases. Pop larger pastry circle into paper cases and divide mincemeat equally between them. Dampen edges of pastry with milk, top with remaining pastry circles and seal well. Brush with milk or beaten egg to glaze and sprinkle with a little brown or Demerara sugar.

Bake in preheated 200°C oven for 20 minutes or until golden brown. Serve warm with cream.

NOW FOR THE TURKEY AND THE TRIMMINGS

Most of us have a moment when Christmas really begins, whether it's listening to Christmas carols, buying the presents, putting up the Christmas tree or making the Christmas cake.

For me it begins with planning the Christmas dinner menu. This menu begins with mixed vegetable soup, a hearty, tangy soup with a hint of spices and fragrant fresh herbs. The main course is a golden roast turkey with a tasty stuffing. To complete the meal, I have included sweet-smelling saffron-infused potatoes, a pasta salad with a refreshing herb dressing, and spiced carrots.

To end the meal, try the rich fruity pudding with an equally rich brandy custard sauce. Stay calm and relaxed. Your only last-minute preparation will be laying out the table and turning on the microwave and the oven.

Celebration Turkey

STUFFING

125 g	day-old bread, crusts removed, cubed
30 g	butter
1	large onion, chopped finely
2-3	shallots, chopped finely
3-4 tablespoons	dry sherry
60 g	smoked bacon, chopped
450 g	good quality veal or chippolata sausages, skins removed
439 g can	unsweetened chestnut purée
1 tablespoon	fresh chopped parsley
1 tablespoon	fresh chopped spring onions
1 tablespoon	fresh chopped marjoram (or 1 teaspoon dried)
1/4 teaspoon	nutmeg
	Salt to taste
1/2 teaspoon	black pepper
1	egg, beaten

TURKEY

51/2 kg	oven-prepared turkey
	Salt and pepper to taste
	Melted butter for brushing
12	rashers of streaky bacon

GRAVY

2 teaspoons	plain flour
1	chicken stock cube, crumbled
300 ml	fresh chicken stock or water
2	bay leaves
2-3 tablespoons	dry sherry
3 tablespoons	double cream or whipping cream

30 g	butter
1	large onion, finely chopped
1	clove garlic, crushed
450 ml	milk
75 g	fresh white breadcrumbs
1/2 teaspoon	ground mace
	Salt to taste

Preheat oven to 200°C. Spread out the bread cubes on a baking tray. Bake for 20 minutes until dry and crisp.

Melt butter in a frying pan, add onion and shallots, and cook until soft. Add sherry and boil for 1-2 minutes. Allow to cool.

Put onion mixture, bacon, sausages, chestnut purée, parsley, spring onions, marjoram and nutmeg into a large bowl. Add bread cubes, salt, pepper and egg and mix by hand.

Rub salt and pepper on inside of the turkey, then stuff neck end only. Shape remaining stuffing into balls and set aside. Truss turkey with string and place on a rack set in a large roasting tin lined with heavy-duty foil. Brush turkey with melted butter and sprinkle with salt and pepper. Place bacon rashers over breast of turkey, then cover with foil.

Roast for 3-3 1/2 hours at 190°C. Remove foil and bacon during last hour of roasting to allow turkey to brown. Half an hour before end of cooking time, place balls of stuffing around turkey.

Remove turkey from oven (make sure it is cooked through first) and leave to rest for about 30 minutes. Transfer to a warm serving place and cover with foil.

To Make The Gravy
Skim off all but 2 tablespoons of pan drippings, then sprinkle in flour and stock cube. Cook for 1-2 minutes, stirring well to scrape up sediment.

Gradually add 300 ml fresh chicken stock, then bay leaves, and bring to a boil, stirring continuously. Add the sherry and cream and continue to cook until the gravy thickens.

To Make The Bread Sauce
Melt butter, add onion and garlic, and cook gently until soft. Add milk and heat just to boiling point. Stir in breadcrumbs, mace and salt. Remove from heat.

Warm sauce over a pan of simmering water just before serving.

Advance Preparation
Turkey can be seasoned two days ahead and refrigerated.

Prepare the ingredients for the stuffing without adding the egg and store in airtight container.

Stuff the turkey on roasting day, mixing the egg into the stuffing ingredients.

Cook the bread sauce on serving day but prepare and measure the ingredients a day ahead.

Mixed Vegetable Soup

2	potatoes, cubed
1 teaspoon	salt
2 tablespoons	corn oil
1	large onion, chopped
3 cloves	garlic, crushed
2	medium leeks, sliced
2 teaspoons	coriander powder
2	zucchinis, peeled and diced
4 sticks	asparagus, cut into 1¹/₂ cm pieces (discard tough ends)
2 sticks	celery, sliced
1	red chilli, seeded and chopped
1 can (410 g)	peeled tomatoes, diced
2 tablespoons	tomato purée
6 cups	fresh chicken stock
2¹/₂ teaspoons	salt
¹/₂ teaspoon	black pepper
2 tablespoons	chopped coriander leaves
1 tablespoon	chopped fresh parsley
2 stalks	spring onion, chopped

Soak potatoes in salt water. Heat oil and fry onion and garlic until soft. Add leeks and fry for three minutes. Put in coriander powder, potatoes, zucchinis, asparagus, celery and chilli.

Cook gently for five minutes. Add diced tomatoes and juice, tomato purée and stock.

Bring to a boil, then reduce heat and simmer gently for 20 minutes, stirring frequently. Add seasonings and chopped fresh herbs.

Advance Preparation
Fresh chicken stock can be made a week ahead. Strain and put in plastic bags and freeze.

Potatoes and vegetables can be cleaned and cut ready for the soup pot a day ahead and refrigerated in airtight Tupperware containers. Don't forget to rinse cut potatoes in plenty of salt water to prevent discoloration.

Saffron Potato Wedges

	Pinch of saffron
2 tablespoons	hot fresh chicken stock
8-10	large baking potatoes, halved
60 g	butter, at room temperature
2 cloves	garlic, crushed
¹/₂ teaspoon	salt
¹/₂ teaspoon	pepper
¹/₂ teaspoon	chilli powder
¹/₂ tablespoon	chopped parsley

Sprinkle saffron into stock. Heat oven to 200°C. Line a baking tray with greased foil. Spread potatoes on foil.

Mix saffron stock with remaining ingredients. Pour over potatoes. Bake for 50-55 minutes until tender. Serves 6.

Advance Preparation (1 day ahead)
Peel and cut potatoes and soak in salted water. Refrigerate in airtight Tupperware.

Prepare saffron and chicken stock and refrigerate.

Mix butter, garlic, salt, pepper, chilli powder and parsley. Put in a small airtight container or plastic bag and refrigerate.

When roasting turkey on the day it is to be served, fold two greased pieces of foil into loaf-tin shapes, put marinated saffron potatoes into the foil and place on the edges of the tray with turkey in the centre. Bake and remove when cooked through.

Pasta Twist Salad

225 g	pasta twists
1 teaspoon	salt
2	tomatoes, cut into 8 wedges
8 slices	salami or ham, cut into 2 cm pieces

SEEDED AND CUT INTO STRIPS

1	green pepper, sliced
1	red pepper, sliced
3	red chillies, sliced

12	green olives (optional)
1 tablespoon	capers

DRESSING

3 tablespoons	olive oil
1 1/2 tablespoons	wine vinegar
1/2 tablespoon	lemon juice
2 tablespoons	fresh chopped parsley
1 tablespoon	fresh chopped spring onion
1/2 tablespoon	fresh chopped coriander
1 tablespoon	garlic salt
3/4 teaspoon	dried oregano
1/4 teaspoon	black pepper

60 g diced cheddar cheese

Cook pasta twists in boiling salted water according to packet directions. Drain well and reserve.

In a large bowl, combine remaining salad ingredients with pasta, mixing well. Pour dressing over pasta. Toss, cover and chill for two hours.

Add cheese. Adjust seasoning to taste, toss and serve. Makes 6 servings.

Advance Preparation
Cook pasta until al dente one day ahead. Drain and stir in extra 30 g of butter. Cool and refrigerate in airtight Tupperware. Reheat in microwave oven on high for 1 minute on day of serving. It can also be prepared a week ahead and frozen.

Slice ham or salami and cheese a day ahead and seal in polythene bag. Refrigerate.

Measure dressing ingredients into a jam jar. Cover and refrigerate. On day of serving, chop and stir in fresh parsley, spring onions and coriander.

Two hours before serving, combine all salad ingredients, pour over dressing, toss, cover and chill.

Spiced Carrots

900 g	carrots
1 teaspoon	salt
1/2 teaspoon	pepper
100 ml	olive oil
40 ml	red wine vinegar
1 teaspoon	ground coriander
1/2 teaspoon	ground cumin
1 tablespoon	fresh chopped parsley
1 tablespoon	fresh chopped basil
1 teaspoon	dried marjoram
1 teaspoon	dried oregano
4 cloves	garlic, sliced
2	red chillies, seeded and chopped

Slice carrots into 5 mm thick diagonal slices. Cook in boiling salted water until just tender. Drain. Sprinkle with pepper.

Mix oil, vinegar and spices, herbs, garlic, chillies and salt to taste.

Mix in warm carrots. When cold, cover and leave in the fridge for at least five hours or overnight, stirring once or twice.

Leave at room temperature for at least 30 minutes before serving.

Serves 6.

Advance Preparation
Make a day ahead and refrigerate in airtight Tupperware. An hour before serving, heat in a microwave oven for 30 seconds.

Claypots

Q: What kind of claypot should I use for cooking a whole duck? Do I need to season the pot before I use it?

A: Use a 30 cm claypot which is glazed inside. (You can buy claypots in Chinese general stores selling household utensils and in some major supermarkets.) Yes, you should season the pot before using it for the first time; this will help prevent cracking during cooking. Soak the pot in water overnight, then dry well and rub the outside of the pot with oil. Pour in half a cup of cooking oil and add water until the pot is three quarters full. Bring to a slow boil for 5-10 minutes, then discard liquid. Your new claypot is now ready for use.

Q: Can you tell me why my claypots keep cracking? I season each new pot, but every time I use one it cracks. What can I do to stop this from happening?

A: Claypots or sandpots are made from porous clay and crack easily if subjected to a sudden change in temperature or not handled carefully. There are a few precautions you can take to avoid cracking. Begin by buying glazed claypots, which are more durable and easier to clean than unglazed pots. Avoid pouring cold water over the pot immediately after cooking, and wash the pot in hot water; a claypot retains heat for quite a while after cooking, and the shock of cold water could cause it to crack. Finally, to avoid hairline cracks, be careful not to knock your claypot against hard objects; store your pot in a rattan basket, and if you are stacking several claypots, be sure to place a thick wad of paper between each pot.

Coconut Milk

Q: I spend a lot of time with my children in England and I often find it very difficult to get fresh coconut. What can I use instead of coconut milk and grated coconut?

A: A good substitute for fresh coconut milk is coconut powder, canned coconut milk (if you're cooking a curry or other savoury dish, make sure you buy unsweetened coconut milk), or blocks of coconut cream. To replace fresh grated coconut, you can use desiccated coconut. Of course, none of these products will give your dish the same refreshing fragrance as fresh coconut.

Q: Sometime ago I tasted chocolate coconut candy. I really liked it but have not been able to get a recipe for it. Can you tell me how to make it?

A: Coconut candy is one of the easiest candies to make, and this chocolate coconut candy is especially delicious.

Chocolate Coconut Candy

3 kg	grated white coconut from 5 coconuts
900 g	sugar
350 ml	evaporated milk
1 (397 g) tin	condensed milk
60 g	butter
1/4 teaspoon	salt
20 g	cocoa, combined with 3 tablespoons water
1/2 tablespoon	vanilla essence
1	egg white, beaten

Put grated coconut, sugar, evaporated milk, condensed milk, butter, salt and cocoa mixture into a large, deep, nonstick saucepan.

Using a wooden spatula, stir continuously for 15 minutes over low heat until mixture bubbles.

Add vanilla essence and beaten egg white and continue stirring for 30 minutes, until mixture forms a sticky mass and leaves sides of pan or until a marble-sized lump of mixture forms a soft ball when dropped into a cup of cold water.

Transfer and divide mixture into two greased 18 x 27 cm lamington trays. Cover the surface with plastic wrap and smooth the mixture by pressing hard with the back of a spoon or rolling it with a small rolling pin. Leave to set and cool.

When slightly cool, cut into squares. When completely cool, dry and hard, separate carefully into pieces. Store in airtight container.

Cookies

Q: Since I am a beginner, I do not understand the use of a cookie tray with nonstick sheets. Can you please explain?

A: Nonstick baking sheets are sheets of siliconised baking paper which don't need to be greased. They are especially useful for cookies that have a tendency to stick even on greased trays or normal baking paper. I use the sheets to line cake tins as well. You can buy them in rolls or sheets in most supermarkets. They are much more expensive than normal baking sheets but can be used several times.

Q: Can you please give me a recipe for shortbread? I bought some from the Cameron Highlands recently and the taste was fantastic.

A: Try this recipe for a rich and buttery shortbread. The addition of semolina gives it a crunchier texture.

Shortbread

180 g butter
80 g castor sugar
175 g plain flour, sifted
80 g semolina
Icing sugar

Cream butter and sugar until light and fluffy. Using a fork, gradually stir in flour and semolina. Draw mixture together with fingertips until you have a soft ball of dough.

Press into lightly greased 20 cm fluted flan tin with a loose base. Lightly roll over with a small roller to even out the surface. Prick surface all over with a fork.

Bake in preheated 160°C oven for 60-70 minutes or until lightly golden.

Leave in tin for five minutes, then mark into eight triangles with a knife. Leave in tin to cool completely. Cut into wedges and dust with icing sugar. Store in an airtight container.

Q: Please give me the recipe for cornflake cookies.

A: Here's a recipe for Orange Cornflake Cookies.

Orange Cornflake Cookies

105 g butter
120 g castor sugar
Grated rind of 1 orange
1 small egg yolk
120 g self-raising flour, sifted
Cornflakes

Cream butter and castor sugar until light and fluffy. Beat in orange rind and egg yolk until well combined. Fold in self-raising flour and mix well. Refrigerate mixture for 30 minutes until batter firms slightly.

Roll teaspoonfuls of mixture in lightly crushed cornflakes. Place on lightly greased trays. Bake in 175°C oven for 15 minutes or until light golden. Cool on wire racks.

Q: Can I use a set of plastic icing tools to make pressed or piped cookies? Should I buy plastic or tin cookie cutters?

A: You can use plastic icing tools to make pressed or piped cookies, provided the nozzles are large enough and have deep, sharp grooves. Some cookie doughs are very stiff and you will have trouble if the nozzles are too small.

As for cookie cutters, any type can be used as long as the size is right and you like the design. Ensure that plastic cutters have sharp cutting edges and are sturdy enough to hold the cookie shape when pressed. Metal ones should also have sharp cutting edges and be rustproof; buy good quality stainless steel or bronze cutters.

NO-FUSS, NO-BAKE COOKIES

Unbaked biscuits are usually made from a rich mixture that improves in flavour with keeping. All you have to do is measure the ingredients accurately to give the mixture the correct consistency.

Chocolate Rice Bubble Crunchies

1¹/₂ cups rice bubbles
1 cup roasted almonds or cashew nuts, chopped
1 cup mixed fruit
1 cup desiccated coconut

100 g white marshmallows
60 g butter

CHOCOLATE TOPPING (MELTED AND COMBINED)
125 g dark chocolate
125 g butter

Grease a 25 x 30 cm Swiss roll pan.

Mix together rice bubbles, nuts, mixed fruit and desiccated coconut in a bowl.

Put marshmallows and butter into a saucepan. Stir constantly over low heat, without boiling, until marshmallows and butter are melted. Add to dry ingredients and stir well.

Turn mixture into prepared pan and press evenly with the back of a spoon. Top with chocolate topping.

Refrigerate until set. Cut into small squares. Keep in an airtight container and store in the refrigerator.

Dried Mango Walnut Crisps

125 g butter
60 g granulated sugar
1 tablespoon golden syrup
120 g dried mangoes, chopped
60 g chopped dates

3 cups rice crispies
90 g chopped walnuts

Line a 28 x 18 cm lamington tin with greased aluminium foil.

Combine butter, sugar, golden syrup, dried mangoes and dates in a saucepan. Stir constantly over medium heat until mixture boils and is well mixed.

Stir in rice crispies and chopped walnuts and mix well. Press mixture into prepared tin. Refrigerate until firm.

Cut into small squares (3-4 cm). Keep in an airtight container and store in the refrigerator.

Chocolate Oaty Fingers

    90 g   butter
    125 g   dark cooking chocolate
    1/2 cup condensed milk
    1/4 cup desiccated coconut
    1/4 cup sultanas
    2 cups quick-cooking oats

Lightly grease a 28 x 18 cm lamington tin.

Melt butter and chocolate in top compartment of a double saucepan over simmering water. Pour in condensed milk and stir until well combined.

Remove from heat and pour into a mixing bowl. Stir in coconut, sultanas and oats; mix thoroughly.

Press mixture into prepared pan. Refrigerate until firm; cut into fingers.

Date and Ginger Slice

    125 g   butter
    1 cup   chopped dates
    1/3 cup sugar
    60 g   preserved ginger, finely chopped
    3 cups cornflakes, lightly crushed
    125 g   dark cooking chocolate

Line base of a 28 x 18 cm lamington tin with greased greaseproof paper.

Put butter, dates, sugar and ginger into a saucepan. Stir over low heat until butter has melted and dates are soft. Add cornflakes and mix well.

Press mixture into prepared tin. Refrigerate until cold and firm.

Melt chocolate in top compartment of a double saucepan over simmering water. Spread chocolate over mixture with a palette knife.

Return to refrigerator until set. Cut into small squares. Store in an airtight container in the refrigerator.

Cooking Oil

Q: Is oil that is used frequently for deep-frying bad for your health?

A: Harmful chemical changes can occur if oil is heated to smoking point. Once oil is used for deep-frying food, it should be cooled and filtered through a coffee filter paper or fine sieve to remove impurities. Oil should be discarded after it has been used a few times as it will affect the flavour of the food.

Q: In your book *Asian High Tea Favourites*, you use corn oil instead of margarine or butter for your cakes. How much butter would equal one cup of corn oil?

A: One cup of corn oil is equivalent to 240 g butter or margarine.

Cream

TASTY TEMPTATIONS IN CREAM CREATIONS

Fresh cream whipped up light and fluffy is such a delicious temptation. Piped or poured onto fresh fruit, pies, puddings and even jellies and ice-cream, cream is sheer indulgence. Cakes, chocolate toppings and sauces, too, are really special when cream is added. It is no wonder that even those who are watching their waistline find it difficult to give up cream.

Real cream is made from milk and the various types are graded according to the amount of butterfat they contain:

Single cream is about 18 per cent fat. It is used for pouring over fruits, and in dishes such as quiches, curries and sauces. It is not suitable for whipping.

Whipping cream is at least 35 per cent fat. Whipped cream will double in volume and is suitable for folding into or swirling onto desserts. It may be piped but does not hold well for long periods.

Double cream is 48 per cent fat. It can be used as a pouring or whipping cream. When whipped it will make 1¹/2 times its original volume. It is most suitable for piping as it holds its shape well. It can be frozen whipped or unwhipped.

Sour cream is made by souring single cream with a natural culture similar to that used in yoghurt. It is thicker than single cream and may be spooned over fruit and baked potatoes or mixed into desserts, sauces and dips. It adds a refreshing tangy taste. Sour cream is not suitable for whipping or freezing.

Thickened creams are equivalent to single, whipping or doubled cream in fat content, but they are homogenised to make them thicker.

Clotted cream, with 55 per cent butterfat, is a thick, rich cream which is ideal for spooning over fruits, pies, scones and puddings. It is not suitable for whipping, mixing into desserts or freezing. It is also not recommended for cooking.

When buying cream, it is important to check on the expiry date, as fresh cream has a short shelf life. Ultra heated cream and sterilized cream come in foil-lined cartons or cans, have a longer shelf-life and may be used instead of fresh cream for whipping or pouring. However, they do not give as good a volume or as light a texture as fresh cream, and the flavour is different.

One of the most important rules to remember when whipping cream in hot weather is to chill the cream, bowl and utensils. An electric mixer with a balloon whisk is very efficient for whipping. For folding, the cream should be whipped until it stands in soft peaks. Over-whipped cream becomes grainy in texture and will have a curdled appearance when piped. (If you over-whip your cream, you can save it by carefully folding two tablespoons of unwhipped cream into every 150 ml of whipped cream.)

If you need to make whipped cream go a bit further, add a tablespoon of milk to every 150 ml of fresh double cream before whipping. Whipped fresh cream will hold its shape better if you add two teaspoons of sieved icing sugar to every 150 ml of cream. If you have some leftover whipped cream, you can pipe out large rosettes and freeze them; they can be used later to decorate cakes and desserts.

Try some of these recipes using the various types of cream.

Pineapple Gateau

240 g	butter
225 g	castor sugar
1 teaspoon	vanilla essence
3	large eggs
	Grated rind and juice of one orange
225 g	self-raising flour, sifted

FILLING AND TOPPING

400 g	cream cheese, at room temperature
75 g	castor sugar
200 ml	whipping cream
1 can (454 g)	pineapple rings
1 tablespoon	Cointreau
75 ml	pineapple syrup
1 teaspoon	cornflour
6	glacé cherries

Grease sides and line base of a 22 cm floral-shaped cake tin with greased greaseproof paper.

Cream butter and sugar together with vanilla essence until light and fluffy. Beat in eggs, one at a time, then orange rind. Fold in flour alternately with orange juice. Pour into prepared tin and level the surface.

Bake in preheated 190°C oven for 45 minutes or until risen and a skewer inserted into the centre of the cake comes out clean. Cool completely.

Meanwhile, make filling and topping. Beat cream cheese and sugar until smooth. Whisk chilled cream in a chilled bowl until fluffy and just stiff. Add cream to cream cheese mixture and stir until blended. Refrigerate.

Split cake in two. Combine two tablespoons of pineapple syrup with Cointreau and drizzle carefully on top of each cake half.

Sandwich and cover top and side of cake with chilled cream cheese topping. Use a fork to create a pattern on surface and sides. Place pineapple rings on surface and arrange cherries in centres of rings.

Put 75 ml of reserved pineapple syrup into a saucepan and bring to a boil. Thicken with cornflour dissolved in a little syrup. Cool and brush over pineapple rings and cherries.

Pipe a decorative border with remaining cream cheese topping. If mixture is too soft for piping, chill again until firm.

Cream Puffs

175 ml water
75 g butter
110 g flour, sifted
2¹/₂ eggs, beaten

FILLING
300 ml whipping cream
¹/₄ teaspoon vanilla essence, optional

Grease two baking trays. Preheat oven to 220°C.

Place water and butter in a medium-sized saucepan. Heat gently until butter melts. Do not allow water to simmer. When butter has melted, increase heat and bring liquid to a full boil. Tip in sifted flour at once and remove pan from heat immediately.

Using a wooden spoon, quickly stir mixture to make a paste. When sufficiently combined, paste will leave sides of pan in a lump of dough. Do not stir once paste is formed. Leave to cool for 5-6 minutes.

Beat eggs in a bowl. Add a little to the paste and beat it in lightly. Pour in a little more egg and beat well. Continue adding eggs, beating well after each addition to make sure that they are thoroughly incorporated. Use all the eggs if necessary to make a smooth but not-too-soft paste. (It should be soft enough to drop from the spoon when tapped but thick enough to hold its shape when piped.) If paste is too stiff, beat another egg and add more to paste.

Fill a piping bag fitted with a large plain nozzle with the paste. Pipe 12 small balls onto each baking tray, pulling bag up quickly to form a peak.

Bake immediately in top of preheated oven for 15-20 minutes until well risen, puffy and golden. To make sure puffs have dried out in the centre, make a small slit in each one and return to oven for 4-5 minutes. When cooked, remove buns carefully from baking tray and leave to cool on a wire rack.

Using a sharp knife make an angled cut into side of puffs to ease them open slightly. Pipe whipped cream or custard into each bun.

To Make Filling
Whip cream in a chilled bowl until it stands in soft peaks, adding vanilla essence if desired.

Fried Chicken with Mushroom Cream Sauce

4 boneless chicken breasts or thighs
1 teaspoon salt
¹/₂ teaspoon pepper

30 g	butter
1 tablespoon	corn oil
2	shallots, finely chopped
1	red pepper, seeded and diced small
120 g	fresh button mushrooms, sliced
2-3	spring onions, chopped
1 tablespoon	plain flour
150 ml	fresh chicken stock
150 ml	single cream
	Salt and pepper to taste

Season chicken pieces with salt and pepper. Heat butter and oil in a large frying pan, add chicken breasts and fry for 10 minutes or until cooked and golden, turning over halfway through cooking. Remove chicken from oil and set aside.

Add shallots and red pepper to frying pan. Cook for one minute. Put in mushrooms and cook for 3-4 minutes. Stir in spring onions and flour and cook for another minute. Gradually add stock and cream, salt and pepper and bring to a boil, stirring constantly.

Return chicken to pan and simmer for 2-3 minutes.

Serve chicken with buttered new potatoes, broccoli and carrots.

Steak with Brandy Cream Sauce

60 g	butter
2	fillet steaks
2 cloves	garlic, crushed
2 teaspoons	French mustard
2 tablespoons	brandy
2 tablespoons	water
	Salt and pepper to taste
3 tablespoons	double or single cream

Heat 30 g of the butter, add steak and cook until done as desired. Remove from pan and keep warm.

Add remaining butter to pan and stir until melted. Add crushed garlic and sauté for one minute. Put in mustard and stir until smooth. Add brandy, water and salt and pepper to taste. When sauce begins to boil, add cream, reduce heat and simmer for one minute.

Spoon sauce over steaks and serve at once.

Q: Sour cream is so expensive. Can I make it myself or use something else instead?

A: Making your own sour cream is not much cheaper, as the ingredients (cream and buttermilk) are also expensive. A good substitute is homemade thick yoghurt. Or you can simulate sour cream by adding 1-2 teaspoons lemon juice to 150 ml of single or double cream and leaving it to sour for about 30 minutes.

Croissants

Q: Do you know of a simple way of making croissants using a food processor? My family especially likes sultana croissants.

A: The food processor makes bread-making a breeze, saving time and muscle. Here's a croissant recipe that is quite easy to handle. For sultana croissants, just sprinkle some sultanas on the pastry before rolling it up.

Croissants

45 g	castor sugar
1¹/₄ teaspoons	salt
300 ml	cold water, from the tap
20 g	fresh yeast (or 8 g instant yeast)
30 g	milk powder
500 g	plain strong flour
290 g	butter
1	egg yolk, beaten with 1 tablespoon milk, to glaze

Dissolve sugar and salt in one-third of the cold water. In a separate bowl, beat yeast into remaining water, then stir in milk powder. (If using instant yeast, stir it directly into the flour.)

Sift flour into bowl of a food processor fitted with a dough blade or dough hook. Add both liquids and turn on food processor for 30 seconds until dough has a soft, smooth consistency.

Leave to rise, covered, in food processor for 30 minutes or until doubled in bulk.

Knock down dough by turning on food processor for 10 seconds. Remove dough and refrigerate for 6-8 hours.

Shape dough into a ball and roll out into a square. Place butter in the centre and fold corners over, ensuring that the butter is completely enclosed and will not ooze out.

Lightly flour work surface and carefully roll out dough into a 40 x 70 cm rectangle. Fold into three, then put in a polythene bag and refrigerate for 20 minutes. Repeat rolling, folding and chilling procedure twice more.

Roll out dough into a 40 x 76 cm rectangle on a lightly floured surface. Using a sharp knife, trim edges and cut dough lengthways into two equal strips. Cut into triangles of desired size. Roll up to form a crescent shape.

Place on baking sheets. Lightly brush with egg glaze and leave to rise for 15 minutes or until doubled in size.

Glaze with egg mixture again. Bake in preheated 225°C oven for 15 minutes or until golden. Cool on wire racks.

Cupcakes

Q. Could you please give some recipes for different types of cupcakes.

A. Here are two for you to try: coconut cupcakes and chocolate chip cupcakes topped with chocolate cream.

Chocolate Chip Cupcakes with Chocolate Cream

300 g	plain flour
2¼ teaspoons	baking powder
½ teaspoon	salt
250 g	butter
50 g	castor sugar
2 teaspoons	vanilla essence
4	eggs
1 cup	milk
180 g	semisweet chocolate chips

Chocolate Cream

180 g	cooking chocolate, chopped
120 g	butter, at room temperature
240 g	icing sugar, sifted
¼ cup	milk
1 teaspoon	vanilla essence
	Chocolate chips or shavings, for decoration

Line 24 muffin cups with paper cases.

Sift flour and baking powder onto a baking sheet and stir in salt. Set aside.

In mixer bowl, cream butter and sugar together with vanilla essence until light and creamy. Beat in eggs, one at a time. Stir in flour alternately with milk. Stir in chocolate chips.

Spoon batter into paper cases until two-thirds full.

Bake in preheated 190°C oven for 20-25 minutes or until tops spring back when lightly pressed.

Cool and pipe surface with chocolate cream. Sprinkle chocolate chips or shavings on top.

To Make Chocolate Cream

Melt chocolate in double boiler over gently boiling water. Cool.

In mixing bowl, cream butter and sugar until light and creamy. Beat in milk, vanilla essence and melted chocolate.

Coconut Cupcakes

125 g	butter or margarine
120 g	castor sugar
1 teaspoon	vanilla essence
2	large eggs
120 g	self-raising flour, sifted
125 ml	milk
35 g	desiccated coconut
	Icing sugar, for dusting

Line muffin cups with paper cases.

Cream butter or margarine with sugar until light and fluffy. Beat in vanilla essence and eggs, one at a time, until soft and creamy. Fold in sifted flour alternately with milk, half at a time, until well blended. Stir in desiccated coconut until mixture is well combined.

Spoon mixture to fill paper cases two-thirds full. Bake in preheated 175°C oven for 20 minutes until golden and well risen.

Cool and dust with icing sugar. If desired, pipe rosettes of whipped cream onto surface and top with chocolate curls or shavings.

Curries

Q: Could you please let me know how to cook vegetable curry.

A: I have a lovely recipe for Mixed Vegetable Curry which I often make without the use of onions and garlic for strict vegetarians. However, for those who are not on a vegetarian diet, this delicious vegetable curry tastes even better with the addition of chicken stock granules. The recipe makes a rather large pot of curry. You'll have enough to give to friendly neighbours.

Mixed Vegetable Curry

4 tablespoons	cooking oil

GROUND INGREDIENTS

25	dried chillies, soaked and seeded
5 stalks	lemon grass, sliced
6	candlenuts, smashed
2¹/₂ cm piece	ginger

VEGETABLE CURRY POWDER (BLENDED WITH A LITTLE WATER INTO A PASTE)

4 tablespoons	coriander powder
2 teaspoons	turmeric powder
¹/₄ teaspoon	black pepper
¹/₄ teaspoon	white pepper

5 cups	coconut milk (4 cups thin and 1 cup thick), from 1 grated coconut
2 teaspoons	salt, or to taste

2 teaspoons	chicken stock granules (omit for vegetarians)
2 teaspoons	sugar
1	carrot, roll-cut
1	brinjal, roll-cut
350 g	cabbage, cut into pieces
10	long beans, cut into 4 cm lengths
200 g	French beans, cut into 4 cm lengths
2 sticks	dried beancurd, soaked and trimmed into 6 cm pieces and deep-fried
2 pieces	firm beancurd, thickly sliced and deep-fried
8	fried beancurd balls, rinsed
50 g	fried vegetarian fish bladder, rinsed

Heat oil and fry ground ingredients until fragrant. Add curry powder paste and cook for one minute.

Pour in thin coconut milk and stir in salt, stock granules (optional) and sugar. When curry comes to the boil, put in carrot, brinjal, cabbage, long beans and French beans. Let simmer for 1-2 minutes. Add remaining ingredients.

When curry boils again, pour in thick coconut milk. Simmer a couple of minutes and taste for salt.

Q: Please tell me how to cook mutton curry (Indian-style) and, most of all, how to get rid of the strong smell of the meat.

A: To minimise the strong smell of mutton, use plenty of ginger, black pepper and spices in the curry. Try this dry mutton curry.

Dry Mutton Curry

800 g	mutton, cut into small pieces
2 tablespoons	yoghurt
3 teaspoons	ground ginger
2 teaspoons	ground garlic
3	onions, sliced
2 teaspoons	black peppercorns, crushed
1 teaspoon	sugar
	Salt to taste
2 tablespoons	cooking oil
1 teaspoon	fennel seeds
5 cm piece	cinnamon stick
5	cardamom pods
4-5 cups	water
12	shallots, peeled and left whole
7	green chillies, split
4	tomatoes, cut into 8 sections

Marinate mutton in yoghurt, ginger, garlic, half the onion slices, black pepper, sugar and salt for 4-5 hours.

Heat cooking oil and fry fennel, cinnamon and cardamom for a few seconds.

Add remaining sliced onions and cook until lightly browned. Add mutton and marinade, and stir well.

Reduce heat and simmer, covered, for 10-15 minutes, stirring frequently. Add water and bring to a boil. Simmer over low heat until mutton is cooked and tender and curry quite dry.

Add shallots and green chillies, and cook for 8-10 minutes. Then add tomatoes and remove from heat.

Q: I would like to know how to cook fish head curry, Indian-Muslim style. Recently I tasted fish head curry at a Chinese restaurant. It was spicy and sourish but did not have much of the curry texture.

A: Here is a recipe for fish head curry.

Fish Head Curry

1	fish head, *ikan merah* or *kurau*, cut into large pieces
1 teaspoon	salt
1/2 teaspoon	pepper
1 tablespoon	tamarind paste mixed in 1/2 cup water and strained
4 tablespoons	curry powder
1/4 teaspoon	turmeric powder
3-4 cups	water
3 tablespoons	oil
2	brinjals, cut into pieces
5	ladies fingers, cut into pieces
8	shallots, sliced
2	green chillies, sliced lengthwise
5 cloves	garlic, chopped
1/2 teaspoon	whole mixed spices
1/2 teaspoon	fenugreek seeds
2 sprigs	curry leaves
	Salt to taste
2	large tomatoes, cut into 8 pieces

Marinate fish in salt, pepper and tamarind juice. Mix curry powder, turmeric powder and a little of the water to make a paste.

Heat pan with oil and fry brinjals and ladies fingers until light brown. Drain from oil and set aside. In the same oil, fry shallots, chillies, garlic, mixed spices and fenugreek until fragrant. Add curry leaves.

Pour in curry powder paste and bring to a boil. Put in fish head pieces and cook until fish is just cooked. Add salt to taste. Add reserved vegetables and tomatoes.

Curry Powder

Q: **Kurma curries are my favourite but I can't find kurma curry powder. Can you please give me a recipe for making it?**

A: Kurma curry powder is a mixture of spices without chillies. It originated in northern India and is used mainly for meat. Here's my favourite recipe for kurma powder.

Kurma Curry Powder

1¹/₂ kg	coriander seeds
300 g	fennel seeds
300 g	cumin seeds
450 g	black peppercorns
150 g	white peppercorns
450 g	dried turmeric roots
10	whole nutmegs, shelled
45 g	cloves
75 g	cardamom pods, shelled
60 g	cinnamon sticks
30 g	star anise

Wash and dry spices in large flat trays in hot sun for 4-5 days, stirring often to ensure even drying.

Roast in moderately hot oven for 10 minutes.

Send to mill for grinding and allow to cool thoroughly. Pack in plastic bags or airtight containers.

Diabetic Cakes

Q: **When I bake a cake for a diabetic, will the cake taste good if I leave out the sugar? Should I add something else in its place?**

A: For diabetic cakes, sugar is replaced with sugar-free sweeteners and more liquid is added. Here is a recipe for a diabetic carrot cake with a creamy cheese topping. It is a lovely cake for a special occasion.

Carrot Cake with Cream Cheese Topping (Diabetic)

225 g	self-raising flour
1¹/₂ teaspoons	baking powder
¹/₂ teaspoon	bicarbonate of soda
¹/₄ teaspoon	salt
	Sugar-free sweetener equivalent to 6 tablespoons (90 ml) sugar
1 teaspoon	ground cinnamon
3	large eggs

150 ml	corn oil
180 g	grated carrots
	Juice and rind of 1 1/2 oranges
60 g	walnuts, finely chopped

TOPPING

300 g	light cream cheese, at room temperature
	Juice and rind of 1/2 orange
1/2 teaspoon	vanilla essence
	Sugar-free sweetener to taste
	Toasted walnut halves to decorate

Line two 20 cm springform pans with greased greaseproof paper. Preheat oven to 175°C.

Put first 6 dry ingredients into a large food processor or a large mixing bowl fitted with a beater. Add eggs, corn oil, carrots, and orange juice and rind and blend gently until almost smooth. Blend gently. Stir in walnuts.

Pour mixture evenly between two tins and smooth the surface. Bake for 25-30 minutes until cooked through, firm and golden. Cool cakes on wire racks.

For the topping, blend cream cheese, orange juice and rind, vanilla essence and sweetener to taste until smooth.

Sandwich cakes with icing and spread rest of icing over top of the cake. Swirl the topping with a teaspoon to create a pattern. Decorate with walnuts.

Dumplings

Q: Can you please tell me how to make transparent vegetable dumplings?

A: *The transparent dough for vegetable dumplings is made from* tang meen fun, *which is non-gluten flour in Cantonese. It is easily obtainable from most Chinese provision stores. Here is a recipe for dumplings using a commercial packet of* tang meen fun *to make the dough.*

Vegetable Dumplings

TANG MEEN FUN DOUGH

225 g	tang meen fun flour
1 tablespoon	tapioca flour
1/2 teaspoon	salt
1 1/2 cups	boiling water
1 tablespoon	lard, corn oil or vegetable shortening

VEGETABLE FILLING

1 tablespoon	oil
1 teaspoon	finely chopped ginger
1 teaspoon	finely chopped garlic
120 g	chopped carrots
60 g	finely sliced French beans
3	dried black mushrooms, soaked and shredded

3 cloud ear fungus, soaked and shredded

SAUCE INGREDIENTS (COMBINED)
125 ml chicken stock
1 tablespoon oyster sauce
1 teaspoon salt
1 teaspoon sugar
1 teaspoon Chinese rice wine
1 teaspoon cornflour

1 tablespoon chopped spring onions

To Make Dough

Sift *tang meen fun* flour and tapioca flour into a mixing bowl and add salt. Stir in boiling water and fat and knead into a smooth dough. Cut into 25-30 even pieces.

Grease a cleaver and surface of table. Flatten each piece of dough into a thin circle with flat side of cleaver or a greased rolling pin.

To Make Filling

Heat oil and lightly brown ginger and garlic. Add carrots, beans, mushrooms and cloud ear fungus and stir-fry over high heat for 1-2 minutes.

Pour in combined sauce ingredients. When the liquid boils and thickens, add chopped spring onions. Spread mixture onto a plate to cool and drain off any liquid.

To Make Dumplings

Put some vegetable filling in centre of dough circle. Fold in half and pinch edges together. Gather outside edge to form pleats. (Or fold into half-moon or crescent shapes, and press edges together.) Continue with remaining dough circles.

Place dumplings in greased bamboo baskets and steam over boiling water for seven minutes.

Eggs

Q: There are many egg sizes available. What size or weight is best for cake recipes?

> *A: Eggs are graded according to weight. Double A (very large) eggs are approximately 75-80 g, A (large) eggs are 70-75 g, B (medium) eggs are 65-70 g and C (small) eggs are 60-65 g.*
>
> *I like to use the Double A and A size eggs for cakes as they beat to greater volume to give cake batters lightness. A whole egg can aerate an equal weight of flour. I use small eggs for cookies.*

Q: What is the correct way of separating the egg white from the egg yolk?

> *A: To separate the yolk from the white, tip the egg yolk from one half shell*

to the other. You can also tip it into your palm and let the egg white run through your fingers. Eggs are easier to separate when they have been chilled in the refrigerator.

Egg separators are also available. They are in the shape of a spoon with slits to allow the egg white to drain through.

Q: Every time I try to make egg pudding the texture always turns out to be a bit thick. What is the correct proportion of eggs to water?

A: *The proportion is 1 large egg to ¹/₂ cup water for a very soft egg pudding. If you like it firmer you can reduce the water slightly. Besides getting the proportion right, make sure the water comes to a rapid boil before putting the dish in to steam. Timing is also important as over-steaming will result in a coarse pockmarked surface.*

Here is my version of Steamed Eggs with Prawns, a firm favourite with young children. Char Siew, or barbecued pork, can also be used instead of prawns.

Steamed Eggs with Prawns

2 tablespoons	cooking oil
3	shallots, sliced
3	large eggs

SEASONING INGREDIENTS

1 teaspoon	salt
¹/₄ teaspoon	sugar
¹/₄ teaspoon	pepper

1¹/₂ cups	water
120 g	shelled prawns, chopped
1	stalk spring onion, chopped
1 tablespoon	reserved oil from frying shallots

Heat 2 tablespoons oil in a saucepan and lightly brown shallots. Drain and set shallot crisps aside. Reserve shallot oil.

Beat eggs gently with a fork, taking care not to create any froth. Stir in seasoning ingredients and water. Add prawns and pour into a heatproof dish.

Steam over rapidly boiling water for 12 minutes or until the egg custard is just set. Sprinkle in reserved shallot oil, spring onion and shallot crisps.

94

Whipping Up Treats with Egg Whites

The egg, high in nutrition, is a remarkable and versatile ingredient which is regarded as practically indispensable in any cuisine.

Many recipes call for the use of only the egg yolk, leaving the egg white behind. What to do with the egg white is a question I have often been asked. It may be less tasty, but it is the healthier part of the egg with its low calorie and cholesterol-free content, and it can be turned into many delectable treats.

Often egg whites need to be whipped to a degree of stiffness that is crucial to the success of the recipe. If the egg white is to be beaten lightly, use a fork. For beating to a much larger volume, you'll need a rotary whisk or an electric mixer fitted with a balloon whisk. Use a sufficiently large bowl if you are whipping two or more egg whites as they can increase six or seven times in volume when beaten under the right conditions. Make sure the egg whites are at room temperature and the bowls and beaters are free from grease. There should also be no traces of yolk in the whites.

For lightly beaten egg whites, the mixture should be foamy and still heavy. When "soft peaks" are specified, the mixture should be a mass of air pockets with rounded shapes which are moist and shiny. Beat a little further and the whites will stiffen and appear moist and glossy. They will hold their shape in soft angular peaks that droop slightly when the whisk is raised. More beating will further stiffen the mixture; it will still appear moist but will have sharp angular peaks. The mixture will not slide when the bowl is tilted.

If beating is continued past this point, the mixture will be over-beaten and become too stiff and dry. The whole mass will break apart into chunks.

Once egg whites are beaten they should be immediately folded into the other ingredients or the air bubbles that you have so carefully worked up will deflate.

Folding should be done carefully with a large spatula or metal spoon so as not to deflate the air bubbles. Always fold the light whites into the heavier mixture, a quarter at a time and using gentle plunging, lifting and turning-over motions.

Egg whites will keep for several days in the refrigerator and for at least three months in an airtight container when frozen. I like to freeze egg whites first in an ice-cube tray, one egg white in each space. When frozen, I remove and store them in an airtight container in the freezer. In this way, I can keep track of the number of whites to be used.

Here are some recipes using egg whites.

Hot and Sour Soup

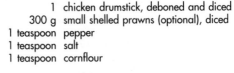

1	chicken drumstick, deboned and diced
300 g	small shelled prawns (optional), diced
1 teaspoon	pepper
1 teaspoon	salt
1 teaspoon	cornflour
9 cups	fresh chicken stock, strained
1	large piece Szechuan vegetable, unwashed and diced
1	carrot, diced
4	dried Chinese mushrooms, soaked and diced
1/2 can	button mushrooms, quartered
1/2 can	straw mushrooms, quartered
10	fresh young corn cobs, diced
3	red chillies, split to remove seeds
1/3 cup	Chinese black vinegar
1	square piece soft beancurd, diced
100 g	frozen green peas, rinsed
4 tablespoons	sweet potato flour, mixed in 1/2 cup fresh chicken stock and strained
2	egg whites, lightly beaten

Mix chicken and prawns with pepper, salt and cornflour.

Pour chicken stock into a deep cooking pot and bring to a boil. Add Szechuan vegetable, carrot, mushrooms, corn, chillies and black vinegar. Allow to simmer for 10 minutes.

Put in chicken and prawns and when mixture begins to boil, add beancurd and green peas. Simmer for another 5 minutes.

Stir in sweet potato thickening and beaten egg white.

Note: *All diced ingredients should measure about 1 cm.*

Meringues

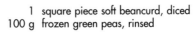

2	large egg whites
125 g	castor sugar (or half castor sugar and half sifted icing sugar)

Line a baking tray with nonstick baking paper.

Put egg whites in bowl of electric mixer fitted with a balloon whisk. Beat until just stiff. Gradually beat in sugar, a tablespoon at a time.

Using 2 teaspoons, shape and drop a full teaspoonful onto the baking sheet. Alternatively, fill a piping bag fitted with a 2 cm plain nozzle and pipe small round or finger- length meringues.

Bake in preheated 110°C oven for 1 1/2-2 hours, depending on size of meringues, until quite firm. Lift off the meringues and dry out. Cool and store until ready to serve.

Serve plain or sandwich with whipped cream or ice-cream. Meringues are also a favourite topping for pies and puddings.

Apple and Mint Sorbet

700 g green apples, peeled, cored and diced
80 g sugar
425 g can custard
1 small bunch mint, washed and finely chopped
3 egg whites
Mint sprigs, to decorate

Put apples and sugar in a saucepan and cook over low heat, stirring to prevent mixture from burning, until soft. Remove from heat and beat to a purée with a wooden spoon. Allow to cool.

Mix apple purée with custard and mint. Turn into a plastic ice-cream container and freeze for 2-3 hours.

Remove from freezer and beat well with a fork until mushy; then freeze for another 2 hours. Remove and beat well.

Whisk egg whites until they stand in soft peaks. Fold carefully into frozen purée with a metal spoon. Put back into freezer and freeze until firm; this will take about 2 hours.

Scoop into balls with a small ice-cream scoop and place in chilled glass bowls or glasses. Decorate with mint sprigs.

Gingko and Water Chestnut Dessert

6 cups water
300 g rock sugar
180 g gingko nuts, shelled, peeled and bitter centres removed
22 water chestnuts, skinned and diced into $^1/_2$ cm cubes
2 egg whites, lightly beaten

THICKENING (COMBINED AND STRAINED)
3 tablespoons sweet potato flour
1 tablespoon cornflour
$^1/_2$ cup water

In a large saucepan, bring water and rock sugar to a slow boil. When sugar dissolves, put in gingko nuts.

Boil over low heat for 10 minutes, then add water chestnuts. Simmer for 10 minutes.

Slowly pour and stir in egg whites and then thickening. When it boils again, remove from heat. Serve hot or cold.

Fish

Q: What fish is suitable for fish and chips?

A: For fish and chips, I would use kurau, garoupa *or red snapper.*

Q: My frying pan is not large enough to hold a whole fish. What is the best solution?

A: The best way out is to cut the fish in half and, after frying, reassemble it on the serving dish and garnish with coriander leaves and spring onions to hide the cut. If you have a spicy sauce to go with it, you can pour it over the fish and cover the cut with chilli strips.

Q: I love eating fish but hate the strong smell. I have tried baking fish with lots of ginger, turmeric powder and other ingredients, but it doesn't seem to help. Is there anything I can do to get rid of the fishy smell?

A: For a start, you must buy absolutely fresh fish. Avoid fish like ikan kembong, ikan bawal hitam, ikan terubok, *or* ikan cencaru, *which* have a strong fishy smell even when they are fresh. Try ikan kurau, garoupa or red snapper. Marinate fish for at least 30 minutes in pepper, fresh herbs, roots and fragrant leaves. You can also bake the fish and camouflage the fishy smell with a good fragrant sauce. Try this recipe.

Baked Fish in Foil

2 slices ikan kurau, about 200 g each

GROUND INGREDIENTS

10	dried chillies
2¹/2 cm	turmeric root
3 cm	young galingale
1 tablespoon	belacan powder
4	candlenuts
2 stalks	lemon grass, sliced
¹/2 cup	pati santan (undiluted coconut milk), from ¹/2 grated coconut
1 tablespoon	cooking oil
1 teaspoon	salt
¹/2 teaspoon	sugar
2 tablespoons	chilli sauce
4	pandan leaves
	Aluminium foil, heavy duty

Marinate fish slices with ground ingredients for at least 1 hour. Refrigerate until cooking time.

Grease foil with cooking oil. Place pandan leaves in centre. Arrange fish and cover with ground ingredients. Fold foil and seal edges securely.

Bake in a preheated 200°C oven for about 12 minutes.

Q: Can you give me a recipe for making fishballs that are spongy, a quality I am unable to obtain?

A: To turn out spongy fishballs, make sure that the fish you buy is absolutely fresh. Buy a good-sized tenggiri, approximately 1.25 kg in weight.

Ask the fishmonger to fillet the fish. Keep the head and bones to make stock or curry. Use a spoon to scrape the flesh from the skin.

From this point onwards I take the lazy and less fishy way out. I put the fish meat half at a time into a food processor fitted with a dough blade.

Blend for 5-6 minutes, gradually adding water (about three fluid ounces in total). Remove and knead in salt to taste.

Q: What does fish maw look like?

A: Fish maw is dried fish bladder. It is cream in colour and flat, in an elongated leaf shape.

Flour

Q: Is sago flour the same as tapioca flour?

A: *Sago flour comes from the starchy pith of the sago palm. Tapioca flour is obtained from the pulp of tapioca roots. Both sago and tapioca flour are used to thicken soups or sauces and to make our local* kuih. *They may be used interchangeably in certain recipes. However, for* kuih, *sago flour gives a smoother texture.*

Q: What is sweet potato flour?

A: *Sweet potato flour is starch flour extracted from sweet potatoes. It is used mainly as a thickening agent for sauces and soups as well as the starchy omelette base in Chinese Stir-Fried Oysters. It produces a less viscous mixture than cornflour.*

Q: What is the difference between tapioca flour and cornflour?

A: *Both cornflour and tapioca flour are used as thickening agents in sauces or soups. Cornflour produces a slightly thicker mixture than tapioca flour.*

Q: I love the taste of green pea biscuits and would like to try making them. How do I make green pea flour?

A: *First, the label "green pea" is misleading because the flour is actually green **bean** flour. To make green bean flour, either roast beans in a moderate oven, stirring occasionally, or fry over low heat in an ungreased pan. Cool thoroughly before sending to the mill for grinding. I think it is easier to buy the flour off the shelf.*

Q: What are the Malay and Cantonese names for rice flour, tapioca flour, wheat flour and plain flour?

A: *Rice flour is* tepung beras, *or* chim mai fun. *Tapioca flour is* tepung ubi, *or* si fun. *Wheat flour* and *plain flour are the same thing* — tepung gandum, *or* meen fun.

Q: Recently, while shopping for flour, I came across flour with the label "bleached" on it. What is the difference between bleached and unbleached flour? Is bleached flour safe to consume?

A: *Bleached flour is flour which has been treated chemically to whiten it. It is safe for consumption, although bleaching does destroy the small amounts of vitamin E that are present in flour. There is no discernible difference between bleached and unbleached flour in the taste or texture of baked goods.*

Q: Can you please tell me what plain, strong flour is?

A: Plain strong flour is sometimes labelled as either high-protein flour or bread flour. It has a high gluten content and is most suitable for bread-making.

Q: Can you explain the difference between high-ratio flour and high-protein flour?

A: High-ratio cake flour, common in the United States and other countries, is now locally milled and easily available in specialist cake shops. It is milled from low-protein wheat flour. This flour has a high absorbency for liquid, sugar and fat — hence the term "high-ratio." Cakes made from high-ratio flour have good volume, tender crumb and very fine texture. High-protein wheat flour or bread flour has a greater gluten (protein) strength and is generally used for yeast breads.

Q: I normally use superfine flour or Hong Kong flour. Which gives a better texture to my cakes? What is the correct ratio of flour to baking powder?

A: Superfine flour and Hong Kong flour are highly bleached all-purpose flours, finely milled from soft wheat. Baked products such as quick breads and pau will turn out whiter than with normal plain flour. Cakes will have a tender crumb and a fine texture. However, you can achieve the same result using normal plain flour; after folding the flour into the cake batter, blend well in an electric mixer at medium speed for three to four minutes.

The amount of baking powder required varies according to the type of cake. To make plain flour equivalent to self-raising flour, use two teaspoons of baking powder for every 240 g plain flour. To obtain better results, sieve the combined plain flour and baking powder a couple of times to ensure even distribution.

Q: Can I use atta flour instead of plain flour for cakes?

A: Atta flour is a fine wholemeal flour. Low in gluten, atta flour produces a heavy and dense texture. Plain or all-purpose flour is more suitable for most cakes and biscuits.

Q: Some Indonesian recipes call for ground rice. What is ground rice?

A: Ground rice is rice flour. It is available at all sundry stores and supermarkets.

Fritters

Q: Could you tell me how to make fried chicken or prawn fritters which stay as crisp when they are cold as when they are hot?

A: *Chicken or prawns deep-fried in batter should be eaten hot to enjoy their crispness. An easy way to re-crisp them is to place them over a rack in a preheated turbo-broiler and grill on medium high heat for approximately five to six minutes. For a good crispy batter, try a combination of two parts rice flour to one part self-raising flour with a teaspoon of baking powder. Blend with water until smooth. The consistency should be slightly thick and not too runny. Season with salt and pepper. It also helps if you dry the rice and self-raising flour in the sun before use. The chicken pieces and prawns should be well-drained after rinsing and towelled dry with kitchen paper before seasoning.*

Q: What do hawkers put into their banana and sweet potato fritters to keep them crisp for so long?

A: *Banana or sweet potato fritter will stay crisp if you use rice flour for the batter. Try four parts of rice flour to one part of plain flour with baking powder and salt.*

Fruitcake

Q: I baked a fruitcake, but it just crumbled to pieces when I cut it. What did I do wrong?

A: *Your crumbling fruitcake could be due to many reasons. The mixture might have been too dry, or there might not have been enough butter or egg to hold the fruit together. Here is a recipe for a fruity, moist and light-textured cake. I bake it in a loaf pan and serve it as a teatime treat.*

Pineapple Fruit Cake

300 g	fresh or canned pineapple, coarsely chopped
375 g	mixed dried fruit
120 g	brown sugar
150 g	butter
2	large eggs

SIFTED INGREDIENTS (COMBINED)

120 g	plain flour
120 g	self-raising flour
1 teaspoon	bicarbonate of soda

1-2 tablespoons	brandy, optional

Grease sides and line base of a 32 x 11 cm loaf pan or 20 cm square cake tin with greased greaseproof paper.

Put pineapple, mixed fruit, sugar and butter in a medium saucepan and bring to a boil, stirring until butter melts. Allow to cool.

Pour cooled mixture into bowl of an electric mixer. Beat in eggs for 2 minutes. Fold in sifted ingredients until well blended.

Turn mixture into prepared pan and bake in centre of preheated 175°C oven for 1 hour, or until skewer comes out clean when inserted into centre of cake.

If desired, drizzle cake with brandy while still hot. Leave to cool in tin.

Q: I have baked several fruitcakes, but my friends always complain that they are not as soft and light as the ones they buy in cake shops. I double-checked the oven temperature with a thermometer, weighed the ingredients carefully, and used a good brand of cake flour. What could be the problem?

A: *Golden fruit cake, if well made, is fruity and moist. Use large eggs and test the cake fifteen minutes before the end of the cooking time. If the skewer comes out clean, the cake is cooked; further baking will dry it out.*

If you prefer an extremely moist fruitcake, stir in three extra tablespoons of brandy to the mixed fruit. Cover and let stand for 3 days before using. Stir occasionally and add a little more brandy if it has been absorbed. Drizzle the cake with more brandy when the cake has finished baking and is still hot. Adding half a cup of chopped canned pineapple is another way of making a fruitcake very moist.

To store the cake and keep it moist, wrap it first in plastic wrap (or in a brandy-soaked cloth) and then in foil. Keep in an airtight container in the refrigerator.

Fruit Salad

Q: Could you give me a recipe for fruit salad? I have tried making it, but it didn't taste very good.

A: *Here is a recipe for an unusual but easy fruit salad: delicious Hot Mango and Banana Salad.*

Hot Mango and Banana Salad

2	large oranges
2 (800 g)	ripe mangoes, skinned and cubed
4	bananas
30 g	butter or margarine
1-2 teaspoons	brown sugar
13 tablespoons	rum
2 tablespoons	lemon or lime juice

Grate rind and squeeze juice of one orange. Peel other orange and slice it thickly across segments. Skin and cut mangoes into diamond-shaped pieces. Peel and thickly slice bananas.

Heat a nonstick frying pan and melt butter or margarine. Stir in sugar, mangoes and bananas. Cook gently for about two minutes until fruit begins to soften.

Pour in rum, fruit juice and orange slices. Bring to a boil, then stir in orange rind. Serve hot.

Fudge

Q: Could you give me a recipe for chocolate fudge for my grand-children in India?

A: This delectable cashew nut chocolate fudge has a great appeal with children.

Chocolate Fudge

120 g	unsalted butter
90 g	cocoa, sifted
465 g	icing sugar, sifted
1 can	evaporated milk
90 g	cashew nuts, roasted and coarsely chopped

Line and oil an 18 cm square tin.

Melt butter in a saucepan. Remove pan from heat and stir in cocoa and icing sugar, then evaporated milk.

Return pan to heat and bring slowly to boil, stirring constantly. Reduce heat and cook until fudge reaches soft ball stage (when a little of it forms a soft ball when dropped into a bowl of cold water). This takes approximately 25-30 minutes.

Stir in chopped nuts and pour into prepared tin. Leave to cool, then chill.

When almost set, mark into squares. Chill until required, then cut into squares. Store, covered in an airtight container, in the fridge.

Q: Can you give me a recipe for a smooth, plain fudge?

A: Here is a recipe for a lovely creamy fudge. You will need an accurate thermometer, and a strong arm for beating the cooled mixture.

Creamy Fudge

3 tablespoons	margarine
3 tablespoons	cocoa powder, sifted
2¹/₂ cups	sugar
225 ml	evaporated milk
1 teaspoon	light corn syrup
1 teaspoon	vanilla essence

In a heavy saucepan, melt margarine. Stir in cocoa powder until well combined. Add sugar, milk, corn syrup and vanilla essence. Cook over medium-high heat until mixture boils, stirring constantly with a wooden spoon to dissolve sugar. This should take about 5-6 minutes. Stir gently to prevent mixture splashing onto sides of pan.

When mixture begins to boil, carefully clip a candy thermometer to side of pan. Reduce heat to medium-low. Mixture should continue to boil at a moderately steady rate.

Cook, stirring frequently, for 10-15 minutes or until the thermometer registers 110°C.

Pour fudge mixture into a large bowl, taking care not to scrape saucepan. Put thermometer in bowl. Cool until thermometer registers 38°C and mixture is thick. This takes about an hour, so check the thermometer frequently. Do not stir during cooling.

Line a baking pan (22 x 12$^1/_2$ x 7$^1/_2$ cm) with foil, extending foil over edges of pan. Grease foil with butter and set aside.

Using a wooden spoon, beat cooled mixture for about 7-8 minutes or until fudge becomes like a soft frosting. It should be thick and glossy.

Pour into pan. When firm, remove from pan and cut into squares. Cover and store in a cool place.

Gluten Balls

Q: How can I make gluten balls?

A: *You will need 600 g high-protein flour, 1 teaspoon salt, and approximately 1$^3/_4$ cups water. Put flour into a large bowl. Dissolve salt in water. Add to flour and form into a stiff dough. Leave to rest for at least 30 minutes.*

Fill a large bowl with water and "wash" dough by kneading and pressing until dough is spongy. Repeat procedure with clean water until the water is as clear as after washing rice.

Leave dough to rest for 15-20 minutes. Drain.

Pinch off small marble-sized pieces of dough and drop into hot oil. Deep-fry until golden-brown and drain.

You can these gluten balls in vegetable stir-fries.

Golden Syrup

Q: Do golden syrup and treacle have to be refrigerated once opened?

A: *Golden syrup and treacle should not be refrigerated as they will crystallise.*

Hamburgers

MAKING YOUR OWN DELICIOUS BURGERS

The hamburger, an American all-time favourite fast food, has also become very popular here.

The hamburger actually originated in Germany, apparently when merchants of the port of Hamburg acquired a taste for scraped raw beef. This eventually led to cooked meat cakes which were then named after the city.

It may be convenient to walk into one of the numerous fast-food outlets for a hamburger or even buy a ready-made one from a supermarket, but it really is quite simple to prepare from scratch this self-contained meal.

Buy good quality minced beef or, better yet, choose the cut of meat you want and have it minced at the shop. Try to avoid excessive amounts of fats or tendons.

Hamburgers can be grilled or shallow-fried. For frying, use a lightly greased nonstick pan (very lean meat will require a little more butter or oil). The pan must be well heated to cook the hamburger quickly. Fry each side for about two or three minutes, depending on the thickness.

To store raw hamburgers, first freeze them well on open trays. Then pack them in wax paper and store them in airtight containers.

Below are recipes for three different types of burgers, including one made with tuna, mushrooms and cheese — a tasty and delightful change from meat burgers, it is crisp on the outside and soft inside when eaten hot. For those energetic enough, I have also given recipes for buns and two types of sauces.

Hamburgers with Herbs

500 g	minced lean beef (topside)
1	onion, finely chopped
75 g	canned or frozen corn
30 g	fresh breadcrumbs
1	egg, beaten
1 teaspoon	salt, or to taste
1/2 teaspoon	pepper
1/4 teaspoon	mixed herbs
1 tablespoon	chopped parsley
1/2 tablespoon	chopped spring onions
1/2 tablespoon	chopped coriander leaves
	A little plain flour
	Oil for frying
8	fresh buns, split
	Butter or margarine
4	lettuce leaves

8 large slices	tomato
8 slices	cucumber
8 slices	red capsicum
	Fried or fresh onion rings
	Light Sour Cream Sauce with
	Mustard (see recipe given)
	Tomato sauce (see recipe given)

In a large bowl mix beef, onion, corn, breadcrumbs, beaten egg, seasoning, herbs and a little flour. Divide into eight equal portions and shape into thin patties, about 10 cm in diameter.

Chill for one hour. Shallow fry for 2-3 minutes on each side until cooked through.

To assemble burgers, spread buns with a little butter or margarine. Place half a lettuce leaf on the base of the bun and add a slice each of tomato, cucumber, red capsicum and some onion rings. Top with hamburger and spread with a spoonful of Light Sour Cream Sauce with Mustard and tomato sauce. Place other half of bun on top and serve immediately.

Chicken Baked Bean Burgers

These mildly spiced delicious burgers make a quick and nourishing meal. Use leftover baked beans as a sandwich filling; just lightly mix in some grated cheddar cheese with a small dollop of hot mustard and a dash of Worcestershire sauce.

400 g	boneless, skinless chicken meat, minced
100 g	canned baked beans, drained and mashed
2 tablespoons	dry breadcrumbs
1	large clove garlic, crushed
1/2	beaten egg
1 teaspoon	paprika
1/2 teaspoon	chilli powder
1/4 teaspoon	each of black and white pepper powder
1 teaspoon	salt
1/2 tablespoon	chopped parsley
1/2 tablespoon	chopped coriander leaves
1/2 tablespoon	chopped spring onion
	Oil for frying

4	hamburger buns, split
2	lettuce leaves
4	tomato slices
4	cucumber slices
	Thousand Island dressing
	Light Sour Cream Sauce with Mustard (see recipe given)

In a medium mixing bowl, combine chicken, baked beans, breadcrumbs, garlic, egg, spices, salt and herbs.

Mix well and shape into 10-11 cm patties. Shallow fry in hot oil for 2-3 minutes on each side.

Sandwich patties between buttered buns with lettuce, tomato, cucumber and a large tablespoon of Thousand Island dressing and Light Sour Cream Sauce with Mustard. If desired, add some chilli sauce as well.

Tuna Cheese Burgers

1 can (185 g)	tuna in oil, drained and flaked
100 g	canned button mushrooms, finely chopped
1/2	egg, beaten with a fork
100 g	grated cheddar or Dutch Gouda cheese
30 g	fresh breadcrumbs
1/2	onion, finely chopped
1	red chilli, seeded and chopped
1/4 teaspoon	salt
1/4 teaspoon	black pepper powder
1 tablespoon	parsley, chopped
1/2 tablespoon	spring onions, chopped
1/4 tablespoon	coriander leaves, chopped
4	fresh buns, split
	Butter or margarine
2	lettuce leaves
4 large slices	tomato
4 slices	cucumber
	Fried or fresh onion rings
4 slices	red capsicum
	Light Sour Cream Sauce with Mustard (see recipe given)
	Thousand Island Dressing or mayonnaise

Mix tuna with mushrooms, egg, cheese, breadcrumbs, onion, chilli, seasonings and herbs. Shape into four patties, approximately 10-11 cm in diameter. Ensure they are compressed firmly as the mixture is flaky and soft.

Shallow-fry tuna burgers in oil in a large saucepan for 2-3 minutes on each side or until golden.

Sandwich patties between buttered buns with lettuce, tomato, cucumber, onion, capsicum and a large tablespoon of Light Sour Cream Sauce with Mustard and Thousand Island dressing or mayonnaise.

Tomato Sauce

2 tablespoons	corn oil or butter
2	onions, chopped
500 g	ripe tomatoes, peeled and finely chopped
2 1/2 cups	fresh chicken stock
1 tablespoon	tomato paste
2 teaspoons	sugar
1 1/2 teaspoons	salt
1/2 teaspoon	pepper
1 tablespoon	chopped parsley
1 tablespoon	chopped spring onions
1 tablespoon	cornflour, combined with 2-3 tablespoons water

Heat oil or butter in a saucepan and cook onions until soft. Add tomatoes and cook, covered, for about 10 minutes, stirring frequently.

Add chicken stock, tomato paste, sugar, salt, pepper and fresh herbs. Simmer gently, uncovered, for 30 minutes or until sauce thickens. Stir in cornflour mixture and cook for one minute. Adjust seasonings to taste.

Light Sour Cream Sauce with Mustard

125 ml	light or whipping cream, chilled
2-3 teaspoons	lemon juice
2 tablespoons	prepared mustard
1/2	onion, minced
1/4 teaspoon	salt
1/4 teaspoon	pepper

Put chilled cream in a chilled bowl and whisk until light and fluffy. Beat in lemon juice to taste, mustard, onion and seasonings. Chill while cooking hamburgers.

Sesame Buns

450 g	high-protein flour
1 teaspoon	salt
2 teaspoons	sugar
20 g	easy-blend yeast
30 g	margarine, melted
175 ml	warm milk, combined with 175 ml warm water
1	egg white, beaten
	Sesame seeds

Lightly grease a large baking tray and line with nonstick baking paper. Preheat oven to 200°C.

Sift flour onto baking sheet. Tip flour into a food processor fitted with dough blade. Stir in salt, sugar and easy-blend yeast. Stir melted margarine into milk mixture and pour into flour mixture. Turn on food processor for 5-6 minutes until you have a smooth dough.

Allow dough to rise for 30-40 minutes or until doubled in bulk. Knock dough down by turning on food processor; process for 1-2 minutes or until dough is smooth.

Remove dough and roll into a long roll. Cut into 10 equal portions and shape into round balls. Flatten buns lightly with a rolling pin or the palm of your hand. Place buns well apart on prepared tray, brush them with beaten egg white and liberally sprinkle with sesame seeds.

Allow to rise for 20 minutes or until doubled in bulk. Bake in preheated 200°C oven for 20 minutes or until lightly browned.

Hari Raya Puasa

COOKIES AND CAKES AS HARI RAYA GIFTS

Hari Raya Puasa, like all Malaysian festivals, is not only a time for entertaining but, more so, a time for giving. Presents made with your own hands will be even more cherished. And if they are beautifully wrapped, you will have delightful surprises for your relatives and friends.

My choice of recipes for three cakes and five cookies was made with the thought of giving in mind. They are easy and can be made well in advance. Fruity Chocolate Cookies, studded with raisins and dried apricots, are irresistible to children. Dried Mango and Hazelnut Cookies are quick-to-make drop cookies. If you like them chewy, bake them until they are just golden. For a crunchy bite, bake them until they are golden brown.

Jam Sandwich Cookies are delightfully buttery; they can either be filled with jam or served plain. Pineapple Cup Crunchies are a version of the ever-popular pineapple tarts, attractively served in multicoloured paper cases with a topping of poppy seeds. And, for the health conscious, the Almond Semolina Cookies are eggless and can be made with margarine instead of butter.

I have chosen three cakes which do not need icing so that they can be easily giftwrapped and transported. To make the cakes attractive without icing, I have used serrated ring and loaf pans to give the cakes some patterning. Fruit and nuts add colour and further enhance the appeal of the cakes.

Here also are some ideas for making your own boxes and wrappings. You'll need the following materials: multicoloured manila cardboard (those with embossed designs are prettier), floral or patterned cellophane paper, bows, ribbons, scissors, sticky tape, glue and a ruler. Each box is designed to hold one batch of cookies from my recipes.

To giftwrap the cookies, carefully place them in a strong transparent plastic bag and seal it to prevent the cookies from going soft. Gather the top of the plastic bag into a knot and secure with sticky tape. Place the bag of cookies into the gift box. Take a sheet of floral cellophane paper and wrap the whole box. Gather the edges at the top and tie with attractive ribbons.

TO MAKE ROUND BOX (See Fig. 1)
1) Cut cardboard to dimensions in Fig. 1. Cut slits in strip B as shown in diagram. Run blunt edge of knife through folding lines for easy folding.

2) Fold rectangular strip into a 15 cm diameter circle with section B flat on the table and section A vertical. Glue ends of A together.

3) Glue one piece of C onto B inside the box and the other piece on the outside.

TO MAKE RECTANGULAR BOX (See Fig. 2)
1) Cut cardboard to dimensions in Fig. 2 and run blunt edge of knife through folding lines for easy folding.

2) Fold A sections flat onto B sections to become A/B sections.

3) Fold A/B and C sections vertical to the base.

4) Fold C1 and C2 sections inwards to overlap and be at right angles to A1/B1 and A2/B2 sections.

5) Fold F sections over C1/C2 with F1 section inside box.

6) Fold A3/B3 and A4/B4 sections inwards to overlap and be at right angles to A1/B1 and A2/B2 sections.

7) Fold G sections over combined A3/B3 and A4/B4 sections with G2 vertical inside box and G3 flat on the base.

8) Cut cardboard to cover dimensions and repeat procedures to make cover.

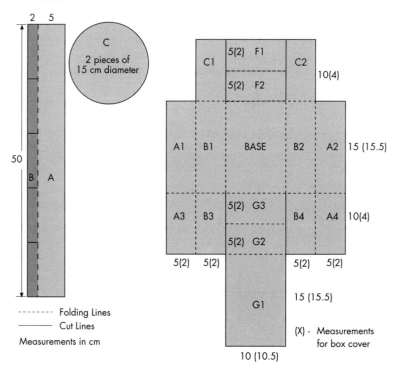

- - - - - - - - Folding Lines
———— Cut Lines

Measurements in cm

(X) - Measurements for box cover

Fruity Chocolate Cookies

250 g   butter
180 g   soft brown sugar
1 teaspoon   vanilla essence
2   small eggs, beaten

SIFTED INGREDIENTS (COMBINED)
275 g   self-raising flour
25 g   cocoa powder
1 teaspoon   baking powder

120 g   raisins
60 g   dried apricots, finely chopped

Cream butter and brown sugar until light and fluffy. Beat in vanilla essence and beaten eggs until well blended.

Sift in combined dry ingredients and then fold thoroughly with the raisins and apricots. Drop teaspoonfuls, spaced well apart, onto greased baking sheets.

Bake in preheated 195°C oven for 10-20 minutes until firm. Cool on wire racks.

Makes approximately 88 cookies.

Dried Mango and Hazelnut Cookies

250 g   butter
175 g   light brown sugar
2   small eggs, beaten

SIFTED INGREDIENTS (COMBINED)
300 g   self-raising flour
1 teaspoon   baking powder

100 g   dried mangoes, finely chopped
180 g   hazelnuts, coarsely chopped
1/2 tablespoon   milk

Cream butter and brown sugar until light and fluffy. Beat in eggs. Sift in flour and baking powder. Then mix thoroughly with mangoes and hazelnuts. Stir in milk until you have a slightly soft consistency.

Using two teaspoons, shape and drop teaspoonfuls of the mixture onto greased baking sheets.

Bake in preheated 190°C oven for 15-20 minutes until golden. Cool on wire racks.

Makes approximately 78 cookies.

Jam Sandwich Cookies

250 g   butter
180 g   icing sugar, sifted
2 teaspoons   vanilla essence

Sifted Ingredients (combined)

240 g	self-raising flour
2 teaspoons	baking powder
120 g	custard powder
1	egg white, beaten
	Sesame seeds
	Papaya or strawberry jam

Line baking trays with greased greaseproof paper.

In the bowl of an electric mixer, at medium speed, beat butter, icing sugar and vanilla essence until light and creamy. Stir in sifted ingredients and beat on lowest speed until well blended.

Place dough between two sheets of plastic wrap and roll out to $3/4$ cm thickness. Refrigerate for 30 minutes.

Using a 5 cm floral cookie cutter, stamp out cookies. Using a $1^1/2$ cm small round cutter, stamp out centres of half the pieces.

Place all pieces on prepared trays. Brush hollowed pieces with egg white and sprinkle on some sesame seeds. Bake in preheated 175°C oven for 15 minutes or until golden.

Cool on wire racks. Sandwich full and hollowed pieces with jam.

Makes approximately 68 cookies.

Pineapple Cup Crunchies

240 g	plain flour
120 g	cornflour
1 teaspoon	baking powder
240 g	cold butter, diced
180 g	castor sugar
1	egg yolk, combined with 2 teaspoons orange juice
	Pineapple jam, rolled into small balls
approx. 120	small coloured paper cases
1	egg white, beaten
	Black poppy seeds

Sift flour, cornflour and baking powder onto a baking sheet and tip ingredients into a food processor. Put in cold butter and sugar, and turn on food processor for a few seconds.

Add egg yolk and orange juice and process again until ingredients cling together.

Remove cutting blade and knead mixture lightly to form a soft dough. Roll into cherry-sized balls. Flatten each ball slightly, place a ball of jam in the centre and wrap the dough around the jam. Seal completely and shape into a ball.

Place in coloured paper cups. Brush with beaten egg white and sprinkle with poppy seeds.

Arrange on a tray and bake in preheated 175°C oven for 20 minutes or until golden brown.

Makes approximately 120 cookies.

Almond Semolina Cookies

200 g butter
100 g castor sugar
1 teaspoon vanilla essence

SIFTED INGREDIENTS (COMBINED)
200 g plain flour
1 teaspoon baking powder

60 g ground almonds
60 g semolina
Castor sugar

Cream butter and castor sugar together with vanilla essence until light and creamy. Beat in sifted ingredients, ground almonds and semolina. Refrigerate mixture for 15-20 minutes.

Shape into half-moons and place on baking sheets. Using a fork, mark a pattern on the centre of each cookie. Bake in preheated 165°C oven for 15 minutes or until golden.

Place on wire racks to cool. While still warm, dredge with castor sugar.

Pumpkin, Prune and Pineapple Cake

5 glacé cherries
2 pitted prunes, quartered
2 tablespoons quick-cooking oats
250 g butter
2 teaspoons grated orange rind
225 g castor sugar
3 large eggs
100 g cold mashed pumpkin
60 g prunes, chopped
60 g dried glazed pineapple, chopped
240 g self-raising flour, sifted
125 ml milk

Grease a 23 cm round cake pan and dust with plain flour. Arrange cherries and quartered prunes and sprinkle oats on the base.

Cream butter, orange rind and castor sugar until light and fluffy. Beat in eggs one at a time until well blended. Beat in mashed pumpkin and chopped prunes and pineapple. Stir in sifted flour and milk.

Spread mixture into prepared pan. Bake in preheated 175°C oven for 50 minutes or until cooked through when tested with a skewer.

Cool cake in tin before turning out.

Golden Date Cake

4 walnut halves
8 glacé cherries
150 ml hot water
225 g dates, chopped
180 g butter
125 g brown sugar
1 tablespoon golden syrup
2 large eggs
300 g self-raising flour, sifted
50 g chopped walnuts

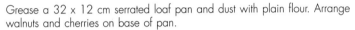

Grease a 32 x 12 cm serrated loaf pan and dust with plain flour. Arrange walnuts and cherries on base of pan.

Pour hot water on dates and leave until cooled.

Cream butter and sugar until light and fluffy. Beat in syrup and eggs one at a time. Fold in self-raising flour, then chopped walnuts and dates (with water).

Spread mixture into prepared pan. Bake in preheated 175°C oven for 1 hour and 15 minutes or until cooked through when tested with a skewer.

Leave to cool in tin before turning out.

Honey Fruitcake

250 g butter
225 g brown sugar
1 tablespoon honey
5 large eggs
200 g raisins, chopped
50 g mixed peel
50 g dried apricots, chopped
90 g cherries, chopped
60 g ground pecans
2 tablespoons orange juice

SIFTED INGREDIENTS (COMBINED)
125 g plain flour
150 g self-raising flour

1 tablespoon apricot jam
Pecans, sliced

Grease a 27 cm ring cake tin and dust with flour.

Cream butter, brown sugar and honey until light and fluffy. Beat in eggs one at a time. Stir in dried fruit, ground pecans and orange juice. Stir in sifted ingredients.

Spread mixture into prepared cake tin. Bake in preheated 160°C oven for 1 1/2 hours or until cooked through when tested with a skewer.

Cool cake in tin before turning out.

Warm apricot jam and pass it through a sieve. Spread jam on surface of cake and sprinkle with sliced pecans.

Herbs

Q: **When cooking with cordyceps and** *tong kwai,* **do I need to put them into a cotton pouch?**

A: *It is not necessary to put cordyceps and tong kwai in muslin pouches as they can easily be removed with chopsticks before serving.*

Q: What are oregano and thyme and what are their uses?

A: *Oregano and thyme are two of the most popular culinary herbs. Oregano is a wild form of marjoram with firm pungent leaves. This zesty herb is used in pasta, rice, pizzas, meatloaf and tomato dishes. Fresh oregano, if available, should be used within 4-5 days. Dried oregano is sold in jars and is easily available in supermarkets.*

Thyme is another pungent Mediterranean herb with small, slender, pointed leaves. It can be added to slow-cooking soups, stews and casseroles, and used in stuffings, chicken, beef and vegetables as well as shellfish and other seafood. Dried thyme is also easily available in supermarkets.

Q: I am interested in Italian cooking but have difficulty obtaining some ingredients, such as fresh herbs, nutmeg and pine kernels. What can I use instead?

A: *It is not easy to buy fresh herbs as they are not grown here. If they are available, they are usually air-flown in and sold in leading supermarkets. Fresh sweet basil (Thai variety) is available at wet markets. Nutmeg, whole or powdered, and pine kernels are available in most supermarkets. You can use dried instead of fresh herbs, but the flavour won't be as good. Dried herbs are sold in small bottles and a wide range is available in most supermarkets.*

Honey

Q: Is it true that honey need not be kept in the fridge?

A: *Honey should not be kept refrigerated as it will crystallise. If possible, store in a cool larder.*

Honeycomb Cake

Q: My recipe for Bee Cake turned out to be a failure. Can you give me another recipe?

A: *The Bee Cake or Honeycomb Cake, as it is more popularly known, is a lovely spongy-textured caramel cake with lots of air-pockets, making it look like a honeycomb. Here is a recipe.*

Bee Cake (Honeycomb Cake)

150 g	granulated sugar
200 ml	water
125 g	soft margarine
1/2 (397 g) can	condensed milk
4	large eggs
150 g	plain flour, sifted
1 teaspoon	bicarbonate of soda, sifted

Put sugar into a heavy-based saucepan and melt over low heat, stirring until sugar turns into an amber-coloured syrup. Remove from heat and slowly add water. Stir until the caramel syrup dissolves into a thin dark liquid. Set aside to cool.

Line the base of a 19-20 cm square cake tin with greased greaseproof paper.

Cream margarine until creamy and light. Beat in the condensed milk.

In a separate bowl, whisk eggs until light and fluffy. Stir into margarine and milk mixture. Mix until well combined. Stir in sifted dry ingredients until well blended. Add cooled syrup and mix well.

Pour into prepared tin and bake in preheated 175°C oven for 1 hour or until cake is cooked when tested with a skewer.

Ice-Cream

ICE-CREAM FOR ALL OCCASIONS

Ice-creams, sorbets and ices, refreshingly cool, light and delicious, are ideal as desserts. And homemade ones, from the simplest to the most sophisticated, can be as good as the commercial products. They are also economical and surprisingly very quick and easy to make.

There are basically two types of ice-cream. One is made with a custard base using egg yolks or cornflour as a thickening agent and the other using light or heavy cream. The cream thickens the ice-cream during the freezing process. Sorbets and ices are made of wine, fruit juices, water and sugar. They have a grainier texture than ice-creams.

Ice-cream and sorbet can be made in a freezer at the coldest setting. Fast-freezing not only saves time but also makes for better-textured ice-creams. (Always remember to return temperature settings to normal afterwards.) It is also important to chill all utensils, mixing bowls, containers and trays.

Here are some simple ice-cream and sorbet recipes.

Vanilla Ice-Cream

2 cups double or thickened cream
1 cup light whipping cream
3/4 cup castor sugar
Pinch of salt
2 teaspoons vanilla essence

In a chilled bowl, whisk creams lightly together with sugar for 1 minute. Add salt and vanilla essence and mix well.

Pour into a chilled deep plastic container and freeze until set.

French Vanilla Ice-Cream

1/2 vanilla pod or 2 teaspoons vanilla essence
150 ml single cream
150 ml full fat milk
3 egg yolks
75 g castor sugar
300 ml carton of heavy or double cream

Put split vanilla pod or essence, single cream and milk in a heavy-based saucepan. Stir and bring to a slow boil. Remove from heat, cover and leave to infuse for 30 minutes. Remove pod, if you are using it.

Place yolks and sugar in a medium bowl and whisk until they are light in colour and thicken slightly. Pour milk mixture into egg mixture, whisking constantly.

Rinse saucepan and return mixture to pan. Have ready a cold bowl with a sieve on top. Place the saucepan over a low heat and stir custard constantly until it thickens and begins to coat back of spoon — this takes about 10 minutes. When froth begins to subside, custard is starting to thicken. Do not boil or custard will curdle. Strain and cool.

Whip cream until it just begins to hold its shape and stir gently into custard. Pour into a shallow chilled freezer tray and freeze until mushy, about 2-3 hours.

Remove ice-cream from freezer and lightly beat with a whisk to break down ice crystals. Do this quickly. Return ice-cream to freezer until firm. This takes about 3 hours.

Lime Sorbet

2/3 cup sugar
1 3/4 cups water
1 1/4 teaspoons gelatine, dissolved in 1/4 cup water
1/2 cup lime juice, chilled
2 drops green colouring
2 egg whites

Put sugar and water in a saucepan. Stir over gentle heat until sugar dissolves. Bring to a boil. Boil for 5 minutes, covered, stirring to avoid crystallisation.

Add gelatine mixture and stir well. Cool and chill. Add chilled lime juice and green colouring and stir well to combine ingredients.

Whisk egg whites until just stiff but not dry. Fold into lime juice mixture. Pour into cold freezer trays or shallow tins, cover with plastic wrap or foil and freeze until the edges are just beginning to freeze and the centre is mushy.

Beat in a chilled bowl quickly with a balloon whisk and return to freezer trays. Repeat process one more time, then freeze for about 3 hours or until well frozen.

Serve scooped in individual glasses and garnish with pineapple, kiwis or other fresh fruit.

Orange Lemon Ice

	Grated rind of 1 orange
	Grated rind of 1 lemon
1³/₄ cups	sugar
4 cups	water
2 cups	orange juice
4 tablespoons	fresh lemon juice

In a saucepan, combine orange and lemon rind and sugar. Stir in water, bring to a boil and boil for 5 minutes. Chill well and, when cold, add orange and lemon juice. Pour into two ice cube trays and cover with plastic wrap. Place in freezer.

When the mixture is frozen to a mushy consistency, remove it to a chilled bowl and quickly beat with an electric whisk until smooth. Return mixture to trays, cover and freeze again. Repeat every hour or until mixture is completely frozen.

Q: Could you give me a recipe for low-fat ice-cream?

A: For the calorie-conscious, ice-cream can be made with yoghurt instead of cream. Here is a recipe for a vanilla yoghurt ice and a delicious low-fat banana-yoghurt ice cream.

Vanilla Yoghurt Ice

3	egg whites
75 g	castor sugar
450 g	plain yoghurt
1 teaspoon	vanilla essence

Whisk egg whites until stiff. Add sugar a tablespoon at a time, whisking constantly, until stiff and glossy.

Fold in yoghurt and vanilla essence. Pour mixture into a freezer-proof container.

Fast freeze for 2 hours, then whisk or blend in a food processor until smooth. Repeat this procedure three times.

Freeze until firm. To serve, place in fridge for 15 minutes before serving.

For coffee yoghurt ice, add 2 teaspoons instant coffee diluted with 1 teaspoon hot water; for chocolate yoghurt ice, add 2 teaspoons cocoa powder.

Banana Yoghurt Ice Cream

120 g white marshmallows
4 tablespoons milk
3 large ripe bananas, peeled
1 tablespoon lemon juice
25 g castor sugar
300 ml thick yoghurt

Chocolate shavings
Mango slices

Cut marshmallows into quarters with scissors dipped in water. Put with milk in a heatproof bowl and place over a saucepan of simmering water. Stir until marshmallows have completely melted. Allow to cool.

Mash bananas with lemon juice and sugar. Blend into marshmallow mixture, then beat in yoghurt. Beat vigorously until smooth and well combined.

Spoon into a well-chilled plastic ice-cream container and freeze, covered, until beginning to set. Remove from freezer and place in a well chilled bowl. Beat vigorously to break up ice crystals. Return to freezer and repeat process.

Freeze until firm. Just before serving, place ice-cream in the refrigerator for 10-12 minutes (for easier scooping) and scoop into ice-cream glasses. Serve garnished with chocolate shavings or mango slices.

Icing

Q: I would be very grateful if you could give me the recipe for chocolate fudge icing.

A: Here's a recipe for a soft fudgy icing which is excellent for a dark rich chocolate cake.

Chocolate Fudge Icing

110 g unsalted butter
30 g cocoa powder, sifted
3 tablespoons milk
285 g icing sugar, sifted

Melt butter together with cocoa and milk in a saucepan. Stir well. Cool and chill for 10-15 minutes.

Beat in the icing sugar until creamy and smooth. Spread on top and sides of a 20-21 cm round cake.

To decorate, mark with a palette knife or fork. Leave to set.

Q: Can you give me the recipe for a hard chocolate icing?

A: I hope you like this chocolate icing recipe. It is enough to cover the surface of a 20 cm round or square cake.

Chocolate Icing

125 g dark plain chocolate, chopped
30 g butter

Melt chocolate and butter over hot water. Cool slightly and spread on surface of cake.

Q: Could you please tell me how to prevent royal icing from discolouring and becoming too hard?

A: Beating in one teaspoon of glycerine for 450 g icing sugar used will stop royal icing from hardening too much. To prevent discoloration, cover the fruitcake with marzipan before icing. (Be sure not to over-knead marzipan as this may cause oil to surface which could also discolour the icing.) Roll out marzipan between sheets of plastic wrap to prevent cake crumbs catching in marzipan and, when placing marzipan on cake, be careful not to get any apricot jam on the surface of the marzipan. Allow marzipan to dry out a little before applying royal icing. Apply icing in two to three layers, the first two thin and the third one thick.

Q: I would be grateful if you could let me have the recipe for marshmallow icing.

A: To make marshmallow icing you will need to use a candy thermometer to prevent crystallisation.

Chocolate Marshmallow Icing

1¹/₂ cups sugar
1¹/₂ cups water
60 g grated unsweetened or semisweet chocolate
1 dozen large marshmallows, cut into eighths and steamed until soft
¹/₈ teaspoon cream of tartar
2 egg whites
Pinch of salt

Put sugar and water in a saucepan. Stir without heating until sugar is dissolved. Then cover and cook for about 3 minutes or until steam washes down any crystals that may have formed on sides of pan.

Remove cover and cook without stirring to 238-240°C (read at eye level to ensure accuracy). Remove from heat and add grated chocolate and marshmallows.

Let this mixture stand until ingredients no longer bubble. Stir in cream of tartar.

In an electric mixing bowl, whisk egg whites with salt until just stiff. Pour in syrup in a thin stream, whipping constantly, until icing has a spreading consistency.

Q: Please tell me how to make a soft butter icing. How do I spread icing evenly on a cake?

A: Butter icing is basically butter and icing sugar, but you can also add milk, sugar syrup, fruit juice or cream. You should come up with an icing that is smooth, spreadable and firm enough for decoration. If the end result is too soft for piping, you can either reduce the quantity of butter or beat in more icing sugar.

To cover and decorate a cake with icing, you must first spread a thin layer of icing sugar all over the cake. Spoon about one-third of the icing on top and spread out evenly. Then, using a ruler or palette knife longer then the width of the cake, draw the icing at an angle of 30° across the top of the cake without applying pressure.

Trim the edges and remove surplus. Spoon a further third around the sides evenly. Then, using an icing scraper or palette knife, smooth and flatten the sides. It will be easier if you have a rotating plate. Hold the palette knife upright at an angle of 45° on the side of the cake and, as you draw it towards you, rotate the plate with your other hand.

Here is a recipe for vanilla butter icing.

Vanilla Butter Icing

180 g	cold butter, diced
210 g	icing sugar, sifted
A few drops	vanilla essence
2-3 tablespoons	cold milk
A few drops	food colouring, optional

Put butter in the bowl of an electric mixer and beat until creamy. Gradually beat in icing sugar, vanilla essence and milk. Continue to beat until smooth.

Add colouring, if desired, and stir until icing is evenly coloured.

Ikan Bilis

Q: Could you tell me how to fry *ikan bilis* — the sweet and hot type usually eaten with drinks?

A: Here's a version of the recipe you requested.

Fried Ikan Bilis in Chilli

60 g	cleaned *ikan bilis*
6-8	dried chillies, seeded and soaked until soft
1 clove	garlic
2 tablespoons	cooking oil
1/2 tablespoon	sugar

Rinse *ikan bilis* quickly and drain well. Spread out on a plate and dry in the microwave on high, or in a hot oven for 5 minutes. You can also dry them in the sun for about an hour.

Pound dried chillies and garlic until fine.

Heat oil in a frying pan and stir-fry *ikan bilis* for 3-4 minutes until crisp and golden brown in colour. Drain well, leaving oil in pan.

Fry ground chilli-garlic paste over low heat for a few minutes. Add sugar, stirring, until it melts. Put in tamarind juice, mix well and simmer for 30 seconds. Return *ikan bilis* to pan and cook for 1-2 minutes.

Jams

A FRUITFUL CHOICE OF JAMS

If your family has a sweet tooth and goes through jars and jars of jam, it is time you made your own. Local fruit is suitable for making jams and is in great abundance throughout the year. Homemade jam has more fruit and is free from artificial preservatives and colouring. You can make it just the way you like it: runny or thick, smooth or filled with chunks of fruit.

Local papayas, mangoes, pineapples, durians, star fruit and strawberries all make excellent and tasty jams. I like the Eksotika papaya, which is a hybrid of our local papaya and the Hawaiian Sunrise Solo. The sweet delicate flesh, rich orange in colour with a tinge of red, makes an appetising jam. As for mangoes, the tart cream-coloured flesh of the popular *harum manis*, elephant tusk or apple mangoes makes excellent flavoured jams. All varieties of pineapples are suitable, but I particularly like the sweet Nanas Sarawak with its pale yellow flesh.

Choose fresh, firm and undamaged fruit which is underripe or just ripe. Fruit which is too ripe lacks sufficient acid and pectin, but you can make up for this by adding some lemon juice.

Granulated sugar, which is easily available, is most economical for jam making. However, preserving sugar, if available, is easier to use and will ensure better results, especially for those not familiar with jam making.

Use a good quality, strong, deep saucepan with a heavy base to prevent the jam from burning and sticking. There are special preserving or jam pans, but they may not be available locally. These pans are wider across the top than the bottom to improve evaporation, and deep enough to allow the jam to boil vigorously. The important thing to remember is not to overfill the pan. It should be half full after the sugar has been added.

A long-handled wooden spoon for stirring is essential. The jam must be continuously stirred while cooking to prevent it from getting burnt.

Jam should be boiled until it reaches a temperature of 105°C, the setting point. A sugar thermometer is very useful to obtain a perfect set. The thermometer should be clipped to the side of the pan but must not touch the bottom. If a thermometer is not available, test for set by pouring a teaspoonful of the jam onto a chilled saucer and leave to cool for one minute. Then push a finger across the surface; if the setting point has been reached, the surface will wrinkle a little. (Turn the heat off while testing to prevent over-boiling.)

It is better to slightly undercook than overcook the jam. Undercooked jam is more fluid, while overcooked jam is more solid and lumpy. You risk burning the jam if you overcook it. If you find on cooling that the jam has not set properly, it is perfectly all right to boil it again until set.

Once the jam is set, remove surface scum with a metal spoon and allow jam to cool slightly before pouring into well-cleaned, warmed jars. After filling, place a round piece of waxed paper on the surface of the jam and carefully wipe off any spillage around the rim of the jar. Cap and tighten lids when the jam is completely cooled.

Pineapple and Orange Marmalade

1	large orange
2 tablespoons	lemon juice
600 ml	water
800 g	pineapple (cleaned weight), coarsely chopped
750 g	preserving or granulated sugar

Wash and dry orange. Cut into quarters, remove pips and shred thinly into a large deep pan. Add lemon juice, water and pineapple. Cover and bring to a boil. Reduce heat and simmer for 40 minutes or until pineapple is soft. Add sugar and stir over gentle heat until sugar is completely dissolved.

Bring jam to a rapid boil and boil rapidly for 30 minutes, stirring frequently until setting point is reached. A teaspoonful on a cold saucer should wrinkle when pushed with the finger while still slightly warm.

Remove any scum from surface with a metal spoon. Leave to cool for about 15 minutes before storing in jars.

Strawberry Jam

1.6 kg	strawberries
	Juice of 1 lemon
1.3 kg	preserving or granulated sugar
25 g	butter

Select fresh and slightly underripe strawberries. Remove stalks and put fruit into a large, deep pan and pour in lemon juice.

Cover and simmer gently over low heat for about 20 minutes until strawberries are really soft. Stir frequently and press fruit against sides of pan to extract juice. Add sugar and stir over a gentle heat until sugar is completely dissolved.

Bring jam to a rapid boil and boil for about 10-15 minutes until temperature reaches setting point. A teaspoonful on a cold saucer should wrinkle when pushed with the finger while still slightly warm.

Stir in butter, which helps to reduce scum. Leave jam to cool for about 15 minutes before storing in jam jars.

Papaya Jam

1.7 kg	papayas (cleaned weight), cut into 1 cm cubes
6 tablespoons	lemon juice
1.1 kg	preserving or granulated sugar

Place papaya cubes in a large deep pan and add lemon juice. Simmer gently for about 30 minutes or until cubes are really soft. Stir frequently to prevent sticking. Add sugar and stir over a gentle heat until it has completely dissolved.

Bring jam to a rapid boil and boil for 30-35 minutes, stirring frequently, until temperature reaches setting point. A teaspoonful on a cold saucer should wrinkle when pushed with finger while still slightly warm.

Remove any scum from surface with a metal spoon. Leave to cool for about 15 minutes before storing in jam jars.

Note: *If you prefer a smooth jam, purée the papaya in a food processor before cooking. Do not add any water.*

Papaya and Jackfruit Jam

1.7 kg papaya, cleaned weight
600 g jackfruit, cleaned weight
1 cup water
5 tablespoons lemon juice
1 kg sugar

Cut papaya into chunks and blend in an electric blender. It is not necessary to add water. Chop jackfruit into small pieces and make a purée with one cup water.

Put papaya and jackfruit purées with lemon juice into a large, deep pan. Cover and simmer, stirring frequently, for about 20 minutes. Add sugar and stir over a gentle heat until it has completely dissolved.

Bring the jam to a rapid boil and boil for about 15 minutes, stirring frequently, until temperature reaches setting point. A teaspoonful on a cold saucer should wrinkle when pushed with the finger while still slightly warm.

Remove any scum from surface with a metal spoon. Leave to cool for about 15 minutes before storing in jam jars.

Mango Jam

2 kg mangoes (cleaned weight), coarsely
chopped
500 ml water
5 tablespoons lemon juice
1 kg preserving or granulated sugar

Place coarsely chopped mangoes in a large deep pan. Add water and lemon juice. Simmer gently, stirring occasionally, for about 40 minutes or until fruit is soft.

Add sugar and stir until it is dissolved. Bring jam to a rapid boil and boil for 15 minutes, stirring frequently until temperature reaches setting point. A teaspoonful on a cold saucer should wrinkle when pushed with the finger while still slightly warm.

Remove any scum from surface with a metal spoon. Leave to cool for about 15 minutes before storing in jam jars.

Note: *If a smoother jam is preferred, purée the mangoes with some of the water in a food processor before cooking.*

TREATS WITH JAM

Here are some interesting ideas on how you can turn the jam you have made into special treats for your family and guests.

Wholewheat Buns

Tired of plain old toast with jam? Well, try these light wholemeal buns which are simple and quick to make. They make a delightful breakfast served with margarine or butter and a thin spread of jam.

225 g	high-protein flour
225 g	plain wholemeal flour
1 teaspoon	salt
2 teaspoons	sugar
15 ml	easy-blend yeast
30 g	margarine
150 ml	tepid milk
165 ml	warm water
1	egg, beaten, for glazing

FOR COATING BUNS

Rolled oats, bran flakes, sunflower kernels, sesame seeds, cumin seeds, black poppy seeds

Lightly grease a large cookie tray or line with nonstick baking sheet.

Sift high-protein flour and wholemeal flour onto sheet of baking paper. Return husks from sieve onto baking paper. Tip into a food processor. Stir in salt, sugar and yeast. Blend in margarine.

Pour warm milk and water into mixture. Process for 5 minutes or until dough is smooth. Allow dough to rise, covered, in food processor for 30 minutes or until doubled in bulk.

Knock down dough and process for 2 minutes or until dough is smooth. Roll out into a long roll and cut into 12 equal portions. Shape each portion into a round, roll in beaten egg and coat with nuts, oats, bran or seeds.

Place buns onto cookie trays. Cover with a tea towel and allow to rise for 15-20 minutes or until doubled in bulk.

Bake in preheated 200°C oven for 20 minutes. Cool on wire racks.

English Muffins

These yeasted muffins have a moist inner crumb and a crispy crust. Serve them for breakfast as a refreshing change from toast or as a quick snack. They should be served hot, toasted on both sides. Then pull them apart with fingers, butter thickly, spread with jam and put together again.

500 g	plain flour
1 level teaspoon	salt
15 g	easy-blend yeast
150 ml	warm milk
100 ml	warm water
1	egg, beaten
25 g	melted butter

Sift flour into bowl of food processor. Stir in salt and yeast. Add milk, water, beaten egg and melted butter. Turn on food processor and blend for 3 minutes or until dough is smooth.

Leave to rise, covered, until doubled in size. Turn out onto floured board. Knead lightly and roll out to 1 cm thickness.

Cut into 16 rounds with an 8 cm cookie cutter. Transfer to a baking tray lined with nonstick baking paper. Cover and leave to rise for 15 minutes or until doubled in size.

Bake towards top of preheated 230°C oven for 5-6 minutes. Turn over and bake for another 5-6 minutes.

Jam Doughnuts

520 g plain flour, sifted
15 g instant yeast
1 teaspoon salt

MELTED INGREDIENTS (COMBINED)

30 g butter
30 g vegetable shortening
90 g sugar

200 ml milk
2 teaspoons grated orange rind
2 large eggs, beaten with a fork
1 egg white, beaten for brushing

Jam of your choice
90 g castor sugar, combined with
1/2 teaspoon cinnamon

Sift flour into a large basin and stir in yeast and salt.

Stir melted fat and sugar into milk. Add orange rind and mix well. Add beaten eggs. Pour into flour mixture. Mix well and knead. Cover bowl and leave to rise until dough doubles in bulk.

Knead dough on a lightly floured board until smooth. Roll out onto a floured board until 3/4 cm thick. Stamp out 5 cm rounds. Gather edges of remaining dough and roll out again. Stamp out again into 5 cm rounds.

Take one round, dent centre slightly with back of teaspoon and fill with one teaspoon jam. Brush another round with egg white and place brushed side down onto jam-filled piece. Pinch to seal and leave on a lightly floured tray. Continue with remaining dough rounds.

Heat oil. Deep-fry doughnuts until golden and puffed up. Drain on absorbent paper and roll in sugar and cinnamon mixture.

Makes approximately 17 doughnuts.

Papaya Jam Squares

250 g self-raising flour, sifted
90 g light brown sugar
1 teaspoon grated lemon rind
1/4 teaspoon salt
180 g cold butter, diced
Papaya jam

Grease a 22¹/₂ cm square pan. Preheat oven to 190°C.

Combine flour, sugar, lemon rind and salt in bowl of food processor, fitted with a cutting blade. Blend in butter until mixture is crumbly.

Remove approximately 220 g of flour mixture and set aside. Pat remaining mixture evenly into prepared pan.

Carefully spread papaya jam evenly on top, leaving 1 cm border around the edges. Sprinkle reserved flour mixture over jam. Smooth and press surface lightly with back of a spoon.

Bake 40 minutes or until lightly browned. Cool in pan on wire rack. Cut into squares.

Pineapple Almond Slice

This unusual slice makes a lovely treat for afternoon tea. It consists of a light crisp pastry base spread with a mixture of homemade pineapple orange marmalade and fresh or canned chopped pineapple, and covered with a moist almond topping.

200 g	plain flour
1/4 teaspoon	salt
90 g	castor sugar
150 g	butter, diced
1	egg, beaten
1/2-1 tablespoon	milk
200 g	pineapple and orange marmalade
275 g	fresh or canned pineapple, chopped

ALMOND TOPPING

125 g	butter
120 g	castor sugar
3	eggs, beaten
60 g	ground almonds
125 g	self-raising flour, sifted
	Grated rind and juice of 1 lemon
2 tablespoons	milk
75 g	flaked almonds

Grease sides and line base of 28 x 20 cm baking pan with greased greaseproof paper.

Sift flour into bowl of food processor fitted with a cutting blade. Add salt and sugar.

Blend for a couple of seconds, then add butter and blend until mixture resembles breadcrumbs. Turn out into mixing bowl.

Add egg and work mixture together with your fingertips, gradually adding enough milk until it makes a soft pliable dough. Chill for an hour.

Roll out chilled dough between two sheets of plastic wrap, then use it to line base of prepared pan. Spread pineapple and orange marmalade on top of dough, then top with chopped pineapple.

Pour almond topping over marmalade and pineapples. Smooth surface and scatter with flaked almonds.

Bake in preheated 200°C oven for 20 minutes. Reduce temperature to 175°C and cook for a further 40-45 minutes. Cool in tin before cutting into rectangular pieces.

To Make Almond Topping
Cream butter and sugar until pale and fluffy, then beat in eggs and ground almonds until well blended. Stir in flour, lemon rind, juice and milk until you have a dropping consistency.

Kaya

Q: How does one make good kaya?

> *A: The old-fashioned method of making a good smooth kaya is time con-suming. I used to watch the old folks do it. The recipe calls for 10 large eggs, 600 g granulated sugar and pati santan (undiluted coconut milk) from three grated coconuts. Put all the ingredients into a double boiler and stir almost nonstop over gently boiling water for approximately 1¹/₂ hours. You have to like kaya very much to be prepared to do this.*

Q: Is there a way to make kaya in the microwave oven?

> *A: Try making kaya in the microwave by cutting the cooking time to 30 minutes. Remember to stir at five-minute intervals.*

Kerabu

Q: Please furnish me with a recipe for kerabu.

A: Here's one of my favourite vegetable kerabu dishes.

Four-Angled Bean Kerabu

300 g	four-angled beans
5	shallots, finely sliced
	Juice of 1 lime
	Juice of 6 small limes
8	bird chillies (chilli padi), sliced
1	red chilli, sliced
3 teaspoons	sugar
1/4 teaspoon	salt
2 tablespoons	roasted grated young coconut (from whites only)
50 g	dried prawns, rinsed, ground and toasted

Cut beans into 4-5 cm lengths. Scald in boiling water until just cooked. Combine with all remaining ingredients. Toss well and serve with rice.

Kuih

NONYA KUIH

These dainty, velvety smooth little mouthfuls make sumptuous teatime treats and great desserts for everyday meals and grand festive dinners alike.

I have always regarded the inventors of *kuih* as clever people indeed to be able to come up with these tempting concoctions from such simple ingredients as flour, eggs, coconut, palm sugar and pandan leaves. Sweet potatoes, tapioca, yams and bananas are all turned into delectable sweet delights.

The Nonyas have perfected the making of *kuih*; it became a matter of family pride to make the best in the village. The ingredients may be simple, but mastering the technique takes plenty of practice. My aunt, a wizard at making *kuih*, can vouch for that.

She tells me that in order to get the right, soft, smooth texture, one must pay a lot of attention to detail. Make sure the flour is finely ground; use fresh coconut milk, made only from the white part of the coconut; never use pandan essence as a substitute for fresh pandan leaves; don't drastically reduce the amount of sugar called for; strain the batter and steam it immediately over rapidly boiling water; if the lid is lifted during steaming, wipe it dry to prevent water from dripping into the batter.

Here are some delicious *kuih* recipes.

Kuih Bingka Beras

SIFTED INGREDIENTS (COMBINED)

110 g	rice flour
50 g	green bean flour
25 g	tapioca flour

230 g	sugar
875 ml	thick coconut milk obtained from 1¹/₂ grated white coconuts
2 tablespoons	pati santan (undiluted coconut milk) obtained from ¹/₄ grated white coconut

Place sifted dry ingredients into a large mixing bowl. Stir in sugar and thick coconut milk.

Strain flour-coconut milk mixture into a nonstick saucepan and cook over medium heat until thick.

Pour mixture into a 20 cm square cake pan. Spread and smooth surface with a spatula.

Brush surface with pati santan and bake in 220°C oven for 45-50 minutes until topping is lightly browned. Cool thoroughly before cutting into small slices.

Kuih Lapis

540 g	sugar
1 cup	water
6	pandan leaves, knotted
600 g	wet rice dough
105 g	tapioca flour
30 g	green bean flour
6 cups	coconut milk made from 2¹/₂ white coconuts
a few drops	red colouring

Put sugar, water and pandan leaves into a saucepan and bring to a gentle boil, stirring to dissolve sugar. Strain and set aside to cool.

Put wet rice dough, tapioca flour and green bean flour into a large mixing bowl. Gradually pour in coconut milk and mix well. Stir in syrup. Strain until smooth and free from lumps.

Divide mixture into two. Leave one half white and add enough red food colouring to other half to obtain a pink batter.

Place a 27 cm round cake pan in a steamer of rapidly boiling water. Pour one cup white batter into pan. Cover and steam over medium heat for 8-10 minutes. When set, carefully pour in one cup of pink batter and steam for another 8-10 minutes.

Repeat procedure, alternating white and pink batter until batter is used up. There should be five white layers and five pink layers. For the final top pink layer, add one to two drops of red colouring to get a deeper shade of pink.

Cool kuih for at least six to seven hours before cutting into small diamond-shaped pieces.

Kuih Talam

150 g	rice flour, sifted and mixed with 325 ml water
90 g	sago flour, sifted and mixed with 325 ml water
5	pandan leaves, cut into 3 cm pieces
250 ml	water
400 g	sugar
a few drops	green colouring

FOR WHITE COCONUT LAYER

100 g	rice flour
1/2 teaspoon	salt
275 ml	santan from 1 1/2 grated white coconuts
400 ml	water

Mix rice flour and 325 ml water in a bowl and leave to soak for 10 minutes. In separate bowl mix sago flour with 325 ml of water and leave to soak for 10 minutes.

Put pandan leaves and 250 ml water in liquidiser and blend. Strain the pandan juice through a fine sieve.

In a large nonstick saucepan, mix rice mixture, sago mixture, pandan juice, sugar and green colouring. Cook over low heat, stirring constantly with a wooden spoon, until batter becomes translucent and thickened.

Pour hot batter into a greased 26 cm round cake pan. Level surface with a plastic spatula. Steam over rapidly boiling water for 30 minutes.

Meanwhile, prepare white coconut layer. Sift rice flour into a mixing bowl. Stir in salt, santan and water. Pour over cooked green layer. Steam again for a further six minutes.

Cool *kuih* thoroughly before slicing into diamond-shaped pieces.

Apam Balik

300 g	plain flour
1/2 teaspoon	salt
225 ml	coconut water
80 g	gula Melaka, chopped into tiny pieces
1 tablespoon	dark brown sugar
5	pandan leaves, knotted
500 ml	coconut milk, from 1 grated coconut
1	egg, beaten
3/4 teaspoon	baking powder
1/4 teaspoon	alkaline water

Sift flour into a mixing bowl and stir in salt. Put coconut water, gula Melaka, brown sugar and pandan leaves in a saucepan. Bring to a slow boil, stirring over low heat until sugar dissolves.

Strain hot syrup into flour and stir well. Stir in half the coconut milk, then beaten egg and remaining coconut milk, baking powder and alkaline water. Strain mixture if lumpy. Set aside to ferment for an hour.

Using **Kuih Bahulu** *mould:*

Heat mould until very hot. Grease well with cooking oil. Lower heat and spoon in batter to fill each mould half full.

When batter starts to bubble and looks like a honeycomb, cover and cook for one minute.

Remove cover, loosen sides with a small butter knife and lift out *kuih* with a satay stick.

Using a **Kuali** *or Nonstick Pan:*

Grease a 22 cm *kuali* or nonstick pan. Pour in one-third of a cup batter and swirl around pan.

Cook for between 30 seconds and one minute on one side only. Remove and fold into half.

Variation: Durian *apam balik* is absolutely delicious, especially if you love durians. Stir about 100 g mashed durian pulp into the batter.

Q: How do I make wet rice dough?

A: First soak rice in water overnight. Grind in a stone grinder or liquidiser. Place watery rice batter in a fine cloth (preferably muslin) bag and tie it up securely. Place a heavy object on the bag to squeeze out excess water.

To make 600 g of wet rice dough, you will need 400-450 g of rice. It is easier to buy ready-prepared wet rice dough in the wet market.

Langkawi Food

CONCOCTING A TASTE OF PULAU LANGKAWI

The food of Pulau Langkawi is a blend of Chinese, Malay, Indian and Thai cuisine. The local Chinese have adapted their methods of cooking to produce Chinese-style sauces with a blend of fiery Thai, Malay and Indian ingredients. The result is a delicious style of cooking.

On a recent visit to the island, I tried a number of dishes. I had fried local *ikan merah*, fresh and plump with a blend of thick, dark soya sauce and lime juice and a generous topping of sliced raw shallots and blistering hot chilli padi. A plate of cuttlefish came in thickened sauce sprinkled with pieces of lemongrass and curry leaves. Absolutely yummy.

We also had king prawns, fresh from the sea. Again, it was smothered with sliced, fresh raw shallots and lots of chilli padi; clearly they have a passion for shallots and chilli padi in Langkawi.

I also tasted a fresh oyster omelette which was very different from the normal sticky stuff. This version was cooked to a soft perfection without the sweet potato flour, and was seared and served on a sizzling hot plate. It was delightfully loaded with fresh local oysters. Truly delicious when eaten with a small plate of soya sauce and chilli padi.

The fish with sambal was different from any that I have tasted. The sambal was finely ground with onion, chillies, lemon grass and lengkuas and was suitably darkened and thickened with thick soya sauce and fish sauce.

It was not easy fishing out recipes from the cooks I spoke to. As they put it, they cook with a "little bit of this" and a "little bit of that". Here, then, are my own versions, which I think are pretty close to the dishes we tried.

Spicy Prawns Langkawi Style

0.6-1 kg (about 15-16)	large prawns, feelers and eyes trimmed
1 teaspoon	salt
1/2 teaspoon	pepper
1/2 tablespoon	cornflour
3 tablespoons	oil
5 cm piece	young ginger, minced with 4 cloves garlic

SAUCE INGREDIENTS (COMBINED)

1 teaspoon	dark soya sauce
1 tablespoon	light soya sauce
1 tablespoon	sugar
1/2 teaspoon	salt
1 tablespoon	lime or lemon juice

10-12	chilli padi, sliced
5	shallots, sliced
2-3 stalks	spring onion, cut into 1 cm lengths

Season prawns with salt and pepper. Just before deep-frying prawns, sprinkle with cornflour. Deep-fry in hot oil for 3-5 minutes until just cooked. Drain. Arrange on a serving dish.

Reheat a clean wok with 3 tablespoons oil and lightly brown ginger and garlic. Pour in combined sauce ingredients and bring to a boil. When sauce thickens, add chilli padi.

Pour sauce over prawns. Sprinkle raw, sliced shallots and spring onion on top, with some additional sliced chilli padi, if desired.

Langkawi Style Sotong Curry

500 g	cleaned, medium-sized cuttlefish, cut into 2 1/2 cm rounds
1/2 teaspoon each	salt and sugar
1/4 teaspoon	pepper
3 tablespoons	cooking oil
2	medium onions, diced
4 stalks	lemon grass, cut into 5 cm lengths
6 stalks	curry leaves
1/2 teaspoon	fenugreek
2 tablespoons	fish curry powder and 4 tablespoons water, mixed into a paste

1/2 tablespoon	*assam jawa* and 3 tablespoons water, mixed and strained
3/4 teaspoon	salt
1/2 teaspoon	sugar
1/2 cup	thick coconut milk from 1/4 small coconut, grated

Season cuttlefish with salt, sugar and pepper for 15 minutes.

Heat oil in a saucepan and cook the onions and lemon grass for 5 minutes until soft and fragrant. Add curry leaves and fenugreek and fry briefly for 30 seconds. When fragrant, put in curry powder paste and cook for one minute. Add tamarind juice and seasonings.

When mixture begins to boil, put in cuttlefish. Cook for 3-5 minutes. Add coconut milk and bring to a boil again. Reduce heat and simmer for 3-5 minutes until curry is thick.

Fish with Spicy Sour Sauce

600 g	red snapper, scaled and cleaned
1 teaspoon	salt
1/2 teaspoon	pepper
1 tablespoon	cornflour
2 tablespoons	cooking oil
1	onion, cut into wedges

SAUCE INGREDIENTS (COMBINED)

1/4 cup	*ikan bilis* stock or water
1 tablespoon	dark soya sauce
1 tablespoon	light soya sauce
1 tablespoon	fish sauce
1 teaspoon	sesame oil
3 teaspoons	sugar
1/2 teaspoon	salt
1/4 teaspoon	pepper
1 tablespoon	lime or lemon juice

10	chilli padi, sliced
2 tablespoons	*ikan bilis* stock or water and 1 teaspoonful cornflour, combined
12	shallots, sliced
2-3 stalks	spring onion, cut into 1 cm lengths
2 sprigs	coriander leaves, cut into 1 cm lengths

Season fish with salt and pepper and leave for 15 to 20 minutes.

Just before deep-frying fish, coat with cornflour.

Heat deep-frying oil until hot and fry fish for approximately 8-10 minutes until cooked through. Remove from oil and place on a serving dish.

Heat oil in a saucepan and fry onion until soft. Add combined sauce ingredients and bring to a boil. Stir in chilli padi. Thicken with cornflour mixture.

Pour sauce over fish. Top with sliced shallots, spring onion and coriander leaves and extra sliced chilli padi if desired.

Marshmallows

Q: I would appreciate it very much if you could give me a simple and easy recipe for marshmallows.

A: To make homemade marshmallows you need an electric mixer with a balloon whisk and a sugar thermometer. Here's an easy-to-follow recipe.

Marshmallows

30 g (2 tablespoons)	gelatine
75 ml (5 tablespoons)	water
275 g	granulated sugar
2 teaspoons (10 g)	glucose powder
1	egg white
2 teaspoons	vanilla essence
	Icing sugar

Line the base and sides of a 16 cm square tin with nonstick baking parchment.

In a small bowl sprinkle gelatine over water. Leave to soak for about 10 minutes. Place gelatine over a pan of simmering water and heat gently until mixture becomes clear. Keep warm.

Over low heat, dissolve granulated sugar and glucose powder in 225 ml water. Bring to a boil and let it bubble and boil until it reaches 128°C on a sugar thermometer. Take the pan off heat.

Whip the egg white until stiff. Pour in the sugar mixture in a slow, steady stream, whisking all the time. Whisk in the liquid gelatine and vanilla essence. Keep whisking until the mixture starts to stiffen.

Pour into the prepared tin and dust liberally with icing sugar. Leave to set in a cool place overnight.

Cut into squares, rolling each piece in sifted icing sugar. Store in an airtight container for up to two weeks.

Marzipan

Q: I would like to make my own marzipan. Can you give me a recipe?

A: Here's a simple recipe for marzipan. You can increase or decrease the amount of sugar to suit your own taste, or try adding different flavourings such as vanilla or almond essence, or rosewater.

Marzipan

250 g	finely ground almonds
250 g	castor sugar
1	egg white, lightly beaten with a fork
a few drops	vanilla or almond essence, or 1-2 tablespoons rosewater, optional

Line a baking tray with greaseproof paper and spread the ground almonds in a thin layer. Toast in preheated 150°C oven for about 10 minutes. Allow to cool.

Combine toasted ground almonds with the castor sugar in a food processor and process for a few seconds until mixture feels like wholemeal flour.

Add egg white and flavouring and beat until the mixture forms a stiff paste. Form into a ball and place in a plastic bag. Flatten into a small square or rectangular block and seal bag.

Leave in refrigerator to mature for two days before using. It will keep well, wrapped tightly in plastic wrap and stored in the refrigerator, for 5-6 weeks.

Measures

Q: I came across a recipe using 0.38 g of ammonia. How many teaspoons do I need to use? I have a problem weighing out that amount.

A: *You do not have to use a scale for this. Just a tiny pinch of ammonia is sufficient for use in most recipes.*

Q: When I use measuring spoons, should I fill the spoon just to the rim or until it peaks?

A: *Measuring spoons and cups are important for accurately measuring dry or liquid ingredients. Unless specified otherwise in a recipe, the correct way to measure dry ingredients is to fill the measuring spoon or cup and then level the surface with a knife. Don't press or shake down the ingredients you are measuring.*

Q: How much is a dessertspoonful?

A: *A dessertspoonful is approximately 15 ml.*

Meatballs

Q: I followed your tips for making spongy fishballs and they turned out great. Now I am keen to make spongy meatballs. Can you give me some tips?

A: *Use very lean meat; dice it and then mince it until very fine in an electric mixer or food processor. Put the minced meat into a deep bowl and add a little tapioca flour or cornflour, and sugar and salt to taste. Mix until meat mixture is a smooth paste. Lift meat from bowl and slap mixture forcefully back into bowl; repeat continuously for three to five minutes. Throwing the meat like this makes the meat very smooth and firm.*

Milk

Q: When a recipe calls for lukewarm milk, should I boil the milk first?

A: *Yes, boil the milk and let stand until it is lukewarm. Use fresh homogenised milk so that the cream will not separate from the rest of the milk.*

Q: When a cake recipe has water as one of its ingredients, can I use milk instead for a richer cake? What type of milk is best for cakes — evaporated, fresh, powdered or UHT milk?

A: *Yes, you can use milk as a substitute for water. Not only does it enrich the taste of the cake, it also helps to keep the cake moist for a longer period of time. Use fresh or UHT milk. Do not use evaporated milk unless specified in the recipe.*

Mooncakes

Q: Can you give me some recipes for mooncakes?

A: *Here are some excellent recipes for mooncakes from a friend who makes perfect mooncakes.*

Lotus Seed Paste Filling

600 g lotus seeds, soaked for 2 hours
1 tablespoon alkaline water
2¹/₄ cups oil, preferably peanut oil
600 g sugar
2 tablespoons maltose

Put soaked lotus seeds and alkaline water in a large saucepan. Add enough water (about 4 cups) to cover lotus seeds. Boil for 7-8 minutes. Drain and wash in clean water. Rub off skins. If using whole lotus seeds, remove green centres.

Put cleaned lotus seeds in a pressure cooker with enough water to cover and cook for 15 minutes until soft. Blend in a liquidiser, with some of the water from the pressure cooker, into a fine paste. Set aside.

Heat a nonstick wok or deep saucepan with 1 ladle of oil. Put in one-third of the sugar and cook on low heat until sugar turns a light golden caramel. Turn off heat. Pour in blended lotus paste and mix well to dissolve caramel. Continue to cook on low heat, stirring constantly. Add 2 tablespoons of sugar and 2 tablespoons of oil every 5 minutes until all sugar and oil have been used up.

Keep cooking and stirring the paste until thick. Stir in the maltose until paste is really thick and leaves the sides of the pan. To test for doneness, cool a lump of cooked paste and form into a round ball. Slice through with a knife. If the knife comes out clean, the paste is ready.

Cool and divide into portions of required weight and form into a round ball for use in making mooncakes. If desired, wrap each portion around a cooked salted egg.

Traditional Mooncakes

PASTRY

300 g golden syrup
120 g groundnut oil
¹/₂ tablespoon alkaline water
¹/₂ tablespoon flour

400 g plain flour, sifted
120 g lotus seed paste
1 whole egg, beaten with 1 tablespoon water, for glazing

Blend syrup, groundnut oil, alkaline water and the ¹/₂ tablespoon flour with a spoon until well mixed. Leave to stand overnight before using.

Sift plain flour into a large bowl (reserve 2 tablespoons of flour for dusting) and make a well in the centre. Slowly pour in syrup mixture and mix well. Do not knead. Divide into portions of approximately 38 g each.

Take a portion of the dough and roll out into a thin circular piece, large enough to wrap around a ball of lotus seed paste (it is easier if you roll out the dough between two sheets of plastic wrap). Shape dough around filling, making sure that filling is completely sealed.

Lightly dust wooden mooncake mould with flour (an easy way is to put some flour into a small piece of thin muslin cloth and tie up the ends of the cloth, and use it for dusting the moulds). Gently tap out excess flour, then press ball of dough into mould. Lightly tap out mooncake and place on a greased baking tray. Brush mooncakes with egg glaze.

Bake in preheated 160°C oven for 10 minutes. Remove tray from oven and brush mooncakes again with egg glaze. Bake for a further 10-15 minutes until golden brown.

Shanghai Mooncakes

250 g   butter
140 g   icing sugar
1   egg, beaten with a fork
1 teaspoon   vanilla essence

SIFTED INGREDIENTS (COMBINED)
400 g   plain flour
50 g   custard flour

Balls of lotus paste (100 g each)

1   egg, beaten, for glaze
Melon seeds or almond flakes

Cream butter and icing sugar and mix in beaten egg and vanilla essence. Mix in combined sifted ingredients.

Divide dough into 50 g portions and roll into balls. Roll out between sheets of plastic wrap. Wrap dough around 100 g balls of lotus paste. Shape into round balls and place on baking trays.

Brush with egg glaze and sprinkle surface with melon seeds or almond flakes. Bake in 200°C oven for 20 minutes until golden brown.

Unbaked White Ping Pei Mooncakes

150 g   kao fun (commercial cooked glutinous rice flour)
120 g   icing sugar
1 tablespoon   groundnut oil
200 ml   ice cold water
a few drops   banana or rose essence

Balls of lotus or red bean paste (90 g each)

Sift kao fun and icing sugar into a mixing bowl. Make a well in the centre. Add oil, cold water and essence and quickly hand-knead into a soft, smooth dough. Leave to rest, covered with plastic wrap, for 30 minutes.

Roll dough into a cylindrical roll. Divide into 7 equal portions, each approximately 70 g in weight. Between two sheets of plastic wrap, roll out each piece of dough into a thin circle large enough to wrap a 90 g ball of filling.

Lightly coat the balls of lotus or red bean paste with kao fun before wrapping in dough. Press into moulds dusted with *kao fun*.

Knock mooncakes out of moulds and store in an airtight plastic container in the refrigerator for up to four days.

Variation: Pandan-Flavoured Ping Pei Mooncakes
Use granulated sugar instead of icing sugar. Put sugar and water into saucepan. Add four knotted pandan leaves and bring to a slow boil, stirring to dissolve sugar. Discard pandan leaves. Cool and chill syrup.

Knead dough with a few drops of pandan syrup to obtain a pleasant light green colour.

Kam Tui Mooncakes

Nuts

135 g	winter melon seeds (*kua-chi*), whole
135 g	small almonds, whole
135 g	olive seed kernels, whole
75 g	walnuts, chopped into quarters
60 g	cashew nuts, chopped into quarters

Ingredients A

2	candied oranges, cut into small cubes
240 g	candied gourd or sugar melon, diced small
180 g	toasted sesame seeds
190 g	castor sugar
1/2 can	Hunan ham (cut into small cubes)

Ingredients B

7 tablespoons	water
7 tablespoons	oil
2 tablespoons	brandy
1/2 teaspoon	salt
1 tablespoon	sesame paste
2 teaspoons	rose jam
2 teaspoons	golden syrup
180 g	commercial cooked glutinous rice flour (*kao fun*)

Put nuts onto cookie tray and roast in a 150°C oven for 45-60 minutes. Allow to cool.

Combine nuts with 'A' ingredients and mix in castor sugar and ham. Combine 'B' ingredients and add to nut and ham mixture. Let stand for 1-2 hours.

Stir in the *kao fun* and mix well. Form into round balls approximately 120 g each. Proceed with pastry and baking as for traditional mooncakes.

Mousse

Q: My twin daughters are celebrating their 16th birthday and have asked me to make them a strawberry mousse cake. Could you give me a recipe, please?

A: Here is the recipe.

Strawberry Cream Mousse

2	large eggs, separated
1/3 cup	sugar
1/4 cup	milk
250 g	strawberries, puréed
3 teaspoons	gelatine
2 tablespoons	water
300 ml carton	double or whipping cream
8	strawberries for decoration

Whisk egg yolks and sugar until thick and creamy. Put into top of double boiler with milk and stir until combined. Stir mixture over simmering water until slightly thickened, then remove from heat.

Put puréed strawberries into bowl with egg yolk mixture and mix well.

Sprinkle gelatine over cold water, dissolve over simmering water. Cool and add to strawberry mixture.

Whip cream in a chilled bowl until soft peaks form, then gradually fold strawberry mixture into three quarters of the cream. (Refrigerate remaining cream for piping). Whisk egg whites until soft peaks form and fold gently into the mixture.

Pour into greased 18 cm baking pan or pudding dish. Refrigerate until firm and set.

To remove from mould, immerse base of pan or dish in hot water. Run a thin-bladed knife around the sides, if necessary to loosen mousse. Turn out onto serving dish. Decorate top with remaining whipped cream and top with strawberries. Keep chilled until ready to serve.

Muesli

Q: I would like a recipe for toasted muesli with dried fruit and raisins.

A: To make your own toasted muesli, put a mixture of oats, wheat bran and oat bran (proportioned according to your taste) onto a baking sheet and lightly toast in a moderate oven for 15-20 minutes. Stir in a handful of mixed dried fruit and raisins. Cool and store in a dry place.

Muffins

TASTY MUFFINS THE EASY WAY

What could be nicer for breakfast than a basketful of warm muffins with generous servings of butter, jam or honey? Or, for a light lunch, muffins are delicious with a bowl of vegetable soup. Served in attractive paper cases, muffins are also impressive for afternoon tea.

Muffins are fast and easy to make. All you have to do is mix the dry ingredients with the liquid ingredients, drop the batter into well-greased muffin tins and pop the whole lot into the oven for 20-25 minutes. Speed is the key to achieving light muffins: mix the ingredients quickly and bake the muffins immediately in a preheated oven.

If you like, you can decorate the surface of your muffins: use a cube of canned fruit sprinkled with sugar, a blob of coarse sugar sprinkled with fruit juice, or a teaspoon of peanut butter, jam or chocolate spread. I find it a good way of using up leftovers in the many jars that clutter up the fridge. You can also sprinkle on some toasted sesame seeds, black poppy seeds, desiccated coconut or finely chopped nuts.

Muffins are best eaten the day they are made or, better yet, when they are still warm. But they also keep well in the freezer in airtight containers; to reheat them, just wrap them in foil and pop them into a hot oven for five to ten minutes.

The muffin recipes I have given here are quick to prepare and healthy too.

Yam Muffins

210 g	plain flour, sifted
2 teaspoons	double-action baking powder
1/2 teaspoon	bicarbonate of soda
3/4 teaspoon	salt
100 g	castor sugar
1 teaspoon	mixed spice
1/4 teaspoon	cinnamon powder
2	large eggs, beaten with a fork
4 tablespoons	melted butter, cooled
200 g	cold mashed yam
1 cup	milk

Sift flour, baking powder and bicarbonate of soda into a mixing bowl. Stir in salt, castor sugar, mixed spice and cinnamon powder.

Add beaten eggs to butter. In a separate bowl, stir mashed yam into milk. Add to beaten egg and butter mixture.

Stir liquid mixture into dry ingredients and mix well, using quick, deft strokes. Fill well-greased muffin tins two-thirds full. If desired, sprinkle finely chopped pistachio nuts on top.

Bake immediately in preheated 220°C oven for 25 minutes until golden brown.

Makes 12.

Wholewheat Muffins

120 g	wholewheat flour
4 teaspoons	baking powder
1/2 teaspoon	salt
1 tablespoon	sugar
1 cup	quick cooking oats or wheatgerm
1 cup	milk
3 tablespoons	honey
3 tablespoons	corn oil or melted butter
1	large egg, beaten

Grease a 12-cup muffin tin or line with pleated paper muffin cups.

Sift flour and baking powder into a large mixing bowl. Return husks to bowl. Stir well and mix in salt, sugar and oats or wheatgerm.

Combine milk, honey and corn oil or butter. Stir in beaten egg and blend well. Pour liquid mixture into dry ingredients and mix quickly.

Fill muffin cups two-thirds full. Bake in preheated 220°C oven for 20 minutes.

Jumbo Oat Bran Muffins

150 g	oat bran cereal
1 1/2 cups	milk
105 g	quick cooking oats

SIFTED INGREDIENTS (COMBINED)

105 g	self-raising flour
1 level tablespoon	baking powder

1/2 teaspoon	salt
90 g	brown sugar
1/3 cup	corn oil, beaten
1	large egg, beaten
60 g	raisins
	Sesame seeds or chopped nuts for sprinkling

Grease 12-cup muffin tin. Preheat oven to 220°C.

In a mixing bowl, mix oat bran and milk. Let stand for five minutes until cereal softens.

Meanwhile, in blender at medium speed or in a food processor, blend oats until fine. Place in a clean bowl. Stir in sifted self-raising flour and baking powder, salt and brown sugar.

Beat corn oil and egg together with a fork until frothy (about one minute). Stir into milk and cereal mixture. Turn on electric mixer and beat for 30 seconds. Stir in flour mixture and raisins.

Spoon batter into prepared muffin cups. Sprinkle with sesame seeds.

Bake in preheated 220°C oven for 20 minutes.

Banana Walnut Muffins

4 tablespoons corn oil
165 g castor sugar
3 medium eggs
3-4 medium-sized bananas, peeled and mashed

SIFTED INGREDIENTS (COMBINED)
125 g self-raising flour
125 g wholemeal flour
3 teaspoons baking powder

1/4 teaspoon salt
1/2 teaspoon vanilla essence
60 g chopped walnuts
60 g raisins or mixed fruit
2/3 cup milk

Lightly grease a 12-cup muffin tin. Preheat oven to 190°C.

Beat oil and castor sugar together, then add eggs and beat for two minutes. Add bananas and mix well.

Add sifted dry ingredients and salt. Stir in vanilla essence, walnuts and raisins or mixed fruits. On low speed, beat in milk.

Fill muffin cups two-thirds full. Bake in preheated 190°C oven for 25-30 minutes or until lightly browned.

Ginger Apple Muffins

2 large eggs
8 tablespoons corn oil
250 g castor sugar
1/4 teaspoon mixed spice
1/4 teaspoon ground nutmeg
2 medium green apples, peeled, cored and grated or finely chopped
400 g self-raising flour
2 teaspoons baking powder
100 g preserved stem ginger, finely chopped
2 tablespoons honey (optional), for glazing

Lightly grease 12-cup muffin tin. Preheat oven to 200°C.

Put eggs into a mixing bowl fitted with a balloon whisk. Beat for 1 minute. Add corn oil, castor sugar and spices and continue to beat until thick and frothy. Beat in apples.

Sift in self-raising flour and baking powder and mix on low speed. Add stem ginger.

Fill muffin cups two-thirds full. Bake for 25-30 minutes until risen and golden brown.

Remove muffins from tin and brush tops with honey.

Blueberry Muffins

350 g	plain flour
1 tablespoon	baking powder
80 g	castor sugar
2	eggs, beaten
300 ml	milk
90 g	butter, melted
1 teaspoon	vanilla essence
180 g	frozen blueberries

Sift the flour and baking powder into a bowl and then stir in the sugar.

In a separate bowl beat eggs together with milk, melted butter and vanilla until combined. Stir into dry ingredients and then gently mix in the blueberries.

Spoon into lightly greased large 12-cup muffin tin until just level with the top. Bake in preheated oven at 200°C for 20-25 minutes.

Leave in the tins for five minutes, then turn out onto a wire rack to cool.

Makes about 12 muffins.

Mushrooms

Q: What is the best way to store fresh mushrooms?

A: Fresh mushrooms should be stored for only 3-4 days after purchase. They should be wrapped in paper and not in plastic as this will cause the mushrooms to sweat and become slimy.

Noodles

HOMEMADE NOODLES ARE THE BEST

The origin of Asian noodles seems to have been lost over the centuries but it is generally recognised that the Chinese were eating noodles by the 1st Century AD. During the period AD 960-1280, special noodle shops are said to have existed in northern China. Of course, everyone is familiar with the story of Marco Polo bringing the art of making noodles from China to Italy, thus giving rise to the famous Italian pastas.

Noodles are generally made by mixing flour with water and adding oil and salt to form a pliable dough. The dough is formed into sheets by either hand-rolling or passing between a pair of steel rollers to desired thickness. The sheets are then cut into strands of different sizes as required. Another method, which requires remarkable skill, consists of twirling and pulling lengths of dough into strands.

Here are some recipes for making and using your own noodles. The flavour and texture of homemade noodles make the effort worthwhile. Have a go at it because it is a lot of fun. Noodle machines are not expensive and are available in most department stores.

Yellow Noodles

600 g	plain flour
1¹/₂ teaspoons	salt
1 tablespoon	alkaline water, combined with 1 cup water
1 teaspoon	salt
6 tablespoons	cooking oil

Sift flour into a mixing bowl and add salt. Make a well in the centre and pour in alkaline and water solution. Bind mixture together to form a very stiff dough. Knead until well combined.

Using a rolling pin, roll out dough on a lightly floured surface until you have a 17 x 30 cm rectangle. Cut the dough into four equal rectangular pieces. The dough is now ready to be passed through a noodle machine.

Adjust knob of noodle machine so that rollers are at their widest setting. Turn rollers slowly and insert a piece of dough. Keep passing dough through machine, decreasing roller spacing each time, until you get the thickness you want. Then pass dough sheet through the cutting machine to make strands. Repeat procedure with remaining dough.

Bring a large saucepan of water to a rapid boil. Add 1 teaspoon salt and 2 tablespoons cooking oil. Scald the noodles for 3 minutes. Drain well and put in a large bowl. Add approximately 4 tablespoons of cooking oil and toss well to thoroughly coat the noodles.

When the noodles are thoroughly cooled, they can be placed in plastic bags for storage in the refrigerator or freezer.

Fresh Egg Wantan Noodles

5 eggs
1 tablespoon alkaline water, combined with 3/4 tablespoon water

600 g plain flour
1/2 teaspoon salt
Tapioca flour for dusting

Place eggs in a bowl and stir with a fork to break egg yolks, but do not beat. Add alkaline water solution to eggs and mix well.

Sift flour into a large mixing bowl and add salt. Make a well in the centre of the flour and pour in egg mixture. Bind into a ball of very stiff dough. Knead dough on a floured surface dusted with plain flour until dough is no longer sticky.

Flatten into a rectangle and roll out until you have an 18 x 30 cm rectangle. Cut into four rectangular pieces. Dust each piece with tapioca flour to prevent sticking. Cover with a dry tea towel.

Adjust knob of noodle machine so that rollers are at their widest setting. Turn rollers slowly and insert a piece of dough. Keep passing dough through machine, decreasing roller spacing each time, until you get the thickness you want. Then pass dough sheet through the cutting machine to make strands. Repeat procedure with remaining dough.

Store in airtight containers or plastic bags in the refrigerator or freezer.

Fried Hokkien Mee

150 g small prawns, shelled
5 small cuttlefish, sliced
1/2 teaspoon sesame oil
1/4 teaspoon each pepper and sugar
1/2 tablespoon light soya sauce
2 tablespoons oil
4 shallots, sliced
120 g chicken or pork fat, diced
5 cloves garlic, minced
6-8 fish cake slices
4 stalks mustard greens, cut into 5 cm lengths
500 g fresh yellow noodles
2 cups fresh chicken stock
2 tablespoons thick soya sauce
1 teaspoon sugar

Season prawns and cuttlefish with sesame oil, pepper, sugar and light soya sauce.

Heat oil in a wok and brown shallots. Drain and set aside.

Reheat a clean wok and add chicken or pork fat. Fry until crisp. Remove crisps, leaving oil behind.

Reheat wok and add garlic, prawns, cuttlefish and fish cake slices. Add mustard greens and stir-fry for a few·seconds. Put in noodles and fry for 2 minutes. Add chicken stock, thick soya sauce and sugar. Stir well, cover and bring to a boil. Simmer for a couple of minutes until sauce evaporates a little. Remove cover and add shallots and crisped fat.

Serve hot with a small dish of *sambal belacan*.

Prawn Noodles (Har Meen)

2 tablespoons	cooking oil
150 g	dried *ikan bilis*, rinsed
90 g	dried prawns, minced
10 cups	water
500 g	chicken bones
1¹/₂ teaspoons	salt
¹/₂ teaspoon	pepper
150 g	boneless chicken breast
250 g	medium prawns, with shells
4 tablespoons	cooking oil
12	shallots, sliced
1 teaspoon	dried chilli paste
600 g	fresh yellow noodles
300 g	beansprouts, tailed and rinsed
150 g	water convolvulus (*kangkong*), cut into 5 cm lengths
3	red chillies, sliced

Heat oil in a large pot and lightly brown *ikan bilis* and dried prawns. Add water and chicken bones and bring to boil. Add salt and pepper and simmer for 45 minutes over low heat. Strain stock and discard simmered ingredients.

Pour strained stock into a clean pot and bring to boil. Add chicken and prawns and cook for 3-5 minutes or until just cooked; remove from pot. Slice chicken thinly and set aside. Shell prawns and set aside.

Heat cooking oil in a saucepan and lightly brown shallots. Drain and set aside for garnishing. Put in chilli paste and stir-fry for a minute over low heat. Pour in strained stock and bring to boil. Add salt to taste and keep gravy hot.

Boil a large saucepan of water and scald noodles for 1 minute. Drain and put on a large dish. Blanch beansprouts and *kangkong* separately in the same boiling water. Place next to noodles.

To serve prawn noodles, place some yellow noodles, beansprouts and *kangkong* in a serving bowl. Garnish with some sliced chicken and prawns. Top with hot stock and serve immediately, sprinkled with crisp shallots.

Mee Goreng

GROUND INGREDIENTS

12	dried chillies, soaked
1	large onion
4 cloves	garlic

4 tablespoons	oil
1	large onion, sliced
150 g	beansprouts
1	large potato, boiled and cubed
300 g	fresh yellow noodles
1	egg
150 g	small or medium prawns, shelled
2	tomatoes, quartered
1 teaspoon	salt
2 tablespoons	tomato ketchup
1 tablespoon	chilli sauce

3	green chillies, sliced
1	whole spring onion, chopped
1/2	cucumber, sliced

Heat 2 tablespoons oil in a wok and fry ground ingredients until fragrant. Remove and set aside.

Heat remaining oil and fry sliced onion until transparent, then add beansprouts and cooked potato, and stir-fry quickly for 1 minute. Put in noodles and fry well for 3-4 minutes.

Make a well in centre of noodles, then add egg, prawns, tomatoes, salt, tomato ketchup and chilli sauce and stir well. Put in the fried ground ingredients and mix well. Just before removing from heat, add green chillies and spring onion.

Serve garnished with sliced cucumber.

Nuts

Q: Should cashew nuts be fried with or without oil? Do they need to be washed and dried before frying?

A: You can either pan roast cashew nuts without oil or deep-fry them in hot oil. Only wash nuts if necessary; just rinse, drain quickly and dry thoroughly before roasting them.

Q: When I'm adding nuts to cakes or cookies, should I toast the nuts first?

A: It's a matter of preference. Generally, nuts are more fragrant and crunchier if you toast them.

Q: I am keen to learn how to roast nuts. My cashew nuts, almonds and macadamia nuts never turn out right, whether I use a conventional oven or microwave oven. Some always get burnt. I have tried washing the nuts with salt water before roasting, adding salt after roasting, and even frying them in a nonstick wok. I cannot go on failing as these nuts are so expensive. What should I do?

A: Preheat oven to 190°C. Spread the nuts in a single layer in a shallow pan and then roast them for 10-15 minutes, depending on their size. Shake and turn them a couple of times during roasting. Nuts burn very easily as they contain a lot of oil, so watch them carefully. Alternatively, you can pan roast them in a dry wok over low heat until golden brown. You can also use a microwave: spread the nuts out on a plate; cook for 4-5 minutes, stirring two or three times during cooking to roast evenly.

Q: What is the easiest way to remove the skin from fresh chestnuts?

A: Make small slits at both ends of the chestnuts and cover with boiling water. Leave for five minutes. With the help of a knife, peel off skins while still warm.

Onion Rings

Q: I love fried onion rings. Can you tell me how I can make them?

A: Here is a recipe for crispy and tasty onion rings.

Fried Onion Rings

2	large white onions, cut across in $1/2$ cm slices
$1/2$ cup	milk, combined with $1/4$ cup water

BATTER

80 g	plain flour, sifted
$1/2$ cup	white wine
$1/2$ tablespoon	sugar
$1/4$ teaspoon	salt
$1/4$ teaspoon	pepper or grated lemon rind
$1/2$	egg white

Soak onions in milk for one hour. Drain and spread on a paper towel.

Dredge in batter with a fork and allow excess batter to drip off. Deep-fry in hot oil until light golden brown. Drain on paper towel before serving.

To Prepare Batter
Combine liquid with all dry ingredients except egg white. Mix well and refrigerate, covered, for 6-8 hours.

Beat mixture until smooth. Just before using batter, whip egg white just until stiff and fold into batter.

Q: Being Muslim, I do not drink alcohol. When making onion rings, can I use water or milk instead of wine?

A: Yes, you can substitute either water or milk for the wine. Try this recipe.

Chilli Onion Rings

4	onions, peeled and sliced
1 cup	milk
1	egg
1/4 teaspoon	chilli powder
1/4 teaspoon	salt
125 g	plain flour sifted

Separate onion slices into rings. Put into a bowl, pour in milk and let stand for one hour. Drain and reserve milk.

Beat egg well, then beat in reserved milk, chilli powder, salt and flour. Mix until batter is smooth and free from lumps.

Dip each ring into batter and deep-fry in hot oil until golden brown. Drain and sprinkle with salt.

Ovalette

Q: Could you let me know what Ovalette is used for?

A: Ovalette is a stabiliser used in baking cakes to help the eggs rise rapidly and stiffly. Stabilisers are acidic and this helps the beaten eggs keep the light, airy, velvety and voluminous texture which is essential for very light cakes, such as chiffon cakes. However, the natural flavour of the eggs and butter is lost if you use stabilisers.

Q: Must Ovalette be refrigerated?

A: Yes, Ovalette is best kept refrigerated.

Pancakes

PANCAKES FOR ALL OCCASIONS

The universally popular pancake or griddle cake is so versatile that it can be served at any meal — as a starter, a main course or a dessert. Pancakes are as old as civilisation. They came about even before baking was known. Over time, different countries developed their own version of making and serving them. The French have crepes, the most well-known being the Crepes Suzette. The Russians have blinis, which are made with flour and yeast. We have our very own Malaysian pancakes: the lacy *roti jala* and the savoury Chinese pancakes we eat for breakfast or tea.

To make soft, delicious pancakes, the consistency of the batter must be just right, the surface of the pan smooth, and the heat evenly distributed and not too strong. A nonstick saucepan or crepe pan, lightly greased between cooking each pancake, is ideal.

You can eat pancakes plain, dotted with butter and drizzled with honey or maple syrup, or rolled up around a sweet or savoury filling. Pancake fillings are limitless — just let your imagination run riot. (Chopped up, seasoned and covered in a sauce, leftover meat and vegetables make excellent fillings.)

My favourite pancake batter recipe uses both water and milk. This makes for more tender pancakes.

Pancake Batter

200 g	plain flour
	Pinch of salt
2	large eggs, beaten with a fork
3/4 cup	milk
1/2 tablespoon	water

Sift flour into a mixing bowl and add salt. Add eggs and stir until mixture is smooth and free from lumps. Gradually stir in milk and water and beat with a whisk into a smooth batter. Allow to stand, covered, for at least 30 minutes. (It can be kept in the refrigerator for up to three hours.)

Heat a small nonstick frying pan and lightly brush with melted margarine or butter. A quick way to do this is to run a chilled block of butter on the heated pan.

Pour 1/8 cup of batter into the pan, swirling it around evenly. Cook over moderate heat for about one minute or until golden brown. Flip over and cook the other side.

Continue with remaining batter. Stack pancakes in a covered dish and keep warm until ready to serve.

Note: Wrapped tightly in plastic wrap, cooked pancakes keep up to a week in the refrigerator or a month in the freezer. To reheat frozen pancakes, thaw at room temperature, then wrap in foil and heat in a 190°C oven for 10-15 minutes.

For a special breakfast, I like to serve soft griddle pancakes with butter, jam, honey and maple syrup for those with a sweet tooth, or with herbed chippolata sausages or bacon and eggs.

Soft Griddle Pancakes

SIFTED INGREDIENTS (COMBINED)
180 g	plain flour
2 teaspoons	baking powder
1/4 teaspoon	bicarbonate of soda
1 teaspoon	bread softener

1/2 teaspoon	salt
2 tablespoons	castor sugar

MILK MIXTURE (COMBINED)
1	beaten egg
200 ml	milk
1 tablespoon	corn oil

Sift dry ingredients into a mixing bowl and stir in salt and sugar. Add milk mixture. Beat well in electric mixer for two minutes. Leave mixture to stand, covered, for 30 minutes.

Drop tablespoonfuls of batter onto a preheated, lightly greased pan or hot plate. Cook for 30 seconds on each side.

Serve hot.

Lacy Malaysian pancakes, or *Roti Jala*, are folded or rolled and eaten with a rich *lemak* chicken curry, such as Curry Kapitan.

Roti Jala

2 cups	plain flour
1/2 teaspoon	salt
2	eggs, beaten
2 1/2 cups	coconut milk from 1/2 coconut, grated

Sift flour into a bowl and add salt. Stir in beaten eggs and coconut milk and beat until smooth. Strain batter if it is lumpy.

Grease and heat a medium nonstick pan on low heat. Put a ladleful of batter into a *roti jala* cup with four funnels and move it in a circular motion over pan to give pancake a lacy pattern. Cook until set.

Turn pancake over onto a dish and continue cooking until batter is used up, greasing pan every now and then.

Fold pancakes into two or fold and roll up.

Another local favourite of mine is a tasty savoury pancake flavoured with dried prawns.

Savoury Pancakes

2¹/₂ cups	plain flour
2 cups	water or thin coconut milk
¹/₄ teaspoon	salt
¹/₄ teaspoon	pepper
75 g	dried prawns, rinsed, minced and pan toasted
2-3 stalks	spring onions, sliced finely
1-2	chillies, chopped
1 tablespoon	lightly browned shallot crisps

Sift flour into a bowl and stir in water or thin coconut milk to make a smooth runny batter. Strain batter if it is lumpy.

Stir in salt, pepper, dried prawns, spring onions, chillies and shallot crisps.

Heat medium nonstick saucepan and lightly grease with corn oil. Pour a ladle of batter, swirl pan to spread it evenly, and fry both sides until lightly browned.

When cool, roll up pancakes and serve with chilli sauce.

Q: Some time ago I was served Peking Duck wrapped in a small, thin pancake. Can you tell me how to prepare these pancakes?

A: The pancakes served with Peking Duck or Crispy Skin Duck are called Mandarin Pancakes. Try this recipe.

Mandarin Pancakes

240 g	plain flour
	Pinch of salt
About 100 ml	boiling water
75 ml	cold water

Sieve flour into a mixing bowl and stir in salt. Make a well in the centre. Pour in boiling water and mix in flour. Add cold water, a little at a time, mixing with a wooden spoon until dough is smooth and just soft enough to work, but not sticky.

Knead for five minutes; then cover with a damp cloth and leave for 30 minutes.

Roll dough into a long sausage and cut into 12 pieces. Flatten each piece with the palm of your hand. Roll out on a floured board until very thin.

Heat a heavy frying pan until hot and cook pancake on both sides until lightly coloured with flecks of brown. It should take 45-50 seconds to cook both sides.

Remove and fold into a triangular shape and wrap in a cloth until ready to serve.

Pandan

Q: Can pandan juice be replaced with bottled pandan flavouring?

A: The fragrance and natural colour of fresh pandan juice cannot be matched by pandan essence. Wherever possible, use fresh pandan juice.

Paprika

Q: Is chilli powder a satisfactory substitute for paprika?

A: Paprika is a sweet, mild spice made from the ground seeds of sweet red peppers. It is used predominantly for its colour-enhancing qualities. In some dishes, you may use chilli powder instead. However, in Hungarian goulash and paprika chicken, for example, paprika must be used to give these dishes their characteristic colour and flavour.

Pasta

Q: I'm vegetarian and would be grateful if you could give me a recipe for a vegetable spaghetti sauce.

A: Try this mixed vegetable pasta sauce. It is delicious with spaghetti or any other pasta.

Pasta with Mixed Vegetable Sauce

2 tablespoons	olive oil
1	medium onion, coarsely chopped
2 cloves	garlic, crushed
250 g	brinjal, diced, salted and drained
250 g	zucchini or marrows, diced
1	red pepper, sliced
1	green pepper, sliced
2	red chillies, seeded and sliced
400 g (14 oz)	can chopped tomatoes
2 tablespoons	tomato purée
200 ml	fresh vegetable stock or water
1 tablespoon	chopped fresh basil, or 1 teaspoon dried basil
2 teaspoons	salt
1/2 teaspoon	pepper
1 teaspoon	sugar
500 g	packet spaghetti or pasta shells
50 g	Parmesan cheese, grated

Heat olive oil in a deep saucepan and cook onion and garlic. Add brinjal, zucchini or marrow and gently fry for five minutes or until softened. Add green pepper, chillies, tomatoes and tomato purée. When the mixture starts to boil, add the stock, basil and seasonings. Simmer for 15 minutes.

Meanwhile, cook spaghetti or pasta shells in a large pan of boiling salted water according to manufacturer's directions. Drain and transfer to a large bowl.

Pour sauce over pasta and serve sprinkled with extra herbs, if desired. Add Parmesan cheese to your liking.

Q: Please give me a recipe for a spaghetti dish. What type of cheese should we use?

A: *I hope you will like this recipe for spaghetti with a beef and tomato sauce. It is my favourite. You can use any grated cheese, such as cheddar or Parmesan. The sauce can be used on pizzas as well.*

Spaghetti with Tomato Beef Sauce

1 kg	minced beef
2 tablespoons	corn oil
4	onions, diced
4 cloves	garlic, minced
6 cans (8 oz each)	tomato sauce
2 cans (6 oz each)	tomato paste
6 cups	water
3 tablespoons	grated cheddar cheese
1 teaspoon	pepper
1 teaspoon	salt, or to taste
1 tablespoon	oregano
	Parmesan cheese to garnish
2 packets (500 g each)	spaghetti
60 g	butter

Brown beef in an ungreased pan and set aside.

Heat oil in a saucepan, add onions and garlic and fry until onions soften. Put in browned beef, tomato sauce, tomato paste and water. Stir well and bring to simmering point. Add cheese, pepper, salt and oregano, and simmer over low heat, uncovered, for 35-40 minutes until sauce thickens.

Cook spaghetti in boiling salted water according to packet instructions and drain thoroughly. Return spaghetti to saucepan, add butter and toss well.

Put spaghetti in serving dish. Top with sauce and sprinkle with Parmesan cheese.

Pastry

Q: What is pastry margarine? Can I use butter or a vegetable shortening instead?

A: *Pastry margarine is a margarine specially blended to produce a tough "plastic" margarine which has a high melting point. You cannot use butter or vegetable shortening as a substitute.*

Q: I use high-protein flour and pastry margarine for my chicken pies. Why does my puff pastry turn out soggy at the bottom and shrink after I bake it? The top is always nice and fluffy.

A: *Use plain flour for making puff pastry. High-protein flour has a much higher gluten content and is more suitable for making bread.*

Q: **I never seem to get my choux pastry right. It always turns out hard or soggy on the outside but not cooked on the inside.**

A: *Like other pastries, the choux or cream puff pastry requires some attention to detail in order to achieve a feather-light crust with a hollow cavity. Success depends on using the right proportion of ingredients and precise measurements.*

The milk or water and butter have to be brought just to boiling point, immediately added to the dry ingredients, then mixed in quickly to partially cook the flour. If beaten too slowly, the pastry can become dry; if over-beaten and overcooked, it will fail to puff. When the dough is slightly cooked, add the eggs one spoonful at a time, beating vigorously.

The dough must be able to hold its shape (a small amount will stand up if scooped up on the end of the spoon).

Use the dough at once. Pipe out desired shapes onto trays lined with greaseproof paper. For a softer crust, you can lightly sprinkle drops of water onto the pastry.

Bake in a preheated 190°C oven. Do not remove from the oven until pastry is golden and quite firm to the touch.

Q: **For "blind baking" of pastry, can the beans used as a weight be reused?**

A: *Yes, you can keep on using the same batch of beans.*

Q: **I have a problem with making tarts. When I roll out the leftover pastry and cut it for a second time, it shrinks while baking. The first batch does not shrink. Why is this?**

A: *Many people face this problem when handling shortcrust pastry. The success of the pastry depends on working quickly and keeping all ingredients cool. Stamp out the pastry as closely as possible the first time so that very little is left over. Lightly gather the leftover bits and place them between two sheets of plastic wrap. Roll out as lightly as possible to avoid stretching the dough.*

Q: **I would like to buy a pastry cutter but am having a hard time finding one. Can you help?**

A: *Pastry cutters seem to be very difficult to find in the shops nowadays. But, although useful, the pastry cutter is not indispensable. You can prepare pastry in seconds using a good food processor fitted with a cutting blade. The golden rule to remember when using the food processor is not to overblend. If you don't have a food processor, you can use two round-bladed or butter knives.*

Pau (Steamed Buns)

Q: I have some questions about making *pau*. What is "Water Lily" flour and is it necessary for making *pau*? Why do my *pau* have a metallic taste and have big holes?

A: Water Lily flour is another name for Hong Kong flour. It is a highly bleached all-purpose soft wheat flour containing eight to nine per cent protein. It is used specially for pau. *Plain flour, self-raising flour and superfine flour can also be used. The metallic taste in your* pau *is from using alkaline water; use plain water instead. The big holes are due to too much yeast and over-proofing.*

Here are two recipes for Hong Kong Pau.

Quick Pau with Spicy Mustard Chicken Filling

240 g	Water Lily flour (Hong Kong flour)
1 teaspoon	double action baking powder
1/4 teaspoon	salt
25 g	vegetable shortening
1 teaspoon	easy-blend yeast

SUGAR MIXTURE (COMBINED)

100 ml	warm water
30 g	castor sugar
1/2 teaspoon	vinegar

CHICKEN MUSTARD FILLING

2	whole chicken thighs, deboned and diced small

SEASONING INGREDIENTS

1/2 tablespoon	oyster sauce
1/2 tablespoon	light soya sauce
1 teaspoon	thick soya sauce
1 teaspoon	hot prepared mustard
1/2 teaspoon	Worcestershire sauce
1/2 teaspoon	sesame oil
1/2 teaspoon	salt
1/4 teaspoon	pepper

1 tablespoon	chilli oil
1	onion, diced
1	red chilli, seeded, coarsely chopped
1 stalk	spring onion, chopped
2-3 sprigs	coriander leaves, chopped
1 teaspoon	cornflour, combined with 1 tablespoon water

Sift flour and baking powder onto a baking sheet. Stir in salt. Pour into the bowl of a food processor fitted with a cutting blade. Add vegetable shortening and blend for 30 seconds until mixture is crumbly. Stir in easy-blend yeast.

Replace cutting blade with dough blade. Pour in combined sugar mixture and turn on the food processor for 1-1 1/2 minutes. Leave dough to rise, covered, for 30 minutes or until doubled in bulk.

Punch down and remove dough. Knead on a smooth surface and shape into a long roll. Cut into 10 even pieces.

Roll out each piece and fill with chicken filling. Wrap and pleat into *pau* shapes. Place on a round of greaseproof paper. Leave to rise for 15 minutes.

Steam over rapidly boiling water for 12 minutes.

To Make Chicken Filling
Marinate diced chicken with seasoning ingredients for 30 minutes.

Heat chilli oil and fry onion until softened. Put in seasoned chicken and stir-fry for 3 minutes or until cooked through. Stir in chopped chilli, spring onion and coriander leaves.

Thicken with cornflour mixture. Leave aside to cool before use.

Hong Kong Pau with Chicken Filling

300 g	Hong Kong flour, sifted
1 teaspoon	baking powder, sifted
6 g (1/2 tablespoon)	easy-blend yeast
a tiny pinch	ammonia powder
60 g	castor sugar
125 ml	warm water, combined with 1 tablespoon corn oil

FILLING

360 g	chicken or pork, cut into 3/4 cm cubes
1/2 teaspoon	pepper
1 teaspoon	sesame oil
1 tablespoon	vegetable oil
2	large onions, diced or chopped
1/2 tablespoon	sesame seeds

SAUCE INGREDIENTS (COMBINED)

1 tablespoon	hoisin sauce
1 tablespoon	oyster sauce
1/2 tablespoon	light soya sauce
1/2 tablespoon	thick soya sauce
1 teaspoon	sugar
1 teaspoon	cornflour, combined with 1 tablespoon water

Put sifted Hong Kong flour and baking powder into a bowl of an electric mixer attached with a dough hook. Stir in easy-blend yeast, ammonia powder and sugar. Turn on the mixer and gradually pour in water and oil mixture. Beat on medium speed for 3-4 minutes until smooth lump of dough is formed.

Knead dough on unfloured board for 1-2 minutes until smooth. Return dough to bowl and cover with a damp cloth. Leave to rise for 40 minutes or until doubled in bulk.

Knead dough again until smooth. Shape into a long roll and cut into 12 even pieces. Roll each piece into a ball. Flatten and roll into 8-9 cm discs. Put a tablespoon of chicken filling in the centre of each and pleat into a *pau* shape. Place on a round of greaseproof paper.

Arrange in a bamboo basket and steam over rapidly boiling water for 12 minutes. Remember to wipe cover of steamer dry before steaming to prevent water from dripping onto *pau*. (If you're using a steamer tray, place a small tea towel on the base to prevent water from wetting *pau*.)

To Make Filling
Season chicken with pepper and sesame oil. Heat a saucepan with vegetable oil and cook onions until lightly browned. Put in chicken and toss until chicken changes colour. Stir in sesame seeds and mix well.

Add sauce ingredients and stir for 1 minute. Thicken with cornflour solution. Cool before using.

Q: When making Hong Kong *pau*, can liquid ammonia be used instead of ammonia powder? Can dry yeast or wet yeast be used instead of easy-blend yeast and, if so, how much should be used?

> A: *Liquid ammonia is usually used for home cleaning and has to be handled with extreme care as it is highly toxic. Use ammonia powder (*chow fun*) which is available at Chinese medicine shops.*
>
> *Dry yeast granules and wet yeast (compressed yeast) can be substituted for easy-blend yeast. However, dry yeast and compressed yeast need to be dissolved in warm water to activate them. Instead of 10 g easy-blend yeast, use 15 g dry yeast granules or 30 g compressed yeast.*

Peanut Butter

Q: Can you tell me how to make my own peanut butter? I tried making it once but it was too thick.

> A: *Here's a recipe for homemade peanut butter.*

Peanut Butter

1 cup	fresh roasted or slightly salted peanuts
2-2^1/$_2$ tablespoons	corn or sunflower oil
^{1}/$_4$ teaspoon	salt or to taste
1 tablespoon	sugar syrup or runny honey

Blend all ingredients in an electric blender until smooth and spreadable. Store in an airtight jar.

Pies

GREAT WAYS TO EAT HUMBLE PIE

The humble pie is anything but humble when filled with a wide variety of sweet or savoury fillings. Great-tasting pies start with a crisp, light and flaky pastry. Although many beginners are quite intimidated by the task, there are really no elusive secrets to making melt-in-the-mouth pastry. Just follow instructions carefully and be sure to use the right proportion of ingredients.

Chill all ingredients before you start, and keep everything as cool as possible while you're making the pastry. Even warm fingers rubbing fat into flour can toughen the pastry dough. Using a pastry cutter or food processor will help cut the fat into the flour quickly and evenly. (If you don't have either, use two small table knives.) Work lightly to incorporate as much air as possible and inhibit the development of gluten. If you're using a food processor, be careful not to overblend or your pastry won't be flaky.

Measure ingredients accurately. Too much flour hardens pastry. Too much liquid makes pastry heavy and soggy, while too little liquid makes it brittle. Too much fat makes it greasy and too crumbly.

Chill the dough in the refrigerator for at least 30 minutes after mixing; this tenderises the dough and helps minimise shrinking during baking. In our humid climate, it also makes it firmer and easier to handle.

Roll out the pastry as lightly as possible with a rolling pin, using very little or no flour. Too much flour toughens the dough.

Choose good, heavy rustproof metal pans for baking. A fluted pan with a removable base or a springform pan is ideal, especially for open pies, so that the pie can be easily slipped out onto a serving dish. Fluted tins also make attractive designs.

Shortcrust Pastry

340 g self-raising flour
1/2 teaspoon salt
210 g cold butter, diced
90 ml ice-cold water

Sift flour into a bowl and add salt. Cut butter into flour with a pastry cutter until mixture resembles fine breadcrumbs.

Make a small well in the centre, add water and mix to a firm dough. Wrap pastry in a plastic bag and chill for 30 minutes.

Roll out pastry between two sheets of plastic wrap to fit springform pie tin. Peel top layer of plastic from pastry and ease pastry carefully into flan tin. Peel off remaining plastic. Trim and neaten edges.

Prick the base with a fork and chill in the refrigerator for 15-30 minutes before putting in the filling.

Walnut Pie

Shortcrust pastry
180 g walnuts
3 large eggs
250 ml dark corn syrup
1 teaspoon vanilla essence
60 g butter, melted and cooled
150 g castor sugar

Line 23 cm pie tin with shortcrust pastry. Prick base with a fork. Chill in refrigerator for 15 minutes. Arrange walnuts on pastry base to cover whole pie.

Put eggs in a mixing bowl and add corn syrup, vanilla, butter and sugar. Whisk with a rotary whisk at low speed until mixture is well blended.

Pour into nut-filled pastry base. Bake in preheated 180°C oven for 50-55 minutes or until a skewer inserted in the centre comes out clean. Cool and serve with whipped cream.

Papaya Pie

Shortcrust pastry
A little beaten egg white

FILLING

600 g ripe papaya, skinned and diced
4 medium-sized eggs
240 g sugar
1/2 cup thickened or double cream
1/2 cup evaporated milk
2 tablespoons melted butter
1-2 teaspoons lemon juice
1 teaspoon lemon essence
Pinch of salt

TOPPING

1 heaped teaspoon castor sugar
1 teaspoon grated lemon rind (yellow part only)
1 teaspoon grated orange rind

DECORATION

1/2 cup whipping cream

Roll out pastry to fit a 20-23 cm fluted flan tin. Brush base of pastry case with beaten egg white. Refrigerate while preparing filling.

To make filling, blend papaya and put into a covered saucepan. Cook over medium heat stirring occasionally until you have a thick purée. This takes approximately 15 minutes. There should be 1 1/2 cups purée. Whisk eggs lightly and beat in cooled papaya and sugar. Stir in remaining filling ingredients.

Pour into prepared pastry-lined flan tin. Bake in 175°C oven for 1-1 1/4 hours until filling is set. Fifteen minutes before removing pie from oven, sprinkle lemon and orange rind topping over surface.

Cool thoroughly for at least two hours before cutting. Just before serving, pipe and decorate with whipped cream.

Pumpkin Pie

Shortcrust pastry
A little beaten egg white

FILLING

900-1,000 g	pumpkin
1/2 teaspoon	salt
180 g	palm sugar, cut into small pieces
90 g	granulated sugar
1/4 cup	water
3	eggs
1 cup	coconut cream (from two grated coconuts)
1 tablespoon	pandan juice

Prepare and line a 20-23 cm flan tin as described for papaya pie.

Peel pumpkin, dice and put in saucepan. Add salt and cook in boiling water, just enough to cover pumpkin, until tender. Drain well. Mash with a fork or blend in a blender.

Combine palm sugar, granulated sugar and water in a small saucepan and melt over low heat, stirring occasionally. Strain syrup.

Whisk eggs lightly and beat into cooled pumpkin. Stir in coconut milk, strained syrup and pandan juice.

Pour into prepared pastry-lined pan and bake in 175°C oven for one hour or until filling is set.

Chill for at least two hours before cutting.

Pie-Tee

Q: The *pie-tee* cups that I have made are difficult to remove from the mould when cooked. Can you please teach me how to remove them.

A: To remove the pie-tee *shells easily from the mould, you have to heat the mould in oil until it is very hot. Then quickly plunge the mould into batter and immediately back into the hot oil again. With a brand new mould (I prefer good-sized brass ones to the steel ones), the first couple of shells may stick. If this happens, lightly loosen the shells with the help of a pair of chopsticks.*

Q: Why don't my *pie-tee* shells stay crisp?

A: As soon as the pie tee *shells are cooled, keep them in an airtight container. Fill the pie tee shells just before serving. Once filled they will soften within an hour.*

Pizza

TOPS WITH HOMEMADE PIZZA

Pizza is a hot favourite with Malaysians. It also ranks high on the popular food list in many other countries. Pizza, I am told, was "created" when an Italian housewife ingeniously put together leftovers to come up with a quick and economical but nutritious and tasty meal. Apparently, she used leftover bread dough for the pizza base and tomatoes, scraps of cheese, and bits and pieces of ham, salami and minced meat for the topping. This dish is now enjoyed by people all over the world.

I like pizza, too. It is easy to make, and the endless variety of toppings that can be used prevents you from getting bored with the dish. I would encourage you to try making it. I have given a simple recipe for pizza dough and a basic tomato sauce flavoured with herbs. The dough is really soft and yet crispy, and can be made in 10 minutes with a food processor.

There are two variations to it: one with plain flour and one with wholemeal flour. To give you an idea of what variations are possible, I have given two toppings, a mixed vegetable topping and a minced beef topping.

Try out these recipes and, once you have mastered them, concoct your own toppings or imitate the Italian housewife and put your leftovers to good use. I am sure you will be able to come up with surprises to delight your family.

Pizza Dough

PLAIN PIZZA DOUGH

500 g	strong or high-protein flour, sifted
1/2 teaspoon	sugar
1 teaspoon	salt
8 g	easy-blend yeast
250 ml	warm water
4 tablespoons	olive oil

WHOLEWHEAT PIZZA DOUGH

250 g	high-protein flour, sifted
250 g	wholemeal plain flour, sifted
1 teaspoon	sugar
1 teaspoon	salt
8 g	easy-blend yeast
275 ml	warm water
4 tablespoons	olive oil

Use the same method for making both types of dough.

Put sifted flour into the bowl of a food processor fitted with a dough blade. Stir in sugar, salt and easy-blend yeast. Add water and olive oil and process for 3-5 minutes until dough forms a soft ball. Leave, covered, for 15 minutes.

Meanwhile, lightly grease two 32-35 cm pizza trays and preheat the oven to 220°C

Turn the dough on to a lightly floured surface. Knead for a minute and divide into two equal portions. Roll out to fit the prepared trays. Brush surface with a little extra olive oil. Bake base (without the topping) for 12 minutes.

Spread the tomato sauce over the half-cooked base and then scatter the topping of your choice over it. Bake for another 15-20 minutes until golden.

Herbed Tomato Sauce

600 g	ripe tomatoes
1 tablespoon	corn oil
1	onion, finely chopped
3 cloves	garlic, finely chopped
2 teaspoons	tomato paste
1 teaspoon	salt
1/2 teaspoon	sugar
1/4 teaspoon	black ground pepper
1/2 teaspoon	dried oregano
2 teaspoons	chopped fresh parsley
1 teaspoon	chopped fresh basil

Bring a saucepan of water to a boil. Put in the tomatoes and scald for 30 seconds. Drain and plunge straight into cold water. Peel off the skin. Chop the tomatoes coarsely.

Heat the corn oil in a clean saucepan and cook the onion and garlic until fragrant. Add the chopped tomatoes, tomato paste, salt, sugar and pepper. Cook, uncovered, for 10-12 minutes over low heat until the liquid is reduced and the sauce is thick.

Stir in the herbs. Set aside to cool.

This recipe makes enough sauce for two 32-35 cm diameter pizzas.

Mixed Vegetable Pizza

	Plain or wholewheat pizza dough (see recipe given)
	Olive oil for brushing
	Herbed tomato sauce (see recipe given)
150 g	broccoli, cut into small florets
150 g	cauliflower, cut into small florets
5 pieces	fresh young corn, diced
120 g	mozzarella cheese, thinly sliced
1	red pepper, cut into 1/4 cm strips
6 tablespoons	grated cheddar or Gouda cheese

MIXED HERBS

1 tablespoon	chopped parsley
1 tablespoon	chopped spring onion
1/4 tablespoon	chopped coriander leaves

Bring a saucepan of water to the boil. Blanch broccoli, cauliflower and young corn. Drop into cold water to stop them cooking and to keep their fresh colours. Set aside.

Divide pizza dough into two equal portions. Roll out to fit two 32-35 cm pizza trays. Brush surface of dough with a little olive oil. Prick surface with a fork. Bake in preheated oven at 220°C for 12 minutes.

Divide and spread tomato sauce on each pizza base. Arrange mozzarella cheese over sauce, followed by equal amounts of cooked vegetables and red pepper strips. Sprinkle generously with grated cheese and mixed herbs.

Bake for 15-20 minutes in preheated 220°C oven until golden.

Mustard Beef Pizza

Plain or wholemeal pizza dough (see recipe given)
Olive oil for brushing
Herbed tomato sauce (see recipe given)

1 tablespoon	corn oil
3 cloves	garlic, minced
350 g	minced beef (topside)
2 teaspoons	tomato paste
2 teaspoons	prepared mustard
1 teaspoon	sugar
1/2 teaspoon	salt
1/2 teaspoon	ground black pepper
60 g	mozzarella cheese, sliced
1	brinjal, thinly sliced
1/2	red pepper, cut into strips
6 tablespoons	grated cheddar or Gouda cheese

MIXED HERBS

3 tablespoons	chopped chives
2 tablespoons	chopped parsley
2 tablespoons	spring onion

Heat oil in a saucepan and add garlic. Stir-fry until fragrant. Put in minced beef and fry until it changes colour. Stir in tomato paste, mustard and seasonings. Cook for 2-3 minutes and then add half of the mixed herbs. Remove from pan and set aside to cool.

Divide pizza dough into two equal portions. Roll out to fit two 32-35 cm pizza trays. Brush surface of dough with a little olive oil. Prick surface with a fork. Bake in preheated oven at 220°C for 12 minutes.

Divide and spread tomato sauce on each pizza base. Arrange mozzarella cheese over sauce, followed by minced beef. Arrange brinjal and red pepper strips on top. Sprinkle generously with grated cheese and remaining mixed herbs.

Bake for 15-20 minutes in preheated 220°C oven until golden.

Q: I would be grateful if you could give me a recipe for a crisp, thin pizza. Most recipes are for the thicker type of crust which my family does not like very much.

A: For a crisp, thin pizza dough, follow this recipe, which uses water instead of milk. Roll it out very thinly. The topping should be sparing as the thin pizza base cannot hold a heavy topping.

Crisp Pizza Dough

2 cups	plain flour
1 teaspoon	sugar
1 teaspoon	salt
1 teaspoon	easy-blend dried yeast
1/2 cup	warm water
2 tablespoons	olive oil

Sift flour into a mixing bowl and stir in sugar, salt and yeast. Pour in warm water and olive oil and mix to a soft dough.

Turn dough onto a lightly floured surface and knead for about 5-8 minutes, or until smooth and elastic.

Place dough in a lightly oiled bowl, cover and let it stand in a warm place for about 1 hour or until doubled in bulk.

Knead dough on lightly floured surface until smooth. Roll out to form a 30 cm diameter circle and place on a lightly oiled pizza tray. Spread with a basic tomato sauce and a topping of your choice.

Bake in preheated 220°C oven for about 25 minutes or until base is browned and crispy.

Popiah

Q: What is the difference between round and square *popiah* skins?

A: Round popiah skins, available in wet markets, are usually used for dishes in which the skins are not fried. The square ones sold in supermarkets are more suitable for fried spring rolls.

Q: What is sweet flour sauce? Can I make it myself?

A: It is easier and more economical to buy sweet flour sauce (hak tim cheong), a thick black sweetened sauce specially for popiah, from Chinese sundry shops.

Q: Can you tell me how to make fresh *popiah* skins?

A: A good cast iron griddle is necessary to make paper-thin popiah skins. It takes considerable practice to acquire the skill of pressing and rolling the soft ball of dough over a hot plate.

Make a soft dough using two parts of sifted plain flour to one part water with a pinch of salt. Cover with a damp cloth and leave for one hour.

Heat a heavy cast iron griddle over moderate heat and rub with an oiled cloth. Take a handful of the soft dough and rub it lightly across the pan to make a thin round sheet about 15-20 cm in diameter.

Cook on moderate heat until the popiah *skin can be peeled off — this takes only a few seconds. Lift off and stack. Cover the* popiah *skins with a damp cloth until required.*

Poppy Seeds

Q: What are poppy seeds?

A: *Poppy seeds are tiny, round, black seeds. They come from the poppy flower but they are free from narcotic properties. They are used in cakes and pastries and sprinkled on bread rolls and pasta dishes.*

Porridge

Q: My husband suffers from ulcers and he has asked me to prepare Chinese porridge. I am Indian, and I am not sure how to do it. Could you give me recipes for vegetarian and non-vegetarian rice porridge?

A: *Here are two porridge recipes for you to try.*

Chicken Porridge

900 g	skinned whole chicken
1 teaspoon	pepper
1 teaspoon	salt
1 teaspoon	sesame oil
approx. 3 litres	water
1 tablespoon	light soya sauce
1 teaspoon	sesame oil
	A dash of pepper
250 g	short-grain rice, washed and drained
2 tablespoons	glutinous rice (optional), washed and drained
2 teaspoons	salt
1 tablespoon	oil
1	chicken stock cube (optional)
	Salt and pepper to taste
10 cm knob	ginger, finely shredded

Rub chicken with pepper, salt and sesame oil and set aside for 30 minutes.

Boil three litres of water in a deep saucepan. Put in chicken and boil rapidly for 5-8 minutes. Reduce heat, cover pan and simmer for approximately 30-40 minutes.

Remove chicken and soak in a bowl of cold water for 10 minutes. Shred chicken and season with light soya sauce, sesame oil and a dash of pepper. Set aside.

Return chicken bones to stock and add water to make 4 litres. Boil with short-grain and glutinous rice, salt, oil and, if desired, a chicken stock cube. Cook over moderate heat for an hour or until it reaches desired consistency. Stir occasionally to prevent porridge from sticking to the bottom of the pan. Stir in salt and pepper to taste; add shredded ginger. If porridge is too thick, add a little boiled water.

Serve porridge in individual rice bowls. Garnish with seasoned shredded chicken, extra-fine shredded ginger and, if desired, chopped spring onions, diced fried Chinese crullers (you tiau), crumbled deep-fried transparent bean vermicelli, and shredded lettuce.

Vegetarian Abalone Mushroom Porridge

250 g	short-grain rice
2 tablespoons	glutinous rice, optional
approx. 4 litres	water
1 tablespoon	oil
1 teaspoon	sesame oil
1 tablespoon	salt, or to taste
500 g	abalone mushrooms, sliced

SEASONING INGREDIENTS
1 tablespoon	ginger juice
1 teaspoon	sesame oil
$1/2$ teaspoon	salt
$1/2$ teaspoon	sugar
$1/4$ teaspoon	pepper
1 tablespoon	light soya sauce
1 teaspoon	cornflour

Bring rice, water, oil and salt to a boil. Cook over moderate heat for an hour or until it reaches desired consistency.

Season sliced mushrooms with seasoning ingredients and steam for 15 minutes.

Serve porridge in individual rice bowls. Add salt and pepper to taste. Garnish with cooked abalone mushrooms, young ginger shreds, shallot crisps, spring onions and some diced fried Chinese crullers.

Potatoes

Q: I'm 13 and would like to know how to mash potatoes. Do they need any sauce?

A: To make good, smooth mashed potatoes, choose floury potatoes. Here's a simple recipe. A sauce is not necessary, but mashed potatoes are delicious with gravy.

Mashed Potatoes

1 kg potatoes, peeled
60 g butter
200-250 ml milk
Salt and pepper to taste

Cut the potatoes into even-sized chunks and bring to a boil in a pan of lightly salted water. Cover and simmer for 20-25 minutes until tender. Drain well, then return to the pan; cover and leave to dry in the residual heat.

Mash the potatoes until smooth. Beat in butter and enough milk to obtain a soft consistency. Season with salt and pepper to taste.

Gravy for Mashed Potatoes

50 g butter or pan drippings (from roasting chicken or meat)
30 g flour
1 cup fresh beef stock, or chicken stock with a dash of thick soya sauce for colour
Salt and pepper to taste

Heat butter or drippings. Add flour and brown lightly, but be careful not to burn it. Gradually stir in liquid, bring to a boil, and stir until thick and smooth. Season to taste.

Prawns

Q: I am on holiday here for one month from Auckland. I have tried Butter Prawns, and I think they are fantastic. Could you kindly give me the recipe for this dish?

A: This is my version of Butter Prawns and it is one of my favourites too. I hope you'll enjoy it as much as I do.

Butter Prawns with Toasted Coconut

500 g large prawns, feelers trimmed
1/2 teaspoon salt
1/2 teaspoon pepper

OMELETTE

2 eggs, beaten
1 teaspoon light soya sauce
1/4 teaspoon salt
1/2 teaspoon pepper

90 g butter
60 g pan toasted grated coconut, blended in electric blender
2 teaspoons sugar
1/2 teaspoon salt

172

 10 chilli padi, finely sliced
Spring onions and coriander leaves,
chopped
Juice of 1 small lime

Season prawns with salt and pepper.

Make thin omelette with omelette ingredients and chop finely. Set aside.

Heat oil and deep-fry prawns until just cooked. Drain.

Heat butter over low heat, put in toasted coconut, sugar, salt, and chilli padi. Toss well and cook until fragrant. Add finely chopped omelette, spring onions, coriander leaves and lime juice.

Add prawns and toss until well coated with omelette mixture. Serve hot.

Q: I enjoy cooking for special occasions. I would be most grateful if you could provide me with the recipe for chilli prawns with cashew nuts as served in Chinese restaurants.

A: Here is the recipe you asked for. I hope you have an enjoyable time trying it out.

Chilli Prawns with Cashew Nuts

500 g shelled prawns, slit and deveined

SEASONING INGREDIENTS

1 dessertspoon	light soya sauce
1 dessertspoon	oyster sauce
1 teaspoon	ginger juice
1/4 teaspoon	salt
2 tablespoons	water
2 teaspoons	cornflour

2 tablespoons	oil
3 cloves	garlic, minced
30 g	dried chillies, cut into 2, washed and drained

SAUCE INGREDIENTS

1 dessertspoon	light soya sauce
1 dessertspoon	oyster sauce
1 teaspoon	ginger juice
1 teaspoon	sesame oil
1/2 teaspoon	thick soya sauce
2 teaspoons	sugar

2 tablespoons	roasted cashew nuts
1 teaspoon	cornflour combined with 2 tablespoons water

Marinate prawns in seasoning ingredients for at least 20 minutes.

Heat oil in wok and stir-fry garlic until fragrant. Add dried chillies and stir-fry over medium heat for 30 seconds.

Put in prawns and cook over high heat until prawns change colour. Add combined sauce ingredients and stir-fry until prawns are cooked.

Stir in cashew nuts and cornflour thickening.

Q: Prawns are delicious, but the prawn entrails spoil the taste. I have tried removing them from the tail end of unshelled prawns without success. Can you suggest a way to do it properly?

A: First, pierce a cocktail stick into the section between the head and the body to detach the entrails from the head. Then pierce the tail end section and holding on tight to the cocktail stick lift with a pulling motion. The entrails will slip out.

Pumpkin

PLUMP FOR PUMPKIN

Mention pumpkin and most people think of the famous American Pumpkin Pie which is traditionally served during Thanksgiving. The American Halloween festival, when pumpkins are hollowed out, carved and made into candlelit lanterns, also comes to mind. But the pumpkin also features in our local cuisine where it is used in curries, custards and *kuih*.

The pumpkin is relatively cheap and very nutritious. It is a good source of vitamins A and C, and is therefore good value for money. The delicious golden orange flesh is versatile enough to be used for both savoury and sweet dishes, such as stews, soups, cakes, custard, ice-cream and, of course, the popular pies.

Pumpkins are easily available locally throughout the year. Look for ripe but firm pumpkins which are heavy for their size and have unblemished skins. They will keep well for a couple of weeks if stored whole in a cool place. Large pumpkins are also sold cut into wedges. Once cut, the pieces should be wrapped in plastic wrap. They keep well for about a week in the refrigerator. Use them as soon as possible as they will quickly lose their flavour or even turn mouldy.

Try these sweet and savoury pumpkin recipes. My favourite is the Spiced Pumpkin Pie, which has a lightly spiced cream filling and a lovely nutty melt-in-the-mouth pastry.

Pumpkin Tomato Soup

1 tablespoon	oil
1/2 tablespoon	butter
2 cloves	garlic, chopped
1	onion, chopped
1	leek, sliced
500 g	pumpkin flesh, cut into 2 cm cubes
2	ripe tomatoes, diced
700 ml	fresh chicken stock
1 1/4 teaspoons	salt or to taste
1/4 teaspoon	pepper
1 tablespoon	chopped spring onions
1 tablespoon	chopped chives
	Single or reduced cream, to serve

Heat oil and butter in a large saucepan and stir-fry the garlic, onion and leek until soft. Put in the pumpkin and cook for about 3-5 minutes and then add the tomatoes. Pour in half of the chicken stock and bring to a boil. Cover and simmer for 25 minutes until the vegetables are tender.

Blend mixture in a food processor until smooth. Strain into a clean saucepan. Stir in remaining chicken stock and seasoning. Bring to a boil and stir in spring onions and chives.

Serve hot with a swirl of cream, if desired.

Spiced Pumpkin Pie

PASTRY

200 g	plain flour
100 g	butter, at room temperature
50 g	castor sugar
50 g	ground walnuts
1	egg yolk, beaten

FILLING

700 g	pumpkin flesh, cubed
75 g	castor sugar
1 teaspoon	flour
1/2 teaspoon	nutmeg
1/2 teaspoon	ground ginger
2	eggs, lightly beaten
250 ml	evaporated milk
1/2 teaspoon	vanilla essence

Icing sugar, for dusting

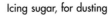

Stir flour into a large mixing bowl and add butter. Using a pastry cutter or two knives, blend until flour is crumbly. Stir in sugar and walnuts and then the egg yolk. Mix gently using fingertips to bind the mixture together. Form into a ball of dough and wrap in plastic wrap. Chill for 30 minutes.

Meanwhile prepare the filling by steaming the pumpkin for 15-20 minutes until soft. Place in a large bowl and mash well. Add the remaining ingredients and mix well. Set aside.

Roll out the pastry between two sheets of plastic wrap and gently ease it onto a 23 cm fluted springform pie tin. Trim edges.

Pour prepared filling into pastry-lined tin. Bake in preheated 200°C oven for 40 minutes or until filling is set and pastry is golden.

Serve dusted with icing sugar.

Pumpkin Scones

250 g	cold mashed pumpkin
45 g	butter or margarine
60 g	castor sugar
1	egg, beaten

SIFTED INGREDIENTS (COMBINED)

300 g	self-raising flour
1 teaspoon	baking powder
1/2 teaspoon	cinnamon powder

1/4 teaspoon	salt
2 tablespoons	milk
1	egg white, beaten, for glazing
	Butter and jam

Press mashed pumpkin through a fine sieve to remove any lumps.

Cream butter and sugar until light and creamy. Gradually beat in egg, then add pumpkin. Fold in sifted dry ingredients and salt. Add enough milk to bind mixture into a soft but not-too-sticky dough. The amount of milk to be added depends on moistness of cooked pumpkin.

Turn dough onto a lightly floured board and roll out to 5 cm thickness. Stamp into rounds with a 5-6 cm scone cutter.

Place on greased baking trays. Brush with beaten egg white. Bake in preheated 200°C oven for 15 minutes until well risen and cooked through.

Serve with butter and jam.

Raising Agents

Q: If a recipe requires 1 teaspoon of bicarbonate of soda and 1 teaspoon of baking powder, can I omit the bicarbonate of soda and double the amount of baking powder?

A: *Baking powder and bicarbonate of soda are both leavening agents. Baking powders are usually a mixture of bicarbonate of soda and another acidic compound like cream of tartar. Bicarbonate of soda is a natural alkaline product which will react with the acids in ingredients such as sour milk, yoghurt, cream of tartar, chocolate and fruits to leaven or raise batters and dough.*

Some recipes call for both baking powder and bicarbonate of soda to ensure that there are enough acids for the leavening action. On the other hand, bicarbonate of soda may be necessary for neutralising the acid ingredients in a recipe to give a tender crumb, while the main leavening action is left to the baking powder. Therefore, depending on the recipe, I would recommend using both baking powder and bicarbonate of soda to get the best results.

Q: Is the soda powder we buy in Chinese medicine shops the same as bicarbonate of soda?

A: *Yes. It is used for tenderising meat in Chinese cooking.*

Q: What is double-action baking powder?

A: *Double-action baking powder, often referred to as combination baking powder, is a leavening agent most commonly used for cakes, quick breads and biscuits. It is called double-acting because it starts working in the cold dough but most of the rising does not begin until the dough comes into contact with the heat from the oven.*

Q: Is the baking powder used in *Asian High Tea Favourites* cookbook double action powder or just normal baking powder?

A: *Unless specified otherwise, baking powder mentioned in any cookbook is normal, "single acting" baking powder.*

Q: What is the function of cream of tartar?

A: *Cream of tartar is a white powder with a tart, slightly salty taste. It comes from certain fruits, such as grapes, and is a by-product of wine-making. It is scraped from the bottom of wine casks and barrels after the juice has fermented. Added to egg whites, its acidity helps to stabilise them when beaten so that they do not deflate.*

Rice

Q: Kindly provide me with a detailed recipe for Yam Rice.

A: I have here a lovely recipe for Yam Rice. It makes an easy-to-prepare one-pot meal.

Yam Rice

300 g	boneless, skinless chicken, cut into 2 cm pieces.

SEASONING INGREDIENTS

1/2 teaspoon	salt
1/2 teaspoon	sugar
1/4 teaspoon	pepper
1 teaspoon	sesame oil
1 teaspoon	light soya sauce
1 teaspoon	rice wine
1/4 teaspoon	cornflour

	Oil for deep-frying
350 g	cleaned yams, cut into 2 cm cubes
6	shallots, sliced
60 g	dried prawns, soaked for 15 minutes and drained
300 g	rice (2 rice cups) washed and drained
2 teaspoons	light soya sauce
600 ml	fresh chicken stock
2 tablespoons	chopped spring onions

Marinate chicken in seasoning ingredients and set aside.

Heat oil in a wok and fry yams for 8-10 minutes or until cooked through. Drain and set aside.

Put in shallots and fry until golden. Drain and set aside for garnishing.

Clean and reheat wok with 3 tablespoons oil and stir-fry dried prawns until fragrant. Add rice and toss for 1-2 minutes. Stir in light soya sauce and mix well.

Remove rice from heat and place in a pot or in an electric rice cooker. Pour in chicken stock. When rice comes to the boil, add yam and chicken. Cook until rice is done.

Just before serving, stir in shallot crisps and spring onions.

Q: My family loves Thai fried rice. Can you give me a recipe?

A: Try this version of Thai Fried Rice.

Spicy Thai Fried Rice

300 g	small shelled prawns
1/2 teaspoon	salt
1/2 teaspoon	sugar
1/2 teaspoon	pepper
3 tablespoons	cooking oil
4	shallots, ground
4 cloves	garlic, ground
2	red chillies, seeded, ground
4 cups	cooked rice
1 teaspoon	salt, or to taste
6	chilli padi, sliced
1 teaspoon	sugar
1 tablespoon	light soya sauce
1 tablespoon	fish sauce
1 tablespoon	chopped basil leaves
1 tablespoon	chopped spring onions
	Basil leaves and strips of chilli for garnish

Season prawns with salt, sugar and pepper and set aside.

Heat oil in a wok and lightly brown ground ingredients. Add the prawns and cook over high heat for one minute, then add rice. Toss well and add salt, chilli padi, sugar, light soya sauce and fish sauce and stir well. Lastly add the chopped basil and spring onions.

Serve hot, garnished with chilli strips and basil leaves.

Saffron

SPICE WORTH ITS WEIGHT IN GOLD

Saffron, made from the bright orange-red stigmata of the autumn-flowering, lilac-coloured blossoms of the *crocus sativus* plant, is the world's most expensive spice, literally worth its weight in gold. Prized since ancient times, saffron has been used in food, in perfume and as a dye for clothes and hair. The Romans used it to perfume theatres, flavour food and as eye make-up.

The stigmata have to be laboriously and carefully hand-plucked from the crocus blossoms with tweezers. They are then toasted or dried in sieves over low heat. Each crocus produces only three stigmata and it takes about 13,000 stigmata to make 25 g of saffron. The *crocus sativus* is now cultivated in Spain, Portugal, Greece, Iran, Kashmir, China, Italy, France and Britain. The finest quality saffron comes from Spain.

Saffron today has a privileged place in cooking around the world: in the French bouillabaisse, Spanish paella, Italian risotto, and Indian pilau. In parts of England, saffron is used extensively in baking; there is even a town, Saffron Walden, named after the spice. Saffron is also used to flavour a variety of sweet rice dishes, semolina puddings and custards.

Do not confuse saffron with turmeric powder, which is very often used instead of saffron but which is a poor substitute. Pure saffron is strongly perfumed and has a unique flavour that is both bittersweet and pungent.

Buy whole saffron (rather than powdered) and use it sparingly. It should be mixed with hot liquid and left to infuse for at least 30 minutes, or preferably overnight, before use. If you add it directly to a dish, crumble it lightly with your fingers and sprinkle it in.

Plaited Saffron Bread

1 teaspoon	saffron strands
100 ml	hot water
2 tablespoons	honey
130 ml	lukewarm milk
90 g	melted butter
650 g	bread flour
1¹/₂ teaspoons	salt
10 g	easy-blend yeast
2 medium	eggs, beaten

EGG GLAZE (COMBINED)

1	egg yolk, beaten
1 teaspoon	milk
	Pinch of salt

Lightly toast saffron strands. Drop into boiling water and leave to infuse for 30 minutes.

Stir honey into lukewarm milk and, when dissolved, add melted butter and mix well.

Sift bread flour into the mixing bowl of an electric mixer fitted with a dough hook. Mix in salt and yeast.

Combine saffron liquid with milk mixture and beaten eggs. Add to flour mixture. Beat to form a smooth, soft dough. Cover with a damp tea towel and leave to rise for 45 minutes or until doubled in bulk.

Knock back the dough and knead until soft and pliable. Divide into 3 even pieces and roll each one into a long sausage. Plait the rolls together, pinching and tucking in the ends. Leave to rise again for 30-40 minutes.

Brush with egg glaze and bake in preheated 220°C oven for 15 minutes or until golden.

Saffron Vegetable Pilau

RICE

1 teaspoon	saffron strands
175 ml	boiling water
1 tablespoon	ghee
1 tablespoon	vegetable oil
2	cardamom pods
2 cm stick	cinnamon

2	cloves
1/2	onion, chopped
1 teaspoon	ginger, chopped
150 g	Basmati rice, soaked for 30 minutes
1 teaspoon	ground coriander
1 teaspoon	cumin seeds
1/4 teaspoon	chilli powder
1 tablespoon	ground almonds
525 ml	water
1	chicken stock cube
1 teaspoon	salt
3 teaspoons	rosewater
	Toasted almond flakes
	Shallot crisps

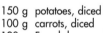

VEGETABLES

1 tablespoon	ghee
1 tablespoon	oil
2 cm stick	cinnamon
1	cardamom pod
1	clove
1 teaspoon	cumin seeds
3 cloves	garlic, chopped
1 teaspoon	ginger, chopped

150 g	potatoes, diced
100 g	carrots, diced
120 g	French beans, diced
2 medium	tomatoes, diced
2	red chillies, diced
1	green chilli, diced
1	red or green pepper, diced
2 tablespoons	yoghurt
1 tablespoon	tomato paste
1 teaspoon	salt

To Prepare Rice

Stir saffron into boiling water and set aside to infuse for 30 minutes.

Heat ghee and oil and fry cardamom, cinnamon and cloves; add onion and ginger and fry until fragrant. Put in rice, coriander, cumin seeds and chilli, and toss until rice is coated with ghee and spices. Mix in ground almonds.

Transfer mixture to rice cooker and add saffron mixture and 525 ml water, chicken stock cube and salt. Cook until rice is done.

Stir in rosewater and divide into 3 equal portions. Set aside.

To Prepare Vegetables

Heat ghee and oil and fry spices, garlic and ginger till fragrant. Add vegetables. Stir in yoghurt, tomato paste and salt. Simmer 3-5 minutes. Divide into 2 equal portions.

To Assemble Pilau

In rectangular casserole dish, spread alternate layers of prepared rice and vegetables, sprinkling almond flakes and shallot crisps on top of each layer of rice. Bake in 50°C oven for 30 minutes.

Sauces

Q: I always have trouble cooking sauces which contain flour. How do you prevent them from turning lumpy? Is there any way to rescue a sauce that has turned lumpy?

A: *The basic ingredients for a white sauce are butter, flour and milk. Melt the butter in a nonstick pan and gradually add the flour; cook the mixture over gentle heat, stirring constantly with a wooden spoon until the mixture comes away from the sides of the pan. Then add the milk gradually, again stirring constantly. Once all the milk has been added, use a balloon whisk and beat until the sauce boils and is thick and smooth.*

If the sauce should turn lumpy while cooking, plunge the bottom of the pan into a bowl of cold water and continue to whisk; the sauce will get smooth again. You can also pass a lumpy sauce through a sieve or pour it into a liquidiser and blend until smooth.

Q: Do I have to put Worcestershire Sauce in the fridge once it's opened?

A: *It is not necessary to store Worcestershire Sauce in the fridge. It keeps well in a cool larder for a long time. Keep a check on the "use by" or "best by" date.*

Q: Is Lea & Perrins sauce the same as Worcestershire sauce?

A: *Yes, Lea & Perrins is a brand name for Worcestershire sauce.*

Scones

Q: I would be grateful if you could tell me why when I bake scones, they sometimes rise unevenly. Can you also give me a recipe for Currant Scones?

A: *If your recipe requires the use of raising agents, the uneven rising could be due to uneven distribution of the raising agents. Another cause could be uneven pressure when rolling the dough, which tends to make the baked scones slanted. But slanting or uneven surfaces are not serious problems if the scones turn out crisp on the outside and light and moist inside.*

Try this recipe for Currant Scones. You can serve them warm with butter, jam or clotted cream.

Currant Scones

240 g self-raising flour
1/4 teaspoon salt
45 g margarine or butter, at room temperature
30 g castor sugar
30 g currants
150 ml milk
extra milk for brushing

Line a baking tray with greased baking sheet. Preheat oven to 220°C.

Sift flour into a bowl and stir in salt. Rub in margarine or butter finely. Stir in sugar and currants. Add milk and mix to a soft but not sticky dough with a knife.

Turn dough out onto a lightly floured board. Knead quickly until smooth. Roll out to a thickness of not less than 2 cm. Cut into rounds with a 5 cm fluted or plain scone cutter.

Place on prepared tray. Brush tops with milk. Bake on top shelf of oven 12-15 minutes until crisp and golden brown. Cool on wire rack. Eat them slightly warm.

Q: I made some pikelets, but they didn't rise even though I used self-raising flour. Some were too hard and some were too soft. What went wrong?

A: Pikelets, also known as griddle cakes, drop scones or Scotch pancakes, should be light and moist. Your problem could be due to your pan or the heat. Use a good nonstick griddle plate made especially for pancakes or a heavy nonstick frying pan. If the scones are pale and too soft then the pan is not hot enough. If over-browned and hard, the griddle is too hot. I hope your next attempt will be successful. Pikelets are lovely served for breakfast or tea and can be turned into great desserts too.

Pikelets (Drop Scones)

120 g self-raising flour
1 teaspoon baking powder
1 tablespoon castor sugar
1 teaspoon butter, at room temperature
1 large egg
125 ml milk
Grated rind of one lemon or orange

Sift self-raising flour and baking powder into the bowl of an electric mixer. Add the castor sugar, butter, egg, milk, and lemon or orange rind.

Turn on electric mixer and beat to a smooth batter for about one minute. Chill and rest batter in the refrigerator for 15-20 minutes.

Heat a pancake griddle or nonstick frying pan. Lightly grease with corn oil.

Drop in spoonfuls of the batter and cook for 1-2 minutes until the scones are golden and the bubbles rising to the surface begin to burst. Turn the scones over and cook for another minute.

Transfer to a tea towel and keep warm. Serve with butter, jam, honey, golden syrup or maple syrup.

Makes 8 pikelets.

Variations
Replace grated lemon or orange rind with $1/2$ teaspoon vanilla essence or mixed spice.

Stir in 50 g sultanas or chopped apricots.

Stir in 60 g finely chopped bananas.

To make into a dessert, top scones with whipped cream, ice-cream or yoghurt together with sliced bananas, kiwi fruit or strawberries.

Semolina

Q: What is semolina?

A: Semolina is a by-product of the milling of wheat. It is granular in appearance and is used to make milk puddings, cakes and biscuits.

Q: Can you give me a recipe for a cake using semolina?

A: Here is a recipe for a lovely semolina cake. It is very rich with butter and egg yolks.

Plain Semolina Cake

180 g	semolina, roasted
500 g	butter, at room temperature
10	egg yolks
300 g	castor sugar

SIFTED INGREDIENTS (COMBINED)

120 g	plain flour
1 teaspoon	baking powder
$1/4$ teaspoon	bicarbonate of soda

2 tablespoons	ground almonds
1 teaspoon	vanilla essence
	Grated rind and juice of 1 orange
1	egg white

To roast the semolina, pan-fry, stirring continuously until very lightly golden. Set aside to cool.

Line a 23 cm square cake tin with nonstick baking paper.

Cream butter for a minute or two, then add roasted semolina. Beat to combine ingredients. Leave to soak in butter for at least 4 hours.

Whisk egg yolks until frothy, then add sugar and continue whisking until mixture is light and creamy. Fold semolina mixture into egg mixture, mixing well. Carefully fold in sifted dry ingredients and then the ground almonds. Stir in essence and orange juice and rind.

Whisk the egg white until just stiff and carefully fold into the semolina mixture. Turn into prepared pan.

Bake in preheated 160°C oven for 1 hr 15 min to 1 hr 20 min or until skewer inserted in the centre comes out clean. Cake will shrink slightly from the sides and take on a golden-brown colour.

Shallots

Q: Please tell me how to make shallot crisps and shallot oil.

A: *Peel shallots, rinse and drain well. Dry thoroughly with absorbent paper or a tea towel. Slice shallots thinly.*

Heat enough oil for deep-frying until smoking hot. Put in sliced shallots and stir-fry continuously over high heat until shallots are just beginning to brown. Reduce heat to low and cook until very light golden brown. Just before removing crisps from pan, increase heat. This will prevent crisps from retaining too much oil.

Pour oil with crisps into a colander placed over a heatproof dish. The shallot crisps must be drained very quickly from hot oil to prevent them from turning too brown.

Spread crisps onto absorbent paper to cool. Store in an airtight jar. The fried shallots will keep crisp for months. Store cooled shallot oil in a separate covered container.

Shortening

Q: What is shortening? Is there any substitute for it?

A: *Shortening usually refers to any edible fat which makes baked goods such as cakes and biscuits "short" or rich. First used to describe animal fat, shortening now includes a much wider range of products, such as blended shortening (using both animal and vegetable fats) and vegetable shortening (solidified vegetable oil).*

Q: Does Crisco need to be refrigerated?

A: *Crisco, which is vegetable shortening, need not be refrigerated. Store in a cool place. However, once the can is open, it will store better in the fridge.*

Q: What is *lemak putih*? Is it the same as Spry?

A: Lemak putih *is vegetable shortening. Spry or Crisco are two brand names that are readily available in supermarkets.*

Q: Can shortening be used in place of margarine or butter for making cookies? Will the taste be affected?

A: Yes, you can use vegetable shortening instead of butter or margarine to make cookies, but butter will give a better flavour.

Soup

Q: Could you give me a recipe for vegetable soup?

A: Try this home favourite which can be prepared in a jiffy.

Onion, tomato and potato soup

5 cups   fresh chicken stock

DICED INGREDIENTS (1 CM CUBES)

1   large onion
1   large potato
2   tomatoes

1¹/₂ teaspoons   salt
1 teaspoon   pepper
2   spring onions, chopped
2 sprigs   coriander leaves, chopped

Put chicken stock, diced onion and potato into a medium-size pot and bring to a boil. Reduce heat to low and simmer for 10 minutes.

Put in tomatoes and seasoning to taste and continue to simmer for a further 10 minutes.

Stir in spring onions and coriander leaves and serve hot.

Q: I would like to know how to make mint leaf and egg soup.

A: Mint leaf soup with eggs is a lovely light refreshing soup. Make a good stock out of chicken bones and use very fresh mint leaves. Here's a simple recipe:

Mint Leaf Soup

2	eggs
1 teaspoon	sesame oil
1-2 litres	fresh chicken stock
	Salt to taste
a large bunch	mint leaves, stems removed
1 tablespoon	chopped spring onions, white part only

Lightly beat the eggs and sesame oil with a fork in a mixing bowl and set aside.

Heat the stock in a large pan. Stir in salt to taste and as soon as the stock comes to the boil, add the mint leaves and simmer for one minute. Stir in the spring onions.

Gradually add the egg mixture in a very slow thin stream. Using a chopstick or fork, pull the egg slowly into strands.

Q: Can you tell me how to make herbal soup?

A: *A good herbal soup depends on putting together the right combination of herbs and giving it time to brew. You can use a double boiler or a porcelain crockpot. Try this Herbal Chicken Soup. It is tasty and nutritious.*

Herbal Chicken Soup

1 (600 g)	kampung chicken, skinned and quartered
1	teaspoon salt

HERBS

15 g	*tong kwei*
15 g	*tong sam*
15 g	*pak kei*
15 g	*yok chok*
10 g	*kei chee*
6	Chinese dried red dates

Rub chicken with salt. Place chicken in an electric crockpot together with the herbs.

Add five cups of water or enough to cover the chicken. Slow cook on high for 3-3¹/₂ hours.

Q: I like chicken soup which is creamy and tasty. Can you give me a recipe?

A: *Here's a recipe for Cream of Chicken Soup using fresh chicken stock. Make a good stock from chicken bones, then strain and de-grease before use. I add very finely diced cooked chicken to the soup instead of blending it with the soup; otherwise the chicken tends to get stringy and spoil the smooth taste of the soup.*

Cream of Chicken Soup

4 cups	fresh chicken stock
1/2	onion, finely chopped
1 stick	celery, finely chopped
1 tablespoon	butter
1 1/2 level tablespoons	flour
1 teaspoon	salt
1/2 teaspoon	pepper
1/2 cup	boiled or steamed chicken, finely diced
1/4 cup	cream
1 tablespoon	chopped parsley

Simmer chicken stock, onion and celery for 20 minutes, covered. Blend in an electric blender and strain.

Melt butter over low heat and quickly stir in flour until blended. Add strained stock and seasonings to taste.

Stir in diced chicken and when stock starts to boil, turn off heat. Stir in cream. Heat, but do not boil. Serve garnished with chopped parsley.

Sour Cream

Q: What is the difference between sour cream and yoghurt? I cannot get sour cream. If a recipe requires sour cream, can I use yoghurt instead?

A: Sour cream is normally a light cream to which a special culture has been added to give it a sour taste. It enhances the flavour and creaminess of many dishes, particularly soups, savoury sauces, dips and jacket potatoes, as well as desserts. You can buy it in most supermarkets.

Yoghurt is made by fermenting milk with a natural bacterial culture. Yoghurt can be used as a substitute for sour cream; the calories will be reduced, but the dish won't be as thick and creamy.

Soya Bean Milk

Q: The soya bean milk I buy from hawkers can be kept for a couple of days, but the soya bean milk I made at home turned slimy and even curdled, despite being put in the fridge.

A: Homemade soya bean milk is usually creamier and healthier than the milk you buy from hawkers. Perhaps you just need to add more water. Here is a recipe.

Homemade Soya Bean Milk

350 g	soya beans, soaked in water overnight
8 litres	water
4-6	pandan leaves, knotted
150 g	rock sugar
500 g	sugar, or to taste
1-2 drops	almond essence, optional

Drain soya beans and gently rub off skins. (You can leave the skin on but the soya bean milk will have a husky flavour which you may not like.) Remove skins and blend beans with a little of the water in a liquidiser.

Pour blended soya bean mixture into a large deep saucepan together with the remaining water and bring to a boil with the pandan leaves. Boil for 5-8 minutes. Remove from heat. Cool a little and strain through fine muslin.

Put strained soya bean milk to boil with rock sugar and sugar. Do not add all the sugar if you like it less sweet. Boil, stirring occasionally, for about 15 minutes until all the sugar dissolves. Stir in almond essence.

Spices

Q: What is the difference between allspice and mixed spice? Are they the same?

A: Allspice grows prolifically in Jamaica where it is widely used in native dishes. It is a member of the pepper family — the berry of the pimento tree. The berries are picked when green and unripe and then dried in the sun to a rich deep-brown colour. Its flavour is a mingling of cloves, cinnamon and nutmeg, with cloves predominating. Allspice can be bought either ground or whole.

Mixed spice is a blend of spices which often includes allspice, ground cinnamon, cloves, ginger, nutmeg and often a pinch of black pepper, although different brands vary.

Mixed spice and allspice are interchangeable and both add a subtle spiciness to sweet and savoury dishes.

Sponge Cakes

Sponge cakes are the lightest of all cakes. Sweet and delicate in texture, they can be made with or without fat. The success of sponge cakes depends on incorporating as much air as possible into the batter. Pay attention to beating eggs and folding in the dry ingredients. The electric whisk is excellent for whisking the eggs and sugar efficiently until light and fluffy. The egg mixture should be stiff but moist and able to hold its shape before folding in the flour.

The dry ingredients can also be folded in with an electric mixer; blend on lowest speed for a few seconds until the batter is well blended with no visible traces of flour. Stop to scrape all batter from the edges of the bowl with a spatula, then turn on the mixer again until just blended.

Once mixed, the batter will lose volume if left to stand, so pour it into the prepared cake pan immediately. Cut through the batter several times to dispel large bubbles, then spread batter to fill all sides and into corners.

Here's a simple sponge cake recipe for you to start with.

Chocolate Honey Sponge Cake

2 tablespoons	good quality cocoa powder, sifted
1/4 cup	milk
1 tablespoon	honey
30 g	butter
4	large eggs, separated
240 g	castor sugar
1/2 teaspoon	vanilla essence

SIFTED INGREDIENTS (SIFT TWICE)

120 g	self-raising flour
1/4 teaspoon	salt
1/4 teaspoon	bicarbonate of soda
1 tablespoon	cornflour

1 cup whipping cream, whipped

Put cocoa, milk, honey and butter into pan, stir over low heat until butter has melted and mixture is blended. Remove from heat.

Beat egg whites in an electric mixer until soft peaks form. Gradually add sugar, beating well after each addition until sugar has dissolved.

Add egg yolks, one at a time, beating until just combined. Add vanilla. Gently fold in sifted dry ingredients.

Return cocoa mixture to heat and bring to a boil. Remove from heat and fold into egg mixture.

Pour mixture into two greased and floured 20 cm cake pans. Bake in preheated 175°C oven for 20-25 minutes or until cake shrinks slightly from the sides of the tin.

When cold, sandwich and decorate cake with whipped cream. If desired, top with sliced fresh fruit.

Q: Could you give me a recipe for a low-calorie cake which tastes as delicious as an ordinary one? I believe sponge cakes are low in calories as less butter is used. Is it true that these recipes do not require baking powder and that pans for baking sponge cakes do not need to be greased?

A: You can turn most cakes into low-calorie cakes by substituting margarine or corn oil for butter. Yes, sponge cakes are low in calories as they can be made without fat, and a true sponge cake is made without baking powder either. Its light texture depends entirely on the air beaten into the eggs. Only a small proportion of flour to eggs is used. There is a high proportion of sugar, which helps in making the cake light.

Sponge cake mixtures are very easily dried and overcooked, so time the cooking to the minute and bake at the recommended oven temperature.

It is not necessary to grease pans for angel or sponge cakes as the cake will rise more easily without a slippery pan. However, for ease of turning out use wax paper to line the base of the cake pan. Pans with a nonstick coating do not need greasing, but a wax paper liner helps to keep too solid a crust from forming.

Try this Lemon Sponge Cake.

Lemon Sponge Cake

6	large eggs, chilled and separated
240 g	castor sugar
2 tablespoons	cold water
	Grated rind of 1 lemon
1 tablespoon	lemon juice
	Pinch of salt
1/4 teaspoon	cream of tartar
240 g	cake flour, sifted

Preheat oven to 165°C. Line bottom of a 25 cm tube pan or two 20 cm round cake pans with wax paper. Place egg yolks in a large mixing bowl and whisk until thick and lemon-coloured.

Gradually add half of the sugar, one tablespoon at a time, and beat until thick and creamy. Combine water, lemon rind and lemon juice and slowly stir into egg yolks.

In a large bowl, with a clean dry rotary whisk, beat egg whites until foamy. Add salt and cream of tartar and beat until soft peaks form. Beat in remaining half cup of sugar, a tablespoon at a time. Continue beating until mixture is stiff but not dry.

Stir a quarter of the egg yolk mixture into egg white. Sift flour on top of remaining egg yolk mixture and gently fold in with a metal spoon. Spoon egg whites over the top and fold gently until well-blended.

Turn into prepared pan. Bake for 50-60 minutes in tube pan or 25 minutes in 20 cm round pans, or until top springs back when touched lightly with your finger.

Invert tube pan or turn out layers on a wire rack to cool. Dust with icing sugar and sandwich with jam or any frosting of your choice.

Q: My sponge cakes look good, but after cooling in the oven the sides shrink even though I have lined the cake tins. Why does this happen?

A: *The main riser in sponge cakes is air. On cooling, the baked cake will contract and pull away from the sides of the pan. If the shrinkage is excessive, the cake has been baked at too high heat. I like to use self-raising flour as it gives added volume.*

Q: What is the difference between sponge cake and chiffon cake?

A: *Chiffon and sponge cakes are both made by the same method, i.e. by whisking eggs and sugar. They contain very little fat and are usually light and airy. The difference is in the baking method. Chiffon cakes are baked in a ring-shaped tube pan. Sponge cakes are usually baked in sandwich tins. They can be sandwiched with jam or cream and dusted with icing sugar.*

Steaks

TIPS FOR HOMEMADE STEAKS

Despite the rich variety of Malaysian cuisine with its diverse and exotic tastes and flavours, many Malaysians still enjoy a good steak. How often have you heard the suggestion, "Let's go for a steak"? Although expensive, having a steak meal in a restaurant has gained popularity. However, it is not difficult at all to create a steak dish to rival the "best in town" if we have some knowledge of preparation and cooking methods.

Two of the simplest methods of cooking steaks are grilling and frying or sautéing. Frying enables one to prepare an interesting variety of dishes, ranging from plain fried steak with salt and pepper to the more famous steaks enriched with wine and cream sauces.

For the best results when cooking steaks, the cut of the meat should be carefully selected and prepared. Choose prime or choice cuts such as:

Fillet: A round steak. Cut across the fillet. It is lean and is the most tender. From these are served the fillet steaks, Chateaubriand and filet mignon or tournedos and medallion.

Sirloin or **entrecote**. Cut from the middle of the ribs or sirloin, it is a boneless slice with good flavour.

Minute steak. A thin sirloin steak without fat

T-bone steak. A large steak from the fillet end of the sirloin, on the bone; off the bone it is known as porterhouse — also large and thick.

Rump. It is usually less tender than fillet. It has a firm texture and the flavour is excellent.

The pan is also important for frying good steaks. Use a good quality, heavy but shallow frying pan. Ensure there is enough fat to give a thin coating on the base of the pan. I like a combination of butter and oil. The butter is for flavour and the oil is to prevent burning.

The pan and fat should be heated to a moderately high temperature, enough to sear and lightly brown the steak as soon as it goes into the pan. This will seal in the meat juices and retain the maximum flavour of the steak. Too high a heat can harden and crisp the outside and too low a temperature will not seal in the juices of the meat.

The cooking time depends on the thickness of the steak. As an approximate guide, a $2^1/_2$ cm thick piece will take a total cooking time of six to seven minutes for rare, eight to nine minutes for medium and 10-12 minutes for well-done. Thin minute steaks will take approximately two minutes cooking time for rare. Halfway through cooking time, the steaks should be turned over if you are not adding sauces. If sauces are added, continue to cook slowly on low heat. Ensure that cooking time does not stretch more than is necessary, as prime steaks will spoil when overcooked.

Steaks should be served on warmed plates and as soon as possible. The golden rule to remember always is that speed of cooking and serving is the secret of success.

Here are two of my favourite steak recipes.

Black Pepper Steak

4	fillet steaks
	Dash of black and white ground pepper
1 teaspoon	salt
3 teaspoons	black peppercorns, crushed or pounded coarsely
50 g	butter (at room temperature), combined with 1 tablespoon oil

SAUCE INGREDIENTS

1/2 tablespoon	plain flour
150 ml	beef consommé
100 ml	whipping cream
2 teaspoons	chopped parsley
1/4 teaspoon	pepper

Season steaks with black and white pepper and salt. Press the crushed peppercorns into both sides of the steaks. Do this firmly so that they do not fall off easily during cooking.

Heat butter and oil in a frying pan and fry the steaks over high heat to seal the juices in the steaks. Cook until browned on both sides, approximately one to two minutes each side or cooked as desired for doneness. Then carry on as follows:

If serving without sauce
Lower heat and cook steaks. It will take about four minutes each side for the steak to be almost done. If not done to your liking, reduce heat again and cook further until done as desired.

If serving with sauce
Push steaks to side of pan. Add flour to pan drippings, cook one minute, then gradually add stock and cook over medium heat.

When sauce thickens slightly, remove steaks onto a hot dish, then add cream to pan and stir over low heat. As soon as it begins to boil, add parsley and seasoning to taste. Spoon sauce over steaks.

Steak with Sour Cream and Mushroom Sauce

2	fillet or sirloin steaks, 2 1/2 cm thick
	Freshly ground black pepper
2 teaspoons	black peppercorns, crushed
30 g	butter
1/2	onion
180 g	button mushrooms, sliced
2 teaspoons	paprika
100 ml	soured cream
1/2 teaspoon	salt
30 g	butter combined with 2 tablespoons oil
	A few shakes of salt
1 tablespoon	chopped parsley

Sprinkle steaks with ground pepper and press crushed pepper on both sides of steaks.

Heat butter in a small saucepan. Add onion and cook until soft and translucent. Increase heat and add mushrooms. Stir in paprika. Cook until liquid evaporates, then stir in sour cream. Add salt to taste and set aside.

Heat butter and oil in a heavy-based frying pan. When hot, add steaks, and cook on high heat for a couple of minutes on either side. Turn down heat and cook for a further two minutes on each side for medium and approximately four minutes for well done. Add salt to taste.

Spoon sauce over steaks. Sprinkle with chopped fresh parsley.

Serve with vegetables or a salad and either boiled herbed potatoes or potato chips.

Sugar

Q: Is there any difference between using icing sugar or castor sugar for biscuits and pancakes?

A: *Castor sugar and icing sugar are both used to sweeten as well as to decorate biscuits and pancakes. Pure icing sugar has the advantage of dissolving quickly and makes a finer-textured biscuit. Castor sugar gives equally good results but it produces a more crumbly texture. Icing sugar is dusted over biscuits and pancakes for sweetening as well as to provide a pretty decorative snow effect.*

Q: What is icing sugar?

A: *Icing sugar is produced by milling selected granulated cane sugar to a fine powder. It is used mainly for cake icing and decorating.*

Q: What is cinnamon sugar? I mixed cinnamon powder with sugar and considered it cinnamon sugar. Is this correct?

A: *Cinnamon sugar is fine castor sugar mixed with ground cinnamon powder. It is used for the coating of doughnuts or biscuits and for the topping of cakes and bread.*

Q: I always have difficulty getting sticky black sugar (gula hitam) out of the bottle. Do you have any tips?

A: *Stand the bottle in hot water until the sugary syrup is fluid and can be poured out easily.*

Q: If I grind ordinary sugar and use it as castor sugar, does it affect the cake, biscuit or bread that I am making?

A: *Generally, it is best to use castor sugar when a recipe calls for it. However, if you have a food processor, you can blend ordinary sugar until it is as fine as castor sugar. But sometimes the result can be uneven, and this affects the texture of the cakes and cookies. Some of the coarser-grained sugar will not melt while creaming and may show up on the cake surface as white specks.*

Swiss Rolls

Q: Can you please give me a recipe for a Swiss Roll?

A: Try this easy Swiss Roll.

Swiss Roll

3	large eggs
100 g	castor sugar
100 g	plain flour, sifted
1 tablespoon	hot water
	Warmed jam, your favourite flavour
	Whipped cream
	Icing sugar

Line a 33 x 22¹/₂ cm Swiss Roll tin with greased greaseproof paper.

Whisk eggs in mixing bowl for 1 minute, then add the castor sugar and whisk until thick, white and fluffy.

Sift in flour and fold as lightly as you can without disturbing the lightness of the beaten egg mixture. Stir in hot water.

Pour and spread into prepared tin. Bake in preheated 220°C oven for 10-12 minutes. Turn out onto a tea-towel sprinkled with icing sugar. Remove lining paper and spread with warmed jam. Roll up carefully with the help of the tea towel.

If spreading with cream, roll up the Swiss Roll without filling. When cake is cold, unroll and spread with cream and then roll up again.

Tarts

Q: How can I make fruit tarts glossy without using Jelifix?

A: You can give fruit tarts a glossy glaze by brushing them with apricot jam. Put a tablespoon of apricot jam in a small saucepan with one teaspoon of water. Bring to a boil and remove from heat. Brush over the fruit tarts while still warm.

Q: I would be most grateful if you could give me a recipe for fruit tartlets, the type with a custard filling and fruit on top.

A: *Try this recipe. It is quite easy to make and you can use the fruit of your choice.*

Strawberry Tartlets

FOR THE BASE

240 g	shortcrust pastry (see recipe on p. 163)

FOR THE CREME PATISSIERE

150 ml	fresh milk
150 ml	cream
1/2 teaspoon	vanilla essence
1	egg
1	egg yolk
50 g	vanilla or castor sugar
22 g	plain flour, sifted
450 g	halved strawberries
1 tablespoon	redcurrant jelly
2 teaspoons	water

Line a 23 cm flan tin or a few small tartlet tins with the shortcrust pastry. Prick the base and chill for 30 minutes.

Bake at 190°C for 10-15 minutes until crisp and golden. Allow to cool.

Make the cream patisserie by heating the milk and cream together with vanilla essence. Remove from heat, cover to prevent a skin forming.

Beat the egg, egg yolk and sugar together until pale and fluffy. Add the flour.

Bring the milk and cream to just below boiling point and pour into the egg mixture. Stir vigorously.

Strain into a clean pan and bring to a boil, stirring constantly. Simmer 1-2 minutes until it has thickened. Leave to cool.

Remove the pastry base from flan tin or tartlet tins. Cover with cool creme patisserie and arrange strawberries in concentric circles on top.

Melt redcurrant jelly with water. Cool and brush over strawberries.

Tea Bread

Q: Could you give me a recipe for baking perfect bread using baking powder as a substitute for yeast as a raising agent?

A: *Breads made with baking powder or baking soda instead of yeast are called quick breads. They are quick to make as the dough is baked straight away. They are a cross between cake and bread. Try this recipe for Milk Tea Bread.*

Milk Tea Bread

SIFTED INGREDIENTS (COMBINED)

265 g plain flour
2 teaspoons baking powder

1/2 teaspoon salt
275 g castor sugar
195 g margarine

EGG AND MILK MIXTURE (COMBINED)

3 large eggs, beaten
1/4 cup milk
1 teaspoon vanilla essence

Grease sides and line base of a 21 1/2 x 10 cm loaf pan with greased greaseproof paper.

Put sifted ingredients, salt, castor sugar and margarine into the bowl of a food processor fitted with a cutting blade. Blend until mixture resembles breadcrumbs.

Combine beaten eggs with milk and vanilla essence. Stir into flour mixture.

Spoon mixture into pan. Bake in preheated 175°C oven for 60-70 minutes or until a skewer inserted into centre of tea bread comes out clean.

Tiramisu

Q: Can you please give me a recipe for tiramisu cake?

A: Tiramisu is a luxurious Italian dessert made with a blend of coffee liqueur, chocolate and an Italian cream cheese called mascarpone. This cheese is smooth in texture with the flavour of whipped cream. You can only find it in selected supermarkets. Here is a recipe for a sponge cake sandwiched with Tiramisu filling. It is deliciously rich yet light.

Tiramisu Sponge Delight

1 tablespoon instant coffee
1 tablespoon hot water
3 eggs
175 g castor sugar

SIFTED INGREDIENTS (COMBINED)

60 g plain flour
15 g cocoa powder

3 tablespoons coffee liqueur
450 g mascarpone cheese
Cocoa powder
Dark chocolate shavings

Grease and line a 23 x 33 cm Swiss roll tin with nonstick baking parchment. Dissolve instant coffee in hot water and set aside.

Whisk eggs and 75 g of the sugar in a large heatproof bowl over a pan of simmering water. Whisk with an electric whisk for 6-7 minutes until light and thick. Fold in sifted dry ingredients and stir in coffee mixture.

Pour into prepared tin and bake for 12 minutes until cooked through when tested with a skewer. Cool the cake, then peel off lining paper. Cut cake into 3 equal pieces and drizzle liqueur over them.

Beat cheese and remaining sugar together. Spread over sponge pieces and stack. Dust with cocoa powder and sprinkle with dark chocolate shavings.

Chill for at least 20 minutes before serving.

Tortillas

Q: I simply love Mexican food. I wonder if you can feature a recipe on how to make tortillas at home. I have searched for a recipe without success.

A: *Mexican tortillas are made with either cornmeal flour or plain flour. They are eaten as a bread or fried to make tacos. They are also rolled around fillings or served with toppings, as in the case of nachos, tortillas and enchiladas. I have two recipes, one for corn and the other for plain flour tortillas.*

Corn Tortillas

275 g cornmeal flour
Pinch of salt
approx. 350 ml warm water

Place cornmeal flour and salt in a bowl. Add water gradually, kneading until a smooth, soft dough is formed. Divide into 14 pieces and leave to stand for one hour, covered.

Place each piece of dough between plastic sheets. Flatten and roll out into thin pancakes, approximately 13 cm in diameter.

Heat an ungreased heavy frying pan. When hot, place a tortilla in the pan. Cook for about one minute or until golden specks appear on the surface. Turn and cook the other side for 1-1 1/2 minutes.

Wrap in warm cloth and keep hot while cooking remainder. If tortillas become cool and dry, moisten with a little water and reheat.

Flour Tortillas

225 g plain flour, sifted
1 teaspoon salt
3/4 teaspoon baking powder
50 g lard or vegetable shortening
approx. 150 ml water

Place flour, salt and baking powder in a bowl. Add lard or shortening and blend with a pastry cutter until mixture resembles fine breadcrumbs.

Stir in water and knead briefly until dough forms a smooth ball. Cover and leave to rest for 15-20 minutes.

Pinch off a ball of dough, approximately 4 cm diameter, and roll out on a floured board to 20 cm in diameter.

Cook in an ungreased frying pan on each side for about 1 1/2 minutes. As bubbles form, press down with spatula until tortilla has brown spots.

Tortilla should be cooked but still soft. Wrap in warm cloth or foil and keep hot while cooking remaining tortillas.

Makes approximately 10 tortillas.

Turmeric

Q: If a recipe calls for fresh turmeric, can I omit it? Will the flavour be different? It is so difficult to get rid of the yellowish stain on my fingers and blender.

> *A: Fresh turmeric has a peppery, spicy aroma and a bitter pungent taste. It gives a bright orange colour and is an essential ingredient in curries. It should not be omitted but may be replaced with turmeric powder.*

Q: Is there any difference between *kunyit* and ginger, or can I use them interchangeably?

> *A: Ginger is very different from kunyit, or turmeric root. You cannot substitute one for the other. Ginger has a warm taste and is used sliced, shredded or minced in stir-fry dishes, steamed dishes, curries, stews, soups and casseroles. Turmeric root, which is bright orange, has a bitter spicy aroma. It is used mainly for its colouring in curries, pickles, chutneys and mustard blends.*

Vanilla

Q: What are vanilla pods and where can I get them?

> *A: Vanilla pods are the fruits of the golden flowered vanilla orchid, a large climbing perennial plant with a fleshy, succulent stem. The plant is native to the tropical rainforest of southeastern Mexico and Central America. In its wild state it may grow to a height of 30 metres, climbing to the tops of tall forest trees.*
>
> *The pods, commercially called beans, have no flavour when picked; the flavour develops during the curing process. The beans are very dark brown and contain tiny black seeds.*
>
> *Vanilla beans, around 10-20 cm long, can be bought whole at cake specialist shops. They can be stored in a jar of sugar, permeating it with their own sweet aroma.*

The beans can be chopped finely or processed in a blender and used to flavour cakes, ice-cream and puddings. The whole pod can also be used to flavour custards and other liquids, then taken out, dried and used again up to three or four times.

Vegetarian Cakes

Q: On the first and 15th day of every lunar month I turn vegetarian. Can you give me a recipe for a vegetarian cake?

A: Here is a recipe for the Eggless Lemon Butter Sponge Cake.

Eggless Butter Lemon Sponge Cake

250 g	plain flour
1¹/₂ tablespoons	baking powder
90 g	light brown sugar
75 ml	hot water
25 ml	malt extract (maltose)
	Grated rind and juice of three lemons
125 g	butter or margarine, melted

Grease sides and line base of two 23 cm round cake tins with greased greaseproof paper.

Sift flour and baking powder into mixing bowl. Add sugar and mix well by lifting and stirring, using a spoon. Set aside.

Combine hot water and malt extract and stir until dissolved. Add lemon juice to malt mixture and mix well. Stir in melted margarine and grated lemon rind to dry ingredients and mix quickly, then immediately add malt and lemon juice mixture.

Beat well for 1 minute, before pouring equal amounts into two prepared tins. Bake in preheated 205°C oven for about 20-25 minutes, or until top is firm and turns golden brown.

Allow to cool before removing from tins. Sandwich with jam or orange marmalade.

Q: I am a strict vegetarian. Can you give me the recipe for a vegetarian chocolate cake?

A: *Here is a vegetarian chocolate cake:*

Vegetarian Chocolate Cake

INGREDIENTS A

200 g	plain flour
2 teaspoons	baking powder
1 teaspoon	bicarbonate of soda
60 g	skimmed milk powder

INGREDIENTS B

1 teaspoon	instant coffee powder
150 g	castor sugar
2 tablespoons	honey
150 ml	hot water

180 g	margarine
1 teaspoon	vanilla essence
30 g	cocoa powder

CHOCOLATE FROSTING

150 g	margarine or butter
120 g	icing sugar, sifted together with
30 g	cocoa
60 g	chocolate, melted
1 tablespoon	milk or water, warmed

Line a 17¹/₂ cm square cake tin with greaseproof paper.

Sift Ingredients A into a baking sheet. Combine Ingredients B and stir until sugar and honey dissolve. Cool.

In the bowl of an electric mixer, cream margarine, vanilla essence and cocoa powder until creamy and well blended. Stir in Ingredients A and B and beat mixture on medium speed for two minutes.

Pour into prepared pan. Bake in moderate oven at 175°C for 50 minutes or until cooked through when tested with a skewer.

Spread chocolate frosting over cake when cooled.

To Make Chocolate Frosting
Beat margarine or butter until smooth and creamy. Gradually add icing sugar and cocoa. Combine melted chocolate and milk or water, and beat into mixture.

Q: I would like to have a recipe for an eggless fruit cake.

A: This eggless fruit cake is rich and delicious.

Eggless Rich Fruitcake

340 g	currants
200 g	raisins
340 g	sultanas
285 ml	water
6 tablespoons	corn oil
1 tablespoon	dark treacle
90 g	brown sugar
1 teaspoon	mixed spice
	Grated rind of 1 lemon and 1 orange
1 teaspoon	cornflour, combined with 2 tablespoons water
395 g	self-raising flour, sifted

Grease the sides of a 33 x 11 cm loaf pan with greased greaseproof paper.

Combine in a mixing bowl fruit, water, corn oil, treacle, brown sugar, mixed spice and grated rind of lemon and orange. Mix well together. Stir in cornflour mixture. Lightly stir in the self-raising flour and mix well.

Spoon cake mixture into loaf pan. Bake for 3 hours in a preheated 125°C oven. After 1/2 hour of baking, cover cake with greased baking paper.

Q: Recently, my son was diagnosed with a skin disease. Because of this, he needs to follow a vegetarian diet. I have experimented with a few recipes but I need more variety. As I am a working mum, could you share some simple and quick recipes?

A: I am sorry to hear of your son's condition. Here is the recipe for a tasty herbal bread which you can easily make for a light snack.

Parsley and Chives Bread

30 g	fresh yeast
250 ml	lukewarm water
450 g	strong plain flour
2 teaspoons	salt
1 tablespoon	chopped parsley
1 tablespoon	chopped chives
2 tablespoons	olive oil

Dissolve yeast in four tablespoons of lukewarm water. Set aside.

Sift flour into a food processor fitted with a dough hook. Stir in salt. Pour in yeast liquid, remaining water, fresh herbs and olive oil. Turn on processor and blend for 4-5 minutes until smooth.

Cover dough with a damp cloth and leave to rise in a warm place for about 1 hour.

Knock back dough and knead lightly on a lightly floured board. Shape into small rounds or as desired and place on a nonstick baking sheet. Cover and leave to rise again for 20 minutes or until it doubles in bulk.

Bake in preheated 220°C oven for 15-20 minutes for small buns and approximately 45 minutes for a whole loaf. Remove onto a cooling rack to cool completely.

Vinegar

Q: Can I use normal white vinegar in recipes that call for either red or white wine vinegar?

A: *The flavours from the wine and the barrels in which the vinegar are made give wine vinegars their subtle flavour. Normal white vinegar is not a good substitute when recipes specially require red or white wine vinegar.*

Waffles

Q: Could you recommend a good waffle maker machine?

A: *There are many well-known brands of electric waffle makers. I would recommend one which has various interchangeable patterns and non-stick plates and which is rectangular in shape.*

Yeast

Q: In your recipe for buns, how much instant yeast do I use as a substitute for $2^{1}/_{2}$ cm fresh yeast?

A: *$2^{1}/_{2}$ cm fresh yeast is approximately 30 g. Use 15 g instant yeast granules.*

Q: Your recipe for Grandma's Pinwheel calls for a $2^{1}/_{2}$ x 5 cm cube of wet yeast, while your recipe for coconut buns calls for a $2^{1}/_{2}$ cm cube. What are the measurements of the wet yeast in grams, and what is the equivalent in grams of one tablespoon of wet yeast?

A: *A piece of fresh yeast which measures $2^{1}/_{2}$ x 5 cm is approximately 60 g and a $2^{1}/_{2}$ cm cube is about 30 g. One level tablespoon of fresh yeast is approximately 15 g.*

Q: Can I substitute fresh yeast for active yeast when making bread?

A: *Fresh yeast can be substituted for active dried yeast in the proportion of two parts (by weight) of fresh yeast to every part of active dried yeast.*

Q: What is the difference between easy-blend yeast and instant yeast? Why is warm water used in recipes which require easy-blend yeast?

A: *Easy-blend yeast is the same as instant yeast. As the name implies, it does not need to be reconstituted into liquid form first. It can be mixed directly with the flour. Yeast needs liquid to make it active. Warm liquid promotes faster action.*

Yoghurt

WHIPPING UP YOGHURT YUMMIES

Natural yoghurt is a thick, white, tangy substance made by fermenting fresh whole milk, low-fat milk, or skimmed milk with a special culture of bacteria. Before the days of refrigeration, it was discovered that the goodness of milk could be preserved by fermenting it into yoghurt. It apparently originated in the Balkans and was introduced into Europe during the 18th century.

Nutritionally, yoghurt is similar to milk, being rich in protein, B vitamins, calcium and phosphorus. It is widely acclaimed as a health food as it contains small amounts of healthy bacteria which help protect the body against infection and the effects of stress. It is also a very versatile product as it can be used in both savoury and sweet dishes.

Commercial yoghurt sold in cartons is readily available in supermarkets. It comes plain or slightly sweetened and flavoured with fruit. When buying the product, always check the expiry date and make sure the carton is not damaged and that the seal on the cover is intact. If the cover is bulging, the product has either not been properly refrigerated or its shelf life has expired.

It may be convenient to buy ready-made yoghurt but it is really not that difficult to make your own. Besides, it is far more economical. To make perfect yoghurt every time, though, you have to understand a few important facts.

Like yeast, the living organism in yoghurt is sensitive to high temperatures. For consistent results, check the milk temperature with a cooking thermometer before adding the yoghurt starter or culture. The ideal temperature is around 41°C to 43°C. But it is not at all essential to have a thermometer as equally good results can be obtained by testing milk with your finger. It should feel warm and not hot.

Once yoghurt is added, leave the milk undisturbed in a warm place for the culture to act. This should take about 8 hours depending on the room temperature. If the yoghurt does not coagulate after 8 hours, it is likely that the temperature of the milk was too high and the culture has been destroyed.

Do not be tempted to use too much yoghurt starter, as the yoghurt will turn sour and watery. To obtain milky and creamy yoghurt, the culture needs room to grow. Yoghurt should never be left to incubate for too long as it will gradually turn sour. It should be refrigerated when it sets into a thick custard-like consistency. Under proper refrigeration, yoghurt will keep for about a week without turning rancid. The surface of rancid yoghurt is slightly pinkish in colour.

To start the first batch of homemade yoghurt, use commercial natural yoghurt as your starter. From then on, save at least a tablespoon of the current batch to serve as a starter for your next batch. The yoghurt should preferably not be more than five days old when used as a starter. Every three months or so, start afresh with commercially made yoghurt as this will have the right balance of culture.

Yoghurt is easily contaminated, so make sure that all utensils and containers have been washed well with hot, soapy water and are absolutely clean.

Here is a recipe for making your own yoghurt as well as some recipes for sweet and savoury dishes that use this versatile product.

Yoghurt

250 ml milk (regular, low fat or skimmed)
1 tablespoon commercial natural yoghurt

Put milk in a saucepan and heat over medium heat until it begins to boil. Remove from heat and pour into a clean heatproof bowl or jar with a cover.

Cool to 41-43°C or until the milk feels comfortably warm to your finger. This takes approximately 40 minutes. The skin on the surface of the milk can either be removed or stirred into the lukewarm milk..

Spoon the yoghurt into the milk. It is not necessary to stir or blend. Cover the bowl and leave it undisturbed in a warm place for the yoghurt to set. This will take approximately 8 hours. The lower the fat content in the milk, the longer the yoghurt will take to set.

When the yoghurt sets into a thick custard-like consistency, place it in the refrigerator. If it is allowed to ferment longer at room temperature, the yoghurt will become more sour. It will firm a bit more when chilled. The yoghurt will keep for about a week.

Yoghurt Garlic Bread

SIFTED INGREDIENTS

250 g high-protein flour
250 g plain flour
2 teaspoons baking powder

1/2 teaspoon salt
3 teaspoons sugar
2 teaspoons easy-blend yeast

175 ml	warmed milk
60 g	melted margarine
150 ml	yoghurt

1	egg, beaten
2 teaspoons	melted margarine
6 cloves	garlic, finely minced

Put sifted ingredients into the bowl of a food processor fitted with a dough blade. Stir in salt, sugar and yeast. Pour and stir in combined milk, margarine and yoghurt mixture.

Turn on food processor and beat for 5-6 minutes until well-blended and smooth. Leave to rise, covered, for 30-40 minutes or until doubled in bulk. Punch down the risen dough.

Turn dough out onto a lightly floured board and knead into a ball. Shape into a long roll and cut into 8 even portions. Shape into balls.

Roll out each ball of dough into a flat circle and pull one end to shape into a teardrop shape approximately 1 1/4 cm thick. Cover and leave to rise for 15-20 minutes.

Meanwhile, preheat oven to 250°C. Place a large greased cookie tray in the oven to heat. Remove hot tray and place risen bread carefully on to it leaving some space in between to allow for spreading. Brush surface with beaten egg and melted margarine and sprinkle with garlic.

Place the tray on the top shelf of the oven and bake for 10-12 minutes until well risen and golden.

Spicy Yoghurt Potatoes

| 500 g | small new potatoes, peeled |
| 2 tablespoons | cooking oil |

1	large onion, finely chopped
1 1/2 cm	ginger root, finely chopped
2	green chillies, finely chopped
2	tomatoes, minced

SPICES (COMBINED)

1 teaspoon	coriander powder
1 teaspoon	garam masala
1 teaspoon	turmeric powder
1 teaspoon	chilli powder

200 ml	yoghurt
1 teaspoon	salt, or to taste
1/2 teaspoon	sugar
20 g	sultanas
1 tablespoon	chopped coriander leaves

Boil potatoes in salt water for 12-15 minutes or until cooked thoroughly. Drain well.

Heat oil in a saucepan and stir-fry cooked potatoes until golden brown. Drain from oil and set aside.

Reheat saucepan and put in onion and ginger and fry until fragrant. Add green chillies and tomatoes and cook for 1 minute. Add combined spices and fry for 3 minutes.

Stir in yoghurt gradually and cook until sauce begins to boil. Put in potatoes, salt and sugar and simmer until gravy is thick. Add sultanas and coriander leaves.

Serve hot with rice or yoghurt garlic bread.

Green Chilli Yoghurt Chicken

1 kg	whole skinless chicken thighs
1 1/2 teaspoons	salt
1 teaspoon	chilli powder
1 teaspoon	turmeric powder
300 ml	yoghurt
2 tablespoons	oil

FINELY MINCED INGREDIENTS

2	onions
2 1/2 cm	ginger
3 cloves	garlic

4	green chillies, finely chopped
1 tablespoon	poppy seeds (kas kas)
3 tablespoons	coconut milk
1/2 tablespoon	lemon juice
1 tablespoon	chopped coriander leaves

Chop chicken thighs into large serving pieces. Marinate with salt, chilli and turmeric powder and yoghurt for at least 30 minutes.

Put marinated yoghurt chicken in a deep saucepan and simmer gently for 15 minutes.

Meanwhile, heat another saucepan with 2 tablespoons oil and fry onions, ginger and garlic over low heat for 5-6 minutes until fragrant.

Put in green chillies and poppy seeds and fry for a further 3-5 minutes.

Stir in coconut milk and then the cooked chicken with all the gravy. Bring to a boil, then simmer, covered for 10-15 minutes over moderate heat until gravy thickens.

Stir in lemon juice and coriander leaves.

Banana Yoghurt Cake with Chocolate Chips

A lovely moist teacake with a delicate tangy taste and well studded with chocolate chips. I make this whenever I have leftover overripe bananas.

125 g	vegetable shortening
240 g	castor sugar
1 teaspoon	vanilla essence
2	large eggs
320 g	mashed bananas

SIFTED INGREDIENTS

240 g	plain flour
1 1/2 teaspoons	baking powder
1 teaspoon	bicarbonate of soda

3 tablespoons	yoghurt
90 g	chocolate chips

Grease sides and line base of a 36 x 11 cm loaf pan with greased greaseproof paper.

Cream shortening with castor sugar and vanilla essence until light and creamy. Beat in eggs one at a time, then mashed bananas. Stir in sifted dry ingredients alternately with yoghurt, one third at a time. Stir in chocolate chips.

Spoon batter into prepared pan, spreading well to corners. Bake in preheated oven at 175°C for 50-55 minutes or until cake is cooked through when tested with a skewer.

Yoghurt Mint Dip

1 cup	yoghurt
1 tablespoon	fresh chopped parsley
1 tablespoon	fresh chopped mint
1 tablespoon	lemon juice
1/4 teaspoon	cayenne pepper
	Dash of ground black pepper
1/4 teaspoon	salt, or to taste

Put all ingredients into a bowl. Beat lightly with a fork until it is smooth and creamy.

Chill until ready to serve.

Q: Can a person suffer from ulcers after eating too much yoghurt? Is it OK to eat yoghurt every day?

A: Far from causing ulcers, yoghurt is recommended for people suffering from ulcers. There is no harm in eating yoghurt every day; in fact, it should do you good. Yoghurt, like milk, is an excellent source of calcium and phosphorous, and a good source of high quality protein and vitamin B.

Q: How long can I keep yoghurt in the fridge? Should I keep it in the freezer?

A: *Yoghurt keeps well refrigerated for up to a week. If you intend to keep it longer, then it should be frozen when freshly made.*

Q: Why is it that whenever I add yoghurt to a curry dish, it curdles? How can I overcome this problem?

A: *To prevent yoghurt from curdling in curries, bring it to room temperature before using it in hot dishes. Stir it into the dish gradually and do not allow it to boil vigorously. You can also mix the yoghurt with a teaspoon of cornflour and gradually stir it into the hot curry over low heat.*